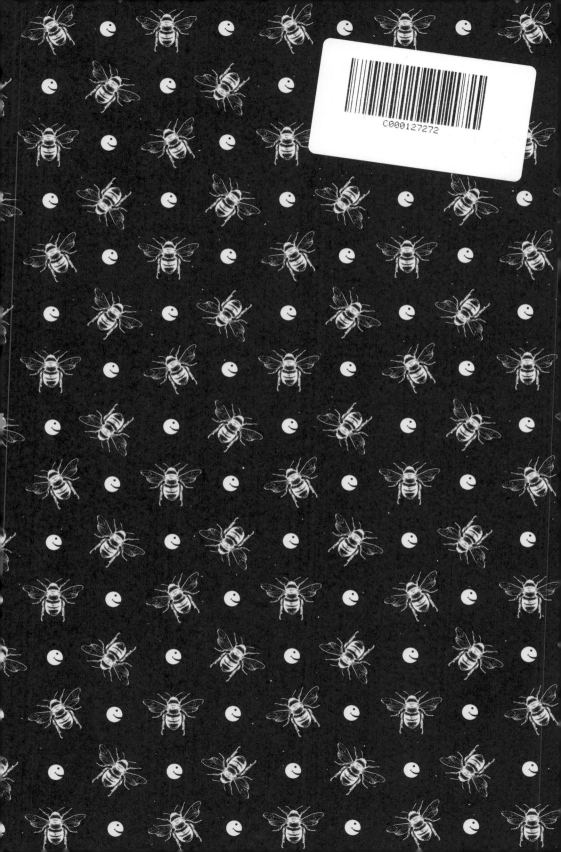

BOZ

Buzzin'

BEZ
Buzzin'

with Andrew Perry

The Nine Lives of a Happy Monday

WHITE RABBIT

First published in Great Britain in 2022 by White Rabbit,
an imprint of The Orion Publishing Group Ltd
Carmelite House, 50 Victoria Embankment
London EC4Y 0DZ

An Hachette UK Company

1 3 5 7 9 10 8 6 4 2

ISBN (Hardback) 978 1 3996 0506 9
ISBN (Export Trade Paperback) 978 1 3996 0507 6
ISBN (eBook) 978 1 3996 0509 0
ISBN (Audio) 978 1 3996 0510 6

Typeset by Born Group
Printed and bound in Great Britain by Clays Ltd, Elcograf S.p.A.

MIX
Paper from
responsible sources
FSC® C104740

www.whiterabbitbooks.co.uk
www.orionbooks.co.uk

Contents

Prologue: Talking to Terry Venables during a
Near-Death Experience   1

1. Salford, Strangeways . . . Morocco   15
2. Happy Days!   44
3. On Top   76
4. Not Straight, but Great   108
5. The New Normal: Just Being Bez   133
6. Rockin' the House   157
7. Every Day Is Like Monday   183
8. Mark Berry MP . . . Who's 'Avin' It?!   207
9. From Es to Bees: Sorted, at Last   231
10. Buzzin' through Covid   254
11. Full Circle   284

Acknowledgements   293

Prologue

TALKING TO TERRY VENABLES DURING A NEAR-DEATH EXPERIENCE

For umpteen reasons, this book should never have happened. I recently turned fifty-eight, and I'm still making a living just being myself in the public eye. I'm still a Happy Monday, I'm on television most weeks of the year and now I'm writing a new autobiography. Suffice to say, none of this would've been foreseeable forty years ago.

You could probably argue that I've been rather a jammy bastard. I've cheated death on a number of occasions, which won't surprise anyone who knows about my dodgy past. I'm like an extremely fortunate feline who's used up his nine lives before he's even left his mother's clutches. How have I survived? I pulled it off, I reckon, from having a love of life, a bit of luck, and a determination not to die. The will to live, and to come through at the other end in one piece.

I've had close calls throughout my life, but the important thing is that I've learned from them all.

My most dramatic brush with the Grim Reaper, however, came about in a relatively innocent, law-abiding fashion in 1999.

I was in a transitional period in my life. The Happy Mondays had split up in drug-addled acrimony, and so had the band that Shaun Ryder and I had formed in the aftermath, Black Grape. The Mondays were just starting to do reunions, I was doing a bit of DJing at weekends for ready money, and finding other stuff to do to keep the wolf from my door was proving remarkably easy.

For two or three years, I had a really good job writing a column for *Front* magazine, a lads' mag that had been set up to rival the mid-90s publishing sensation *Loaded*. All I had to rustle up was 700 words every month, and I got paid one English pound per word - 700 quid! It was good cash!

For one of the first columns, the editor put me together with this gangster fella who was a big East End debt collector and hard man, most famous for running the security at Ronnie Kray's funeral - he even carried the coffin. He's quite a fucking mad character. He's got a giant painting of himself on a horse that's rearing up, with his missus on the back, naked. I found him a likeable guy and fun to hang about with.

I wanted to go out with him in London, so me and a few of my mates from Manchester - larger than life characters, some of whom have passed away now - went up there to meet him. This geezer had a white Rolls-Royce and stuck a magnetic number plate over the legal number plate, saying 'BAD BOY 1' on it. We kept shouting, 'Bad Bwoy I!' the Rastafarian thing, and he kept saying, 'No, it's Bad Boy *One!*' He had all these fake guns in the back of his Roller, God knows why, so we were hanging out of the windows waving these replica Tommy guns about, and we ended up getting him kicked out of all the clubs he took us to, including one of his own places, because we were snorting coke off the tables and bars.

My one mate was doing that thing to someone where you go really fast between their fingers with a knife, stabbing the table, and he actually stuck the knife right through the centre of their hand - on purpose. He's nuts, one of them little angry men.

So I was writing this monthly column about crazy times like these, and as always I was looking for a new blag. I really fancied getting into motorbikes with it, so I suggested to *Front* that we have a little section in every issue where we test the latest models. They loved the idea, and we went through a period of test-driving motorbikes, which we basically got given on a free loan.

One particular month we got two Triumphs – a Daytona and a Speed Triple – two brand-new models that were about to come on to the market. The Speed Triple went to this kid who was helping me blag all the bikes, because he was actually a proper motorbike journalist, and the Daytona was for me.

That weekend, I had a DJ gig up in Scotland, so me and the journalist kid ended up doing a run up to Edinburgh to try out these new Triumphs long-distance. We had all the kit imaginable, which had also been blagged off the bike company for photo shoots and what have you, and we had waterproofs on as well because it had been raining that week.

Unfortunately, this was in the days when I was still smoking weed, and *heavily*. One of my mates, who for legal reasons I shall call Jim, always says that he had a really lucky escape here, because on the way up I called in at his place in Hull, to get a load of weed off him. We got really stoned together – which I can see now was not my smartest decision – and then I started getting my shit together ready to complete the journey on this Daytona.

'Why don't you hop on the back and come with us?' I said to Jim, as I was stumbling about pulling my waterproofs back on.

He was looking at this monster of a bike, grinning and shaking his head.

'No, I don't think so,' he replied, which turned out to be a much better decision.

On the final leg of the journey, we were doing stupid speeds out on these country roads leading into Edinburgh. I was chasing up after the other kid, who was a much better rider than me. At one point, he nipped around two cars. I went after him, but I didn't have enough time to brake going into the bend. I tried powering through the corner, and I lost the back end of the bike - it's called a highside, I've since found out - went into a skid, and ended up sliding across the road backwards into a stone wall.

Most people, when they have a bad accident, are lucky enough not to remember a single bit of it. However, there's nothing I don't remember about mine. I actually remember every minute detail, possibly because I was so busy trying to save myself. I was doing everything I could to prevent myself from crashing. Even when I was sliding across the road backwards at high velocity, I remember thinking to myself, 'I've got to hunch up before I hit the wall!'

What saved my life was the rucksack on my back, containing all my going-out gear for that evening's DJ gig, which acted as a sort of airbag, and took some of the brunt of the impact.

Even so, I still smashed my pelvis in five places, broke all my ribs and punctured my lung. There also was a big hole in the back of my helmet, although it did its job and saved me from any head injury. If it hadn't been for the rucksack, the accident would have been so much worse. The damage I suffered would've been that much more severe, and I possibly would've snuffed it.

So I was there lying on this grass verge, and the journalist came back on his bike.

'Come on, Bez, get up!' he went, like I'd just tripped over on the pavement or something.

'Do you think I'm lying here for the fun of it!' I replied, or at least think that I replied. 'What do you think I've been trying to do for the last five minutes?'

I could hardly breathe because of the punctured lung, and there was no way I was getting up on account of the smashed-up pelvis. By the time the ambulance arrived I was going into shock, but I focused all my energy on staying awake until it actually pulled up. As soon as I knew that it had and they'd put me in there and I was safe, I said to the ambulance geezer, 'Right, I'm getting my head down now, if that's okay?' and I went off to sleep.

When I regained consciousness, I was actually in hospital in Edinburgh, and a few of my mates had come up to see me, but the very next day I fell into a coma because I caught the MRSA hospital superbug, a really fucking nasty one, and I stayed in the coma for the next month. While I was in the coma I was having multiple organ failures, heart failures – all sorts of shit was going down. Obviously, they couldn't operate on me. I was that ill, I was given the last rites, and my next of kin were informed that I had a one in four chance of making it through the night.

Through all my time in this coma, I was having mad dreams. I was aware but not aware, if you know what I mean. I thought I was in some hospital tent deep in the fucking Malaysian jungle, like a scene from *M*A*S*H*, being looked after by some Chinese-type people. I was aware that loads of friends had come to see me to say goodbye, because they'd been told I was supposed to be dying that night. I was aware of their presence, and who they all were, and I could make out

5

all of their voices, but then I could hear ocean waves crashing on a nearby beach. I could also hear a campfire burning outside what my delirious mind was telling me was this hospital tent in the jungle that I was shacked up in, and then I was also hearing all this tribal music playing, which was apparently actually coming from my friends' ghetto blaster. I was saying, 'Fucking hell, I can't believe you've come all this way to visit me!' because I thought I was in the Malaysian jungle.

Debs, the mother of my two eldest sons, was telling me that I had to piss, because I hadn't pissed for days, and they said to her, 'If he doesn't piss he's gonna die!' I started pissing, because I needed to piss, but I was still in a coma, so I don't know how I knew that this was still going on.

All the doctors and specialists were buzzing in and out to check on me, but none of them seemed to think I was going to pull through. Out of desperation, my mum and Debs called in this woman, who was some kind of New Age healer. She put these crystals all over my head, and started giving it the reiki shit, 'woo-oo-oo-ooooo!' up and down my body. The consultant was going to my dad, 'This fucking woman, I don't know what she thinks she's doing!' and he was explaining everything that they had done for me, and the next minute, I've sat bolt upright out of this coma, with all my broken bones and everything, and I was fucking *up*! This hippie woman had brought me out of the coma.

Obviously, that was a good thing, but then they all started panicking, and they put me back into a medical coma, because the shock of me coming round might have been too much.

You wouldn't believe how much I was hallucinating. The wildest ones were when I came out of the coma. At that point, I was still too ill to have any operations, because I was having all these organ failures. I was getting rushed about from one hospital to the next. I was having heart failures, I had heart surgery. There was that much of this shit going down, the file they had on me was thicker than the Bible.

For weeks, I was lying there hallucinating, and I can still remember all these visions vividly. That Scottish comedian, Billy Connolly, used to visit me on a regular basis, hanging about at the end of my bed in a wheelchair, doing wheelies in it and all sorts. I used to see him a lot, but I've never met him in my life - not before or since - but he was being a proper Billy Connolly, telling jokes and stories, while doing tricks in his wheelchair.

I'd have these mad conversations with him. One time, I'd just had my first drink of water after coming out of the coma - he wasn't really there, remember, I was just hallucinating that he was! - and Billy was down the end doing his wheelies as usual, and I was telling him how I was never going to drink anything but water ever again, because this water tasted so fucking good after being in a coma that long. It was like the fucking nectar of life going down you, you could feel the magic of it inside you.

So, Billy was going, 'Bez, I'm going to bring some water in for you from my loch at the bottom of my garden!' He came in the next day - I used to think that he was going out with one of the nurses that were looking after me - and he brought me this dirty brown water in a bottle and told me how this was the best fucking water in the whole of Scotland, and he got it from his loch.

Around that time, I'd been getting into ayahuasca, the potent psychoactive brew from South America. It's meant to be the most potent hallucinogenic on earth. We were calling it Daime Tea, and I got a bottle of Daime off Billy Connolly as well. They had done a healing thing on it, and I was having little cups of it, so on top of everything else I was doing, all that hardcore medication, I was drinking Daime-ayahuasca in the hospital. It might have done some good for me, because there was a placebo effect in knowing that they had done a little healing ceremony on it. I think that helped in my psychological recovery.

Even without that, the doctors couldn't believe how much I hallucinated. I - was - off - my - fucking - HEAD! They said, 'We've never ever, *ever* encountered anybody who hallucinates as much as you do.' On top of the morphine, I was also eating these little ganja cakes that my partner had made for me, because I wanted weed and I couldn't leave my bed. Plus, I was on the drip, so I was constantly squeezing the little trigger for intravenous morphine - a hundred times a second! The journeys I used to go on inside my own brain . . .

I was like Michael Gambon in *The Singing Detective*, with all this shit going on at my bedside. I've seen kids climbing on the roof of the hospital, all sorts, climbing up the walls, and I was saying to the nurse, 'You've got to tell them kids!' I was really concerned for their welfare, but obviously there was nobody there.

Some days, I just didn't want to believe I was in hospital. In my head, I was having full days out, going on adventures around Salford. I was convinced it was true, but it was all totally fabricated in the mind! I was telling the nurses all about it.

'I've just been out for the day.'

'You've been nowhere, love.'

'Yes, I fucking have!'

'Well, get out of bed then!'

'Aaargh!'

I couldn't move. I think I was probably a bit of a pest. I used to tell all the nurses they were sadistic bitches, when they used to come and give me bedbaths, because I was in that much pain. The pain was unreal.

Very honestly, I thought I was gonna die, and I got in a panic because I couldn't remember my Lord's Prayer, until a mate brought me the Cliff Richard version, and we were singing along, 'Our Faaaather, who-ooo art in heav'n,' which was a bit of a comedy moment. After my mate had gone home, I used to play it over and over again in the hossie, hoping I would be able to remember it in my hour of need. So Cliff helped save my life as well.

I was four months in hospital over New Year 1999-2000, so I missed the biggest party of the century, which is unlike me. I don't think I'd even actually had the chance to line up my itinerary for the big night - the best nights out are the ones you don't plan.

Truthfully, I'd started to face up to the possibility that I wasn't going to make it, because I kept getting rushed about from one emergency to the next. On Millennium Eve itself, Debs brought my two sons for a visit, and one of them was saying to my mate Winker, who had also stopped by that day, and who kind of looks and sounds a bit like me, 'Can't you just lie in bed and be my dad for the night, and let him come out with us?' I wished I could've swapped places with him, but I couldn't.

That night, seeing that I was in hospital in Edinburgh, the whole craziness of Hogmanay unfolded on the streets outside:

all the fireworks were going off, and I could see them out of the window in real life, and pretty much simultaneously on the telly in the corner of my room. The following morning, New Year's Day, we got haggis for breakfast and it was the best haggis ever. Haggis is one of my favourite foods anyway – it's not awful, it's offal! – and in the circumstances this one tasted unbelievably good to me.

Through all that time, I was getting amazing support, all these letters and phone calls from friends, celebrities and well-wishers. I had Eric Cantona phoning in to talk to me, and that *wasn't* a hallucination – that was for real!

One night, the former England football manager Terry Venables phoned me up, and he was on for two hours, maybe more. We'd both just been involved in some TV ads for Admiral sportswear, but I hardly knew the guy really. I was actually in the worst pain I've ever been in, I could hardly bear it, and he kept me talking on the phone, told me his whole life story, about all his time with England, and the guy Alan Sugar with the computers who owned Tottenham during his spell in charge there. He was telling me everything. If I was a journalist, and I was in a good state of mind, I would probably have got the best story ever on record. He talked about everything, the Euros, it was fucking amazing, and it totally distracted me from the pain I was in. Looking back, I can't believe he did that for me.

The funniest one was when Shaun Ryder came to visit. He knew I was in a bad way, and there was quite a strong chance I was gonna die. He'd started this urban myth that I was racing some superbike world champion, and I was just screaming round the final bend to beat the fucker when I totalled my wheels and landed up in hospital.

The whole hospital knew he was coming, and all the nurses were getting really excited. I was saying, because I know what he's like, 'Fucking hell, that's *if* he comes . . .' He did actually turn up but, like I predicted, it wasn't within the stipulated visiting hours. He actually materialised at four o'clock in the morning, like a bat at the window - you know, with the little ears! Like a vampire! I'll always remember seeing his head appear at the door, like fucking Dark Lord Morgoth. For some reason he brought me all these VHS cassettes, so we sat there watching them through into the morning, some really good films like *The Matrix* and that vampire movie *From Dusk Till Dawn*. We had a right laugh about it, because I knew that if he was going to come, there's no way he'd take the regular route.

Like I said, all told I was in the hospital for about four months. Eventually I got discharged, and went back to my home in Glossop, on the outskirts of Manchester, to recuperate. I got myself back up on my feet as quickly as I could, but not without a struggle and a whole load of physiotherapy. I used to have dreams about walking. In one of them, there was a boat out at sea, and I had to walk across a platform that was wobbling - mad walking dreams about impossible situations on platforms over wobbly, wavy seas. I was that determined, though, I was up on my feet within two weeks of the final operation I had, and they said they'd never seen that before. There are those who still haven't even got up after a month or two, after the kind of ordeal I'd been through. But I forced myself.

However, it wasn't over yet, as I ended up with a really bad addiction problem. People might not believe it, but I'm really good at giving things up. It's one of my strong points! But this was without question the toughest test I've ever faced on that front, because when I got discharged from hospital, they basically packed me off with a load of morphine. Very quickly, I got addicted to Oramorph, Gabapentin and other painkillers and morphine-based tablets. With the Oramorph, at the beginning when I was in physical agony, I could open the packaging, put the dispenser in my mouth, pop the thing and drink it - I had this whole little technique of getting my morphine down me. At first I might've needed it, but by the end there it became something else.

It was fucking double-strong stuff. I had medicine bottles of it, so much really strong medical morphine. I was giving bits of my stash to Shaun, who at the time was a heavy heroin addict, and it was even knocking him right out.

The worst thing about it was, it didn't make me feel good in the least. I was angry, frustrated, sleeping constantly. I was grouchy, being really horrible to all the people around me who I loved, none of which was 'me' at all. It was actually Joe Strummer from The Clash, who'd become a friend during Black Grape days, who flagged up to me that I wasn't my usual self.

It took me a while to realise that I was properly addicted to the morph. I was looking at myself, and I decided - this is fucking not me, I've got to give it up, and I just went cold turkey on everything - gabapentin, Oramorph, and this long list of fucking tablets, which I'd been left addicted to after the accident. I gave them all up at once. I've since read that you shouldn't do it that way, that it could be dangerous giving everything up in one go, and certainly from that moment of giving them all up, I didn't sleep for a whole month. Proper insomnia. It was driving me crazy, a month of sheer hell, but I was determined to get all that shit out of my life.

One night, Debs got an aromatherapist massage woman to come around. I was really losing the plot, not able to cope, and she gave me this aromatherapy full-body massage, because I was still in pain as well as not sleeping, and I didn't even remember this woman leaving. I fell asleep and woke up two days later. Two days' sleep after a month of being awake!

From there, the journey went on. The first time I went onstage with the Mondays again was in July 2000, not too long after I'd cut all that shit out and started walking again. I'd only just got rid of my crutches, and I was back giving it loads with my maracas supporting Oasis at Wembley Stadium. I remember thinking to myself, 'How the fuck am I going to get through this?' - after all, I could hardly stand upright - but I managed to do it while experiencing a world of pain, and hiding my grimaces behind this rather cool goggle mask.

After that, going on tour and gigging was like physiotherapy for me, because by the end of that tour I had danced myself back into action, from being almost a cripple to being able to have full movement again. So my actual physio was being on Es and off my nut onstage! That was actually very beneficial for me, as a form of physiotherapy, and I kind of forced myself better very quickly through doing it.

The accident was definitely a turning point in my whole journey on this planet. It taught me one thing: you have to live your life to the fullest every day, because you never know when you'll take your last breath. So it was a funny time, but it was a good time as well, because I never took life for granted ever again.

Now, every time I walk out the door and speak to anyone who means anything to me, I always tell those people that I love them, because the biggest worry for me out of the whole experience was all the people I hadn't told that I loved them before the accident happened. I could've gone off without them ever knowing. So that's what I took from it: I always tell everyone I love them now, little things like that.

In the first hours and days after I came out of the coma, I didn't think I'd be able to walk again, and now I live a full active life. A lot of people tend not to be so active after such a life-changing event, but I've forced myself to do it. I'm doing things constantly. I do training, ice skating, snowboarding, boxing, bike riding – all these activities – because I know if I stop, I'm just going to seize up.

Even twenty-plus years later, I have still got the effects of that accident. I live in constant pain with it, and my legs and my pelvis have never worked as well as they used to. I don't feel like I can run. I force myself to do things that my body is trying to tell me not to do.

The surgeons who put me back together again were amazing. One of them actually got in touch recently because he sees everything that I'm up to, all the Mondays tours and reality shows on TV, and he can hardly believe what he's seeing. He said, 'I've done too good of a fucking job putting you back together again, mate, haven't I!'

Chapter 1

SALFORD, STRANGEWAYS . . . MOROCCO

Another thing I'm good at is doing things wrong. I don't really know what people's perception of me is (I don't spend a lot of time thinking about that stuff), but my main motivation in writing this book is to record what I've done in my life, so that my kids and grandkids know the absolute truth about what happened in each and every case, while I can still remember it. So that they understand what drove me, for better or worse, and the book will always be there for them almost as a guide to what *not* to do.

And for anyone else reading, I think it's a good story that's worth telling. My life hasn't been that usual.

In my first book, *Freaky Dancin'*, which was published in 1998, I went into all my criminal activity as a teenager - inciting street battles at school, thieving with a perilous lack of forward planning, getting thrown out by my parents, living homeless, landing in Strangeways for a stretch and eventually falling into the drugs trade. All those stories have been told. I don't mind going into it again in brief - maybe there'll be a few crazy flashbacks here and there - but I certainly don't want to big up that side of my life too much, because I don't want my youngest kid and my grandkids reading about stuff like that and thinking that it could be a viable way of life for them.

I don't want to promote a life of criminality, because I don't agree with it and don't want to be seen endorsing it, or glamorising it. or boasting about what I got up to in any way. It's nothing to boast about. I went through it and it was shit. My involvement only taught me one thing: that it's really not a way to live your life. At one stage I did think I could make a living out of it, but the reality was different, a complete disaster. I ended up in prison. Later on, I got held hostage, and drug deals were constantly going wrong.

It's not really the lifestyle that people imagine it to be. It's full of stress, and for that reason you could never actually enjoy the money you made from it. I always had this feeling of being on the run. It was a shit way of living, and it only led to misery. All I found out was, it's not the way for me.

To be clear, my attitudes towards drugs per se haven't changed too much. Everybody knows that prohibition doesn't work, but society has obviously got its reasons for enforcing it - if you've learned your lessons from the past, then obviously you're doing it for a reason. But everybody knows it doesn't stop people taking drugs. That's been proven throughout human history, so they obviously maintain that prohibitive environment for another purpose - to create an enemy. People need an enemy.

I wasn't ever dealing any hardcore drugs, just moving on hash mostly, and a bit of weed, and I don't even really class those as drugs. I was just providing a service, but ultimately, after many years of anxiety and mishap, I decided: 'I'm Bez from the Happy Mondays, I realise that this isn't the right path, and I don't have to participate in that rubbish any more to earn a living.'

*

To be truthful, I don't overanalyse my life. I never waste time pondering on things I've done, I'm always looking forward. I prefer creating to pondering, but I do think I understand the psychology of what made me behave the way I did: I was in full-on rebellion mode ever since I was a toddler. That's when I can remember it all starting, and that's been my mindset ever since, and I've carried that energy with me to the present day.

I'm a full-blown anarchist. The only thing that worries me about becoming more of a normal member of society these days, paying my tax on time and appearing on primetime TV, is that I can't fucking say I'm an anarchist any more! Have I become just a normal conformist? That's a worrying thought.

What set me on my dissenting course were two clashes with authority when I was just five years old. When I was a child growing up in Manchester, my old fella was a copper and tried to give me a very strict upbringing. Both my parents were Scousers, my dad Tony Berry originally hailing from Norris Green, and my mum Norma from Fazakerley, before they got married and moved to Manchester when Dad joined the force.

I was born Mark Berry in a hospital in Bolton on 18 April 1964. We lived in various places in Swinton, Walkden and in the suburbs right on the edge of Salford, which was its own city back then, before it was incorporated into Greater Manchester. We'd be in police houses, which they used to have back in the day to accommodate the constabulary – you got the job and they gave you accommodation. They were just like corporation houses, or council houses, but specifically for the force. I was only a kid, so I'm not too sure what the deal was, but I think you still had to pay rent, as with a council house.

By no means were we rich, but we weren't poor either. My dad had worked from a very young age; at fifteen, he was jumping from ship to ship in Liverpool Docks delivering telegrams. With the police, he drew a good working-class wage, and no more, while Mum brought in extra income via various jobs as a telephone operator and an auxiliary nurse. In my upbringing, I certainly wasn't deprived in any way. We always had food on the table. My sister Michaela and I got clothes bought for us and we'd go on family holidays, mostly camping in England or Scotland. We had a good level of living, and we never went without. We were comfortable.

My dad and mum are still together to this day, thick as thieves, and they were bonded as strict, old-fashioned disciplinarians, each from that kind of background, and so that was how I was brought up. Their social conditioning during the war was very institutionalised. They had no understanding of contemporary culture, even less so today – anything modern was just alien to them. Mum just agreed with my dad, and she never questioned him. My dad was the man, and she was the woman, in a very traditional relationship.

In the 70s, Dad rose up the ranks to become a chief inspector in the anti-terrorist squad, and he was that typical hard-drinking policeman, right out of *Life on Mars*. As a copper, Dad obviously had a narrow view of the world, which soon conflicted with my own. He dealt with some of the worst elements of society, you could say, and that definitely coloured his outlook. My view was obviously a more happy-go-lucky type, without much care about things. I just got on with doing whatever I wanted to do, which was normally causing trouble. I understand now that part of my character from an early age, as young as I can remember, was about rebelling against this disciplinarian environment I was being brought up in.

Early on in life, I showed a thirst for adventure, a desire to escape. Very young, I got caught making off to visit my nan in Liverpool. One of the neighbours found me going up the East Lancs Road in my pedal car, because I knew that my nan and grandad lived up the far end of it. What I didn't realise was that it was thirty miles away. In my head, it was just down the road, and I was off for a visit in my pedal car!

Another time as a toddler, I was apparently hanging out of the upstairs window, shouting at everybody downstairs, and my dad had to sneak up from behind and rescue me before I plunged onto the tarmac below. There would be more and more incidents of this nature, like the time we were playing in this croft with all these garages for the houses nearby. We used to walk over the roofs there quite regularly, jumping from garage to garage, only on this occasion I landed a bit too heavily on the window panel in one roof, went straight through and landed on this little sailing boat in the garage amid a shower of shattered glass.

Later on, in my teens, I would often stay with my grandparents when my parents couldn't cope with me. I always trace back my upstart inclination, my tendency towards outright rebellion, to a couple of events which occurred at the ripe age of five.

One of these formative experiences came just a couple of days after I'd started at St Peter's C of E Primary School in Swinton. My mum had given me some money for a snack at break time, and she'd told me to buy a packet of crisps with it. When break time came, buzzing with excitement about this rite of passage towards independence and self-determination (via Mum), I picked out a packet of crisps and handed over the money, but then the teacher in charge tried taking the crisps back off me.

'Listen,' I said, snatching it back, 'me mam told me to buy crisps with this money and nothing else.'

'Yes, but you don't have enough money for a bag of crisps,' the female teacher tried to explain, and showed me all this other shit I could have for that amount - puffy cheese balls and what have you.

'No,' I doggedly replied, 'Mam said I've got to buy crisps with this money and nothing else.'

Outside the tuck shop, the queue was building up with hungry little pupils, and the teacher in charge told me I had to choose something else, and again she tried taking the crisps out of my hand.

That was it, the red mist came down. I'd been told I was having crisps and I'd settle for nothing less, so I just sank my teeth right into her hand and bit her as hard as I could to stop her taking my packet of Golden Wonder.

The teacher ran out of the shop screaming, and all the other kids came swarming around, telling me that I was properly for it. They were all saying I was going to get the cane, but I had no idea at all what that was. I thought I was going to get put in a cage made of bamboo, and have fruit and veg thrown at me. That's how young I was!

I actually ended up not getting into big trouble on this occasion. A letter got sent home to my parents, and to my surprise that was pretty much it, but this incident was already almost the beginning of the end of my schooling. The die was cast, the precedent was set, and from that moment on it seemed to be my calling to be constantly in trouble with school and any form of authority. All of my schooling life was dogged with trouble of one kind or another, until I left school, as soon as I was allowed, aged sixteen.

Growing up in the 1970s, around our way there was still that educational regime where we got thrashed every day, and that became normal to us. Sometimes the teacher would pick you up by the ear and give you the board duster, beating you with it in front of the whole class, and that was *normal*, you know what I mean?

What I can categorically say is that this institutional violence had no positive effect on your discipline whatsoever. The threat of being brutally thrashed didn't stop you, and sometimes it was even a badge of honour, to go and get the cane or the pump or whatever they were using that day. You didn't bat an eyelid to it. Like, 'Ha, so what?'

What I did learn through it is that violence is not a good way to gain what you want. You can try and rule by fear, and it does work with some people, obviously - fear can be a great way to get control over people - but when the target individual is already in full-blown rebellion against the authority that's trying to beat the fear of God into them and make them do as they're told, and they're just not having it - then, it really doesn't work. That's how it was with me. I grew up towards the end of the era where thrashing kids was the norm, I took a lot of thrashings, and it didn't bother me whatsoever. I still had the capability to cause chaos in the classroom. I was a problem child, and they couldn't bully me.

The irony was that, while I was constantly in trouble, I was well liked too, because I always had a nice smile, and was always well mannered and polite. The teachers struggled with me because, as well as being unruly, I was a pleasant kid. I had these moments when I was totally out of control, but

I was always very nice with it! It's a thing I still appreciate today, someone with good manners, and I always drummed that into my own kids, to be well mannered and decent to others.

In this atmosphere of mischief and retribution, though, my education just never got off the ground. I spent a lot of time wagging. Bunking off and roaming the neighbourhood was good for my social life, and for copping off with girls once I got into my teens, but clearly it had a negative impact on my academic progress.

I did enjoy some subjects. I used to enjoy geography and science, but I was shit at maths and English. I've always been a terrible speller. I've just never been able to do it, and I couldn't write my own name until I was seven. I was over the moon when I first managed to do it. In class, I would try to avoid writing anything down, and it got to a point where I used to pretend to write, but I wasn't actually writing words, just scribbling nonsense across the page. When the teacher came around and looked over, it looked like I was writing, but I hadn't actually written anything but doodles that I'd shaped to look like writing. Somehow, I got away with it, and I don't think I ever actually got challenged for it.

My sister Michaela, by contrast, who was eighteen months younger than me, started to do really well at school. I loved my sister, she was great. She only ever told on me once, when I bought us a load of sweets with a few pennies I'd scrounged and we couldn't eat our tea at home. She never told on me again because she saw the consequences of it with Dad's punishment, so we were always friends after that.

In our family, every now and again, we throw up this highly intelligent being, and that was very much the case with

Michaela, because she went on to study at Oxford University and become a City lawyer renowned within her field.

But then you get people like myself! You know them kids you read about who are nightmares? I think that was me. Before they had labels for such children, I was just a nightmare. But I loved my sister.

Salford in the early 70s felt old-fashioned even at the time. We were still a nation of shopkeepers back then, and all the shops were like an extension of the front room. You had your paper shops, your butcher, your baker - a shop for everything, and all of them used to be bustling with customers.

Though school was hardly enjoyable, I always think of my early years as good times, getting up to all sorts of adventures. Growing up, we were never indoors. We were always outside. We didn't have computer games back then, we used to go everywhere collecting eggs, building dens, and going to Woolworths to shoplift all the stuff to put in them. The summer of 1976 was really hot, of course, so I was out all the time playing football and other games.

Up to when I was about fourteen or fifteen, I used to go to Middlewood Scout Camp in Walkden, with a group called 5th Worsley. It wasn't far from where I was living, on the borders of Salford and Bolton, kind of Boothstown way. I would go out for weekends there in the woodlands with a few of my mates, and that's where I learned all my camping techniques - some good life skills that have come in handy in later life, like putting together a proper campfire. I loved camping out, smoking cigs and getting up to the usual mischief as a teenager.

Otherwise outside the classroom, I used to play for the local youth club football team, and on Fridays we'd go to the local youth disco at Turners, which was this little hut at the top of our road. That was where I first danced to punk and New Wave records. In the daytimes, I used to ride skateboards and bicycles. All I ever wanted was a new bike. I never got bought anything extravagant as a kid, so I used to have to make my own. In them days we used to go out foraging for stuff. A lot of us used to make our own bikes. We didn't just go and buy one from a shop, we all built our own. We'd go out and scavenge bike frames, and cobble together the other parts as best we could. Some of the bikes we used to make were death traps, to be sure, but we didn't grow up pampered, that's for certain.

I had to work for every penny I ever saw. I used to have to wash my dad's car, change the tyres around on the wheels, do paper rounds - all these jobs - for pocket money. The first bike I ever bought, a racer, cost me £35 second-hand, and I had to pay it off at a pound a week after I'd earned that sum doing my paper round. It had big cowhorn handlebars, little short mudguards, and only a back brake, not a front one. I rubbed it all down, sprayed it with paint, got the Brasso out, polished up my wheels. I was proud of it, and I'd paid for it all myself.

We'd ride motorbikes down at the slag heaps, because there was a lot of coal mining around us. The bikes weren't our own, because you could always find stolen motorbikes in the bushes, where people had hidden them to go back and ride them another time. We'd go searching in the undergrowth, find a dumped motorbike and race around the slagheaps for the afternoon. Everything was robbed. There was a big culture of theft. Not everybody was actually doing it, but it was a big thing, a lifestyle of shoplifting and robbing all around you.

The first time I've ever done a burglary, I was about seven or eight. A mate and I went into the school next door, Christ the King's, and we nicked all the chalks and a few footballs. We found loads of 50p pieces in the nuns' office, and the kid who I was with made me put it back because that was proper stealing, so I had to go back on my own later to get the money! That was my first breaking-and-entering type job, and the mad thing was, the school was right next to Mum and Dad's house, and that same afternoon I was right outside on the pavement, drawing stuff on the tarmac with the chalks I had just got back from thieving next door. We weren't very clever with it.

I was never good at anything in the classroom. I wished I was. I always admired people who're good at shit. I've never been good at anything apart from getting out there and enjoying myself. That was my thing, and my behaviour definitely got worse once I got to secondary school, at Wardley High in Swinton. I arrived there in the mid-70s when it was in transition from a grammar school to a comprehensive, and our year's influx of pupils was one of the first under the new system. We hadn't had to pass the eleven-plus exams to get in there, and we were also the worst they'd ever known for behaviour. They got us lot in and they never knew what hit them or how to deal with us.

Today, I think I could've been good in English, but unfortunately I gave up on that after a story I put together for creative writing landed me in deep water. They get you to write these stories at school to get into your psychology and see what you're up to, and what's going on in your head. Obviously, I wrote a story based around my reality – a fictional story based around some kind of truth going on in my life. It was all about going out and having gang fights, street battles with kids from the next school along – this degenerate teenage gang culture that I was just starting to get involved in. My dad read this essay I'd written, and that was it, I had given away all my secrets. It got me into so much trouble, I swore I was never going to write another story again. I stopped writing because I didn't want them to have a window into my mind.

When you get into a gang, it doesn't really feel like a gang as such. It's just a group of friends from an area having a fight with another group of friends from another area. More often than not, you knew everybody you were fighting with. It's the wrong word to use, gangs. It's just certain areas against other areas, territorial, not a gang as such. We would fire rockets at each other, throw fireworks - set up all our rockets and shoot them across at the other lot, trying to blast them to pieces. We used to get a really good armoury up and have really good fun doing it.

People used to get hurt, but then one time, a lad got stabbed quite badly after a big stand-off in a shopping precinct and that brought it to an end. The incident actually made the daily papers, it was that bad. It had got huge, the stakes kept getting higher, until it was totally out of control. That's when you started hearing about knives coming into it - people carrying blades and other weapons. I never did carry a knife, because if you carry a knife, at some point or another you're going to end up using it. I knew a lot of people who did carry them, though. Some of them still do, and they're my age, in their fifties! Now, it's escalated to the point where you've got a gun culture as well, kids running around with shooters on top of it all. It has become something else.

Back then, I guess you'd have probably called me a problem child. I was always the problem, everywhere I went. If I'd behaved that way nowadays, I probably would've got diagnosed with one of the D's that they have knocking about, like ADHD, dyslexia . . . and what's the other one? Is it LSD? Ha!

I know that Shaun Ryder went out and got himself tested, and he found out that he's got all these fucking things. A lot of adults in our generation have discovered in later life that they've had these problems going on, which kind of explains some of their conduct in their youth. I'm not interested in knowing, because I'm not looking for an excuse for it, and it wouldn't make a fucking iota of difference to my life, finding out. Back then they just thought you were nuts!

In that era around Manchester, it seemed like there were a lot of unruly kids. From my reading later on, I believe it could possibly have been vaccine damage - don't get me started on that one! But maybe that's one explanation for why our generation was so fucking mad! That's how I remember those early years - fucking bedlam.

By secondary school, I was involved in a lot of criminal activity. There are many kids who grow up in my sort of environment who don't resort to crime. Regardless of your background, it's a choice you make when you're young. You either do it or you don't. I did it because I thought it was easy money, I didn't have to work, and I could get what I wanted through that lifestyle, which turned out to be not a good decision.

But that was how we grew up, there was a lot of it about, and it was the path I took, which after a series of narrow escapes and probations, led to me getting locked up when I was about sixteen.

By that point, I was no longer living at home. As soon as I was old enough to be legally free of my mum and dad's responsibility, I was kicked out of the house. My criminal activity and general rebelliousness obviously caused problems. We didn't see eye to eye at all, but as you can imagine it wasn't easy coming from a strict disciplinarian background, and then you had me thrown into the mix, who as a child possibly had behavioural difficulties, or whatever label they might give me these days. My mum always thought there was something wrong with me!

I didn't have much contact with my family for quite a number of years, until later on in life. I broke contact with everyone for a while. I just didn't want to bother them with whatever I was up to. I thought it better to leave them out of it.

I'm glad to say that we're all over with that now, as a family. The nice thing for me is that, in my adult years, my dad has apologised to me, saying that he never understood me as a young man growing up, as a teenager, as *me*. He said he didn't understand my character back then, and the person I was, so that was a good moment. He actually apologised, and that I will take, and appreciate. I never spoke much about him in the other book, because some things are best left personal. We've gone through highs and lows, like all families, but suffice to say that I get on really well with my old fella now. We've got a totally different relationship.

Getting kicked out of home was the making of me. I'm glad it happened because from then on I had to stand on my own two feet and take care of myself in my own haphazard way, and I went on my own journey. I always survived, sometimes quite well - but in a funny way, not perfectly. I got into loads of trouble, I was a bit of a delinquent, but that was my path and I wouldn't have done it any other way.

After I left home, and once school was thankfully over at sixteen, I stayed for periods with both of my nans, in Liverpool and Wigan, but I soon wound up as a lodger with a mate's mum, Mrs McGuire. I eventually converted her garden shed into my own luxury den, with thick shag-pile carpet, and all the latest TVs and stereos. Girlfriends used to stop by and end up wanting to stay the weekend. It was ace!

My plan for getting upwardly mobile in my newfound independence was to turn over the clubhouse at Worsley golf course, which was a short hop down the disused railway line that ran on the other side of our garden fence. One night, me and an accomplice – who, unbeknown to me, had already made one failed B&E attempt at this property – broke in and pinched twenty golf bags stuffed full of Slazenger jumpers out of the club shop. I also trousered quite a bit of money out of there – a few grand.

For several weeks, I lived a life I'd always dreamed of, with cash to burn and personal freedom, but eventually someone must've grassed me up. The police came for me and found some of the missing jumpers in my room, and I got sent to a probation house in Eccles. After I did a runner from there and spent a few nightmarish weeks dodging the law, I finally got caught and sent down for six months at a detention centre in Stoke called Werrington House. It was the first time I ever made front-page news, with the headline: SHED DWELLER IN £6,000 RAID.

Up to the day I got locked up, I'd been going through a really bad spot: I was on the run, kipping under bushes, hiding out wherever I could. I was almost glad to get locked up because I was fucking starving. Sometimes the only thing I would manage to eat in a day would be a meat pie. Other times I'd literally go without. I used to lie there at night dreaming of food, but then, once I was inside, I had a bed for the night and three meals a day.

It's obviously not the best place in the world to be, but it also wasn't a punishment for me either. You get what they call the 'short sharp shock', all that boot-camp stuff of having to be spotlessly clean and tidy, but I didn't really get anything positive out of it. I certainly didn't come out of it feeling reformed. It didn't reform me in any way whatsoever. No authority reformed me. I eventually reformed myself. It didn't have any effect on my life apart from, you just don't want to go back there if you can help it.

There's this perennial cycle of people reoffending and going back to jail: I've read that 75 per cent of inmates reoffend – so that's only two or three out of every ten who never go back. Nowadays you've got three- or four-generation families who know nothing else. As a deterrent to crime, it really doesn't work.

The way we do things at the moment, the whole engineering of society needs to change, and that's how you prevent crime. It's easy to do, it could be done, but the fact is that nobody wants to solve the problem. They don't want everybody to be successful, do they? They want to build more prisons the size of small towns – super-prisons, they're calling them, like giant sausage factories – which are a lucrative privatised industry in themselves.

The alternative to prison, and the way to start really changing things, is to make sure that people don't go down that path in the first place. If you made everyone a worthwhile member of society, then you wouldn't have people committing crime – at least not in such huge numbers. You start from the beginning and change the whole way you do things in this world: you end the whole system of money and hierarchy so everyone can contribute. With no money involved, there would just be manpower, and that'd be the only resource that would cost anything. This has always been the thing I've spent my days fantasising about.

After my own release, it was literally only a couple of weeks before another botched job saw me put on remand for ten weeks in Strangeways, in the young offenders' side of the prison, pending my court hearing coming up. All I can say about Strangeways is, it was a very sad place that I don't care to remember too much. Many of the young people in there have got a lot of issues, and there's a lot of violence involved. Many aren't coping well in the situation they've put themselves in. There's a lot of self-harm – there was always somebody setting themselves on fire in the cells. It was a crazy place. These days, apparently, they have it all sectioned off, one part for the gang bangers, another part for a different group, etc., so it's probably a different place from what it was forty years ago, but it's a place that you wouldn't want – or at least I wouldn't want – to revisit.

After an agonising wait in that madhouse, I was eventually sent down for another stretch at Hindley, a closed borstal in Wigan. That was just like Ray Winstone in *Scum*: 'Who's the fuckin' daddy? *I'm* the fuckin' daddy!' Again, this establishment was extremely violent. There were a lot of troubled kids, all fighting for position. I've seen many terrible things going down in there, but you just get your head down, and get on with it, and for me it wasn't a problem. I couldn't say that I enjoyed being locked up, but I didn't have an awful stay in that one. I made good friends, and I got on with doing the time. The only thing about it was, you got locked up in a cell at the end of the day, and you couldn't go out at night.

It wasn't too boring either, because you were kept busy doing stuff throughout the day, and I had a little radio to listen to at night. Also, I was a reader, and a prolific one, which maybe not many people know about me. It's one of my favourite methods of escapism, particularly in periods of my life when I'm not experiencing the best of times. If I'm down or suffering moments of low energy, I'll get lost in a book, and take on someone else's reality for a bit.

All the useless information I have at my disposal has been gleaned through all the pointless reading I do. The funny thing is, I'm a prolific reader, but I still can't spell for toffee, which is weird. Sometimes I go through months of just reading. I kind of enjoy it, but I've read that it might not be a good thing for me to overindulge in, for who I am as an Aries.

It's normally a bad sign if I find myself stuck in a book, because something has usually gone wrong somewhere. I hate using the word 'depression', because it's bandied about too much and often misapplied. It's a clinical term that people use too lightly, so I would say it's more that I'm going through one of my lower vibrations, and literature is my escape.

When I was in prison, I read maybe three or four books a week. Back then, I think Harold Robbins was my favourite, because you got some sexual adventure in there.

Another book that had a massive influence on my life around that time was *Ringolevio* by Emmett Grogan. It's kind of the author's life story, and I think it's the best cultural book you'll ever read. Like myself, he was always in trouble as a kid, taking drugs, doing robberies and other misdemeanours, but he went on to become part of the San Francisco Diggers, a group of radical activists around the time of Flower Power. He had this thing called the free frame of reference: he actually built a big frame, and everything in it was free, so he was giving out free food, clothes and information to people in the community.

Reading about all the stuff he got up to totally changed my life. That guy became my hero, and I set out to live my life like he did. I suppose I tried to emulate his life, but not exactly. In the end he overdosed on a subway train when he was only in his mid-thirties, so I never wanted to emulate that part.

When I got out of Hindley, I started getting involved in drug-taking, and I had a thing about injecting – anything, really, mostly speed. I had no money and I was tempted to resort back to criminality, but I was trying not to do that sort of thing, so I would spend weeks reading and coming down, rather than going out robbing. It was a choice I made: I could either go out thieving, breaking-and-entering and all sorts of bad shit, or I could get my fucking head down with a book and read my way out of it. I used books in moments like that, and I reckon that was a good decision.

Music was always important for me, and I loved the whole journey of discovery that you go on, finding your way through different artists and genres. The first record collection I got was an inherited one, aged seven. When stereos came out in the late 1960s, my Uncle George decided to upgrade, and he passed on to me his old mono record player, which was like a suitcase where you lifted the lid up and there was a turntable inside. To go with it, he also gifted me his old mono records, which was basically all the classic 60s music – a huge cache of seven-inch singles and a couple of albums, including a mono original of *Sgt. Pepper*, 'Pinball Wizard' on 45, all the Who tunes, and loads of Merseybeat stuff.

I used to spend hours sat in my bedroom religiously going through all these records, stacking up the singles so they'd each drop down onto the deck and blare out of the built-in speaker underneath. There was a Buddy Holly compilation, too - that one I particularly fell in love with. It was such a great present so early on in life.

Pretty young I discovered ska, and then Bob Marley, and all the reggae music, and then when I was about thirteen my mate's brother introduced me to punk music, which suddenly alerted me to the fact that there was a punk explosion going on. This kid was quite a few years older and he looked cool as fuck. I got talking to him, and he was telling me about all the different punk groups. I actually borrowed my first ever punk record off him - I'm pretty sure it was the single of 'Anarchy in the U.K.' by the Sex Pistols.

By the time I got to secondary school, everyone used to be in Smokers' Corner playing their seven-inches on little portable record players - battery-powered Dansettes with one speaker, with the little Perspex lid that you'd lift up. We'd sit there puffing away, listening to all the latest New Wave and punk. It was a great era to grow up in, because ska and northern soul were both massive in our teens as well - you grew up in that culture in the North-west, and we'd hear it all at the youth-club discos at Pembroke Hall Market in Walkden. This was more for your mid to late teens and was the next step up from Turners on our road. Every club used to have its own northern room - and then you had the ones into all the metal.

Musically we had the best choices, and it used to be such a massive part of youth culture back then. You'd go into other people's bedrooms and listen to their record collections, while scoring your red Leb, which was the main type of hash that you could buy where we were. It came from the Lebanon in these little red-brown sticks, hence the name. We'd also go up to Moss Side on the bus to buy pound wraps of weed, or a piece of Lebanese. Travelling about scoring, you got into that bedroom culture where you were all sitting about getting stoned listening to records. You'd be discovering music through getting stoned and getting vibed up on what your mates were listening to.

I've been smoking weed from when I was in my early teens. When I was in borstal, I was one of the few people who was getting weed brought in, by my mates. There were a few kids from Moss Side who'd obviously got some weed lined up, but I was the only one with hash in the whole jail.

Back then in the early 1980s, there were smokers around, but it wasn't a massive cultural thing like it is now. A lot of people I knew back then used to frown upon it. I started growing weed as well - I was one of the first home-growers! I didn't know anybody else who was doing it, apart from a good friend of mine who I grew up with. We had this book, *The Great Books of Hashish*, about all the hashes of the world. It's the daddy of books about marijuana. I'd love to get it back again, that book, but, at the time of writing, there's only one copy on Amazon for £250!

The fella who wrote it, Laurence Cherniak, was a fucking innovator, a man who loved his hash, and he travelled the world to all these sources of the best hash known to mankind. Me and my mate used to flick through the pages and learn about all the different types and tastes, looking at pictures of these great bits of hash. Your red Lebanese, your Moroccan black. That was our dream: we wanted to go to the source of where the best hash originated. Temples, remote villages . . . It was all in this book, your guide to the world's hashish, telling you exactly where to go to find it. We wanted to be connoisseurs, and we loved the idea of smoking only the very finest hash in the world.

Alongside that journey of discovery, I went on the usual journey that everybody went on with music. I remember when I first heard The Velvet Underground's *White Light/ White Heat* album, that really blew my head off, and the first Velvet Underground album with the banana on the front, which was an out-and-out drug album. You couldn't believe that anyone was actually making that sort of music, at the same time as we were having the Beatles explosion with *Sgt. Pepper*, which was going on over the pond. You know, in the early 60s we had 'Love Me Do' and 'I Wanna Hold Your Hand', and then a couple of years down the line you had this lot completely off their heads. I couldn't believe it!

On a different tip again, all my friends used to go up to the Wigan Casino - we've always had that dance culture in Manchester, and it ended up influencing a lot of the bands later on. I first went in the Casino with this other kid; we were thirteen-year-olds, really young, whizzing our tits off on chalkies - they were amphetamines, like slimming tablets, three for a pound. When you took a load of them, you'd have all this chalk hanging around the side of your mouth like a big white chalky foam, which got worse as the evening wore on. We were selling them, decked out in our Wranglers - we didn't even have the northern soul gear on! We used to get black bombers an' all, two quid each. Those were the days! After that, we got into amphetamine in a big way. Speed was a huge part of the culture, because it was the cheapest drug. It wasn't like today where everyone sniffs coke. Everyone was on factory-made amphetamine.

When we were growing up, there were a lot of different looks going about - the northern soul look, mod, rude boy, all these different looks going down - and the one you chose sort of distinguished you with a certain identity. But me, I enjoyed all music. At the local disco, there would be the northern room, and then you'd have the rock one, playing Led Zeppelin and *2112* by Rush for the greasers who loved all that shit, but I used to spend time in both rooms, because I loved all of it.

Talking about all this now, it makes me really sad, because I've lost so many record collections over the years. You didn't think about it at the time, did you, that it might be worth something to you in the future - either financially or emotionally? Loads of them I just gave away. I gave all my punk vinyl to a cousin - a huge collection of seven-inch singles, gone forever, because I'd moved back into ska, around the time of 2 Tone.

One of the first bands I saw was The Specials at Salford University, just after they'd released their first album, which was pretty crazy. My very first gig was the Salford Jets, a local punk band fronted by Mike Sweeney, a Piccadilly Radio presenter who used to play around the local pubs. They weren't massive, but they had records out, like, 'Gina, by Christ you should have seen her . . . in a Cortina . . . walking around down town, looking at the squares'.

In a way, though, my musical journey kept going on hold because I was locked up a lot. I never saw Joy Division, for instance, which I probably would have, because they were obviously the big new band in Manchester at that time. Still, in borstal and detention centres, we all used to have our little portable transistor radios on at night in our cells, and everyone used to be dancing in their cell window, busting moves on a Friday night, pretending we were out on the town.

Back then, actually being in a band myself wasn't ever something I imagined doing, apart from when you used to pretend to play along on a tennis racket in your mate's bedrooms.

That was about as far as it got with me. One year, when I was five or six, I got a guitar for Christmas, and I picked up this guitar, and I ended up smashing it up on the first day because I couldn't get anything out of it - pure frustration.

I didn't have a very musically orientated family. Nobody in the house played an instrument. Dad was into fucking Elkie Brooks, all that type of shit singer-songwriter music, so that's just the way it was.

After Mum and Dad kicked me out, I'd literally lived homeless between the ages of sixteen and twenty-two - six years, a long time. After all that, I had nowhere to live, and I seemed to be on this irreversible path of criminality. I was always in and out of trouble, doing time in detention centres, borstals, halfway houses, living on the streets, sleeping under bushes, sofa surfing - all the usual young offender's locations.

How I coped with homelessness on the mental-health level was, I always believed that there was something amazing around the next corner. That's how *I* kept going, how I dealt with it - and there usually was. I don't know about other people's psychology, what works for them. I didn't feel like I had to look after my mental health or anything like that. I didn't think of it that way. I still always got on with enjoying myself, and going out.

I didn't ever think to myself I was hard done by. Sometimes, when I was starving, like dreaming of eating a meat pie when I didn't have a penny to my name, I would have those rough moments. But I always knew and believed that something better lay ahead. I never hung about waiting for it. I was always out being active. I tried getting work, doing odd jobs and carrying on as normally as I could - it was just that I was homeless.

We didn't have things that you have these days like Coffee4Craig, the homeless charity that I'm now a patron for. That would've been amazing for me when I was a kid, because I could've gone in and got food, got showered, got clothing, got clean and got help - maybe even got rehoused - but because I was always such a kid in my head, I never had that capability to sort that bit out for myself. It took me ages to figure out that side of life.

I was just always looking for that thing that was going to change my life forever. I simply kept on believing. And sure enough, something good would happen, just as I'd hoped.

When I got out of jail, all I knew was, I just didn't want any more of that incarceration for myself. I didn't want to fall back into that old criminal lifestyle again, stuck with the same people, doing the same things, ending up in and out of prison for the rest of my life - so I decided to do something about it.

After I came out of Strangeways and Hindley, I went off travelling, and at that point I had never even left the country before. I'd heard of people who had gone off travelling, from the lads, kind of thing, so that was what I decided I was going to do as soon as I got free. I wanted my freedom, I wanted to get out of town because I knew that the world was a bigger place than the view I had of it at the time.

The previous summer, one of my mates had been out to the town of Kavos in Corfu, working by day painting and decorating holiday apartments, and partying by night, which sounded more than alright by me in my precarious state.

Within a matter of days of my lightning decision, I'd got a passport together, and paid £39 for a one-way ticket to Corfu with Magic Bus, this cheapo transportation company that went into Europe. Suddenly me and a couple of mates were off, all with next to no plan, and no money - I actually left the country with a £50 Giro and little else to my name. These days I wouldn't dream of undertaking what I did and going where I went without a penny. The mere thought of it is really daunting to me now, but when you're that young, you just do it, don't you?

The other two didn't last very long, because they could only eat English food, like egg and chips, and when you're on the move and starving, I quickly learned that you have to eat local food and engage with the culture, or else you're not going to survive. They didn't cope very well with that, so after Corfu I ended up travelling on my own, because I didn't want to go home. It was a great way to travel, actually, because I'd meet up with girls, different people from all over England and Europe. I went with a French girl for a while, going all over to different places, with different people, and I loved it.

I suppose you could say that I've been on the road ever since, through the job I do. I've never stopped travelling. I always seem to be on the road to somewhere.

From Corfu, I tried to get into India via the Turkey-Iran border, but Iran was at war with Saddam Hussein's Iraq, so I went right down to Portugal and Spain, and over to Africa instead. I went absolutely everywhere! I did really well with the girls, it was kind of mad. In France I ended up with two ballerinas. I got one of them in trouble driving about in Porsches. We had a huge adventure that could never have happened if I'd have sat on my arse where I grew up.

In Torremolinos, I had a top-quality smoke with this kid from northern Morocco. He started telling me about how his family actually grew the shit we were zoning out on, and that if I liked it that much I should go and visit them. Thus it was that I ended up on my own, totally penniless, shuttling all the way down to a *pension* in Tétouan, a few miles south of the Strait of Gibraltar. I was now a good way off the tourist trail, and my welcome spliff rated as easily the strongest dope I'd ever puffed at that stage.

As the kid had told me, from this humble B&B his family ran a little ganja export business. It took a good couple of weeks of me dropping subtle hints that I'd love to see where they grew their crops, before eventually they took me under their wing and drove me out there. It was like your dream come true - heaven on earth! Suddenly we were riding through gigantic fields of ganja, smoking pure kif pipes, and in the end they trusted me enough to get me helping some Dutch fellas load up their little rowing boats full of hash, to ship out to Europe.

After some weeks in my idea of paradise, I decided I was ready to go home again. Still completely without cash, I hung around for a few days in the harbour area, and I'm not proud to say I was robbing off the Moroccans while I waited for Nan and Grandad Berry to send me money for my return fare to Blighty. The police and general public in this town could see what I was up to, unwashed and prowling around, and they weren't happy with me, chasing me all through the streets, which was quite frightening. You don't want to end up in a Moroccan jail, so I scarpered and lived in a cave for a while, out of cash and starving, while I waited for that life-saving letter from my grandparents to get me out of there.

But of course, it was an amazing adventure that I really loved and never for a second regretted. I saw so many incredible things, and perhaps the greatest thing about it was returning home and seeing how absolutely nothing had changed. It was like everyone back here was sat in some weird time-warp. Nothing had gone on in their lives, only the same old shit. I had been on this mad odyssey, just because I was feeling the itch because I'd never been abroad before. I'd seen a huge chunk of continents that I've never known about, been with girls from right around Europe, seen magical fields of green in Morocco, then I got back six months later, and everyone was still sat in exactly the same place in the pub that I'd left them in.

My prospects back in Manchester, however, were not good. I came home with a load of hash, and a few bits and bobs of hash oil, but again I was as skint as fuck, and almost immediately I fell into the old routine of crime – the only way I knew how to make money. I didn't do anything normal, chiefly because I was that young and I had nobody to guide me in how to do the sensible stuff.

Through criminal channels, though, things quickly started looking up when I bagged quite a bit of money from doing a snatch. I got put onto this opportunity by some people who at the end of each week carried money to the bank for a Manchester business, and I ended up robbing a week's takings.

With that filthy lucre, I managed to get myself together to rent my first ever flat, a little bedsit place on Half Edge Lane in Eccles, and buy all these top new clothes. All of a sudden I was living the life of a well-dressed delinquent, and it was during this spending spree that the meeting happened that would change my life forever.

Everyone was telling me about this kid, Shaun, and that us two had to get together, and that when we did we'd be a force to be reckoned with. It turned out that people had been telling Shaun the same thing, that they could see the potential of some sort of madness going off between us.

The funny thing was, I know it sounds mad, but while I was in the mountain cave in Morocco, I was having weird visions, because I'd drunk some contaminated water, I think, and it had sent me into a fever. In my delirious dream state, I was hearing this music, and everyone was in their doorways dancing, and it was like they were dancing *my* dance, how I like to move.

This dream of the whole nation dancing like me.

And then it actually happened.

Chapter 2

HAPPY DAYS!

The brothers Ryder swerved into the pub car park in younger bro Paul's canary-yellow Ford Escort, affectionately known to everyone as the Egg. In the passenger side, Shaun William Ryder sat grinning with an enormous spliff, before bounding out to shake hands and lead the charge into the boozer, where a long afternoon's drinking ensued to celebrate receipt of the first copies of Shaun's debut single as leader of the Happy Mondays - called 'Delightful', and released that very day on Tony Wilson's Factory Records.

From that first sighting, I thought Shaun was a really cool dude. The people who'd been saying we had to meet each other were saying it for a reason, because we had an instant liking for each other, and everything they'd imagined came to fruition as we became really close mates really quickly.

I can see now that we have complementary personalities. He's a Leo and I'm an Aries, which makes us natural bedfellows for friendship (apparently). A Leo is someone who craves to be the centre of attention, which is why a lot of Leos become singers onstage. I've got a Leo dog, and it's unbelievable the pains that he'll go through to make sure he's the centre of attention over my other dog. He'll go to extraordinary lengths - and he's a dog and doesn't know anything about astrology. Me, I'm as daft as a ram, and for whatever reasons, those two personalities just seem to fit together quite well.

Meeting Shaun was the pivotal moment in my life, because literally overnight it completely changed from then on, and I was hanging out with Shaun and Paul's band the whole time.

I soon learned that I already knew all the other three members of Happy Mondays from school at Wardley High. Mark Day, the guitarist, was a year or two above me, and Gaz Whelan, their drummer, and keyboard player Paul Davis were in the year below. We'd never hung out, any of us, but we all knew who each other was. Everybody knows each other at school, don't they, and I was pretty renowned in our school anyway for being the troublemaking type. Our year was legendary for the carnage we caused around the place: flooding toilets, terrorising teachers in lessons, and having pitched battles with rival schools. Gaz and Paul's year, the next intake, was almost as bad as us, but not quite, and as such they used to look up to our year. We led by example, our lot, in how to be completely degenerate.

Shaun, who was a year or two older than me, and Paul, who's just a week younger, both went to the Roman Catholic school down the road, St George's. Even though we had mutual friends, somehow we kept missing each other over the years, but me and Shaun soon made up for lost time, every few days tucking into a batch of lively black microdots. On one psychedelic-tinged bender, I was hustled through the entrance into Factory's postmodernist designer nightspot, the Hacienda, tripping my nuts off, with Shaun assuring the bouncers, 'He's not drunk . . . he's in our band!'

It's hard to know how much time elapsed in between, but on 27 October 1985 I saw the Happy Mondays play a gig for the first time at Corbieres, a cavern-themed downstairs wine bar on Half Moon Street, and I was totally, utterly blown away.

They'd got this groove, and everyone in the place - maybe 150 friends and family - was going apeshit. I'd just come back from travelling, I'd been in and out of prison, and here they were living this rock 'n' roll life in a band, pursuing their own dream. It was everybody's idea of a perfect existence either to be a footballer or a musician. That was what you clung on to as a kid, so it was really impressive to me that people I knew were actually in a band. Three of them even went to my school, and now they had a record out, and were playing gigs where everyone danced and lost their shit.

I, meanwhile, was still trying to sort my life out, and until that fateful day meeting Shaun I'd been slipping back into my old thieving ways.

One of those first nights on the tiles, however, Shaun said to me, 'We can do anything we want, Bez!' It was like he was opening the doors for me, and just telling me to go on through.

I didn't have an eye on being in a band at all - theirs, or anyone else's. I was just like a friend, supporting my mates. When I became a member, it was a pure case of right place, right time. There was no cunning plan - it could never have worked that way. It just happened out of the blue. That's what makes me smile about it all these years later, because I had no conception of ever landing up on that path, because musically I was no good whatsoever. It was the last thing I'd ever have thought of as a career goal.

It'd been another few months of us knocking about together when the Mondays were lined up to play at the Hacienda supporting New Order, who were being filmed by Channel 4's live music show, *The Tube*. Unfortunately, their cameras weren't rolling for this historic set in Happy Mondays folklore so there's no point searching on YouTube. New Order, going back to their early days with Ian Curtis as Joy Division, was a massive band for us in Manchester, and I couldn't believe I was getting in free to see them play, with my mates opening for them. Extra supplies, above and beyond the usual, were obviously required.

Throughout that afternoon, I was out on the town, and I managed to score a hundred white microdots and a hundred black microdots, and by early evening when I arrived at the pub across the road from the Hacienda, the City, I'd already necked one tab. By the time we went over for the Mondays' set, I'm pretty sure Shaun and I had both dropped a white one and a black one each - a bit of yin and yang going on - and we were completely flying off our nuts.

On arrival backstage - my first time ever in a proper dressing room, with lightbulbs around the mirrors, and all the trimmings - Shaun was on the ropes, and feeling like he needed a bit of moral support.

'You've got to come up onstage with me, Bez!' he goes, to everyone's merriment.

'Fuck off, are you fucking mad?'

The banter between us went on for a few minutes, but the time was fast approaching when the band was due onstage.

'I can't go on, I'm that off my head,' goes Shaun. 'You're gonna *have* to come on with us!'

He knew that I was in the same frame of mind as he was, and after a bit more to-ing and fro-ing between us, with me being called a soft cunt if I didn't go on, I finally agreed to do it. Just as I was going on, I grabbed a pair of maracas that were lying around, jumped up there and started shaking them about, and danced right through the whole gig, in my own particular style of the moment. Throughout, Shaun was giving me a sidelong grin, with an evil glint in his eye.

And that set the tone for the next forty years. It was a complete life-changer, and no mistake, because I've never been offstage since that moment.

I don't know if there was always a performer in me, but there was always a blagger . . .

The buzz of my impromptu performance lasted for many hours of aftershow partying. When I got home, I had a blister in the middle of my hand the size of a 50p piece, from all the shakin'. Lying in bed, I couldn't stop laughing. I was still fucking penniless, just surviving on selling speed to my friends. Now I was on acid, and I had just been supporting New Order, our neighbourhood idols. I couldn't stop cackling, the madness of it all, and I laughed myself all the way to sleep.

The funny thing was, the next day, somebody said to Shaun, 'Oh, that was really nice of you, letting that kid with special needs come onstage with you' – which was me on acid, shaking me maracas!

From that night on, Tony Wilson was actually saying that I should join the band. I think I might've reminded him a bit of Ian Curtis, with the spasmic dancing, but it wasn't something that Tony and Shaun had discussed prior to that Hacienda gig, because Tony didn't know me from Adam till that moment. I'd been going to the Hacienda and getting in for nothing as a Happy Monday, but it wasn't in any way official.

The first time Tony mentioned it was when the Mondays were at Strawberry Studios recording a second single, 'Freaky Dancin'', with Bernard Sumner from New Order producing. I was always pretty starstruck back then. I'd met Bernard once or twice. The first time, he was coming around to pick up a bunch of us from my little flat in Eccles, and I had all these people hanging around, waiting to catch a glimpse of him before we all piled into his motor and went off to the Hacienda. Everyone was still massive Joy Division and New Order fans round our way in the mid-80s, so to have Bernard come and pick you up from your flat - fucking hell, that was a magic moment!

I'd never got to see Joy Division, because I was in jail when all that stuff was going on, including Ian Curtis's suicide. I'd missed a lot that went on in music when I was between the ages of sixteen and nineteen, because I spent so much time inside, so I had a lot of catching up to do when I came out.

It was funny that day at Strawberry, which was 10cc's place out in Stockport, because you wouldn't believe how hungry we all were - we were starving, and we spent a lot of time pining after food in them days. At the end of this break in the session, Bernard threw his Chinese takeaway in the bin, and we were all fighting to get his leftovers out of there.

At some point, Kevin Cummings, a local snapper for the *NME*, came down to take individual photos of each band member for the single sleeve, and then some group pictures for the press. Tony Wilson had come down to check out how recording was going, and while they were taking pictures in all the usual band poses, he told me to get in there and have my photograph taken with them, with my maracas, and that kind of clinched it that I was in the band. I also had my mugshot on the sleeve, like an equal contributor.

I was now officially a Happy Monday.

*

The great thing about me and Shaun all these years later is that his memory of things is totally different to mine. We can tell a story of the exact same occurrence, and we'll disagree right the way through it, over every detail and development. We have two completely different views of the same events, and if you put them together you get a perfect and fully formed version of, well, something verging on the truth. Maybe!

He likes to spin out stories, does Shaun. He loves to hold the stage, and you don't get a word in edgeways, so I'm going to let him in here to say how he saw the early days of our friendship, and my joining the Mondays . . .

SHAUN: How it all starts really is that Bez, Mark Day, Paul Davis and Gaz Whelan all went to the same school. Theirs was the right-foot school, they were all Protestant, Church of England, and me and our kid went to the left-foot Catholic school down the road. We all lived around the same-ish area, and I'd seen them knocking about since they were little kids. Bez I'd heard of, but I'd never actually met him, and I don't even think I'd seen him.

I started the band in 1982 when I was nineteen, and by about 1983/84, Bez had been away, and he was a bit down on his uppers, but we all were, and we all scored drugs in the same places.

My theory is that one of the reasons us lot all ended up together in the band, and as pals, was because if you tested every one of us, we'd all have some fucking condition or other. In later life now, I've been diagnosed with ADHD. Bez, he won't have it, but I know for a fact that he is ADHD'd up to fuck! He's like, 'I'm normal, X! I'm not like you with HDCBC!' But the thing is about people with

50

conditions: when you're too odd to mess around with other people, or you're a bit nutty and always causing trouble, you end up attracting each other. So I think that's what pulled us together as a band. We were all that trouble-making kind of kid that nobody understood yet, and who liked drugs and music.

In my flat at that point in 83/84, I'd stashed these little six-ounce Kashmir eggs. The hashish from Morocco came in these flat nine-ounce bars, but the hash from Kashmir came in six-ounce eggs – they looked like loads of rabbit shit stuck together in the shape of an Easter egg. So I was holding these eggs at mine with the guy who was the main 'head', and usually we'd cut ounces off them to sell. Of course, we didn't have mobiles in them days, so this guy calls me on the landline to tell me that he's bringing this character Bez around, to lay one of these six-ounce Kashmir eggs on him.

Now, at the back of my flat lived the head of the drug squad in Salford, but that made it a good place to be, right? It was really deep, know what I mean – no one's gonna think someone with fucking ounces and ounces of Kashmir eggs is going to be in the back yard of the head of the drug squad!

So I told the guy, 'I don't want you bringing that fucker round to my place, right?' because I already had an impression of Bez by then, from the rest of the band and what I'd heard around our area, and that was that he was too loud – not in a shouty way, just that he would attract unwanted attention.

You'd hear all these rumours about him, how he'd been away in Morocco. As far as I was concerned, this dude

Bez – that everybody knew around the area, who was a fighter and a robber and got locked up in Strangeways when he was sixteen, but was a good lad, and an 'ead, and one of the boys, and dead funny – he might blow my cover, because my place was getting a bit on top.

So I'm like, 'I don't want that fucker anywhere near my flat!' and then the guy turned up with him anyway! And from the very first moment, we got on like a house on fire.

Basically, after turning up at mine, Bez never went home – not even that night, because he ended up crashing with me. Even though it turned out that he'd got this place fixed in Eccles, very soon after that he ended up basically moving in, and we used to sort of use both places. Then he somehow lost the place in Eccles and he ended up staying at mine, so we were knocking around together all the time.

We got on because we've got a lot of things in common. Like, obviously, we was both into drugs, and we're both quite adventurous. Also, in the 70s and 80s, you couldn't be into all sorts of music. You either had to be a punk or a New Romantic or into heavy rock, glam-rock or soul – into Motown, a northern-souler. It was very regimented – you had to be something. I suppose a lot of people were too scared to say, well, I like Bowie, Roxy and Motown, at the same time as I like Showaddywaddy and The Sweet. It just didn't go. But we liked fucking Chas & Dave as well as fucking Brian Eno, and we didn't mind letting anybody know that.

How Bez ended up onstage, here's the truth! We were doing a lot of acid, and Happy Mondays did one of them 'battle of the bands' shows at the Hacienda. There were bands copying Madness, and bands copying Orange Juice, but there weren't many bands doing their own thing. We were all tripping our nuts off, and I says to him, 'Get onstage, come and dance!' How people now think of him dancing – when we used to go out to nightclubs, before we even went to the Hacienda, if he was dancing in the local nightclub, that was how he danced. You wouldn't even class it as dancing really, but he looked good, and he looked cool, and when we were doing the battle of the bands, I said, 'Get onstage!'

He kind of was onstage already, stood at the back, because he had been knocking about with us for a few months, coming to the various shitty little gigs we were doing. So then he came properly onstage, and he ended up with a pair of maracas in his hands, shaking away, and that was it. After that he was in the band, and the rest of the lads fucking hated it! They didn't like it, and I suppose it carried on like that, them not liking it, but he looked good, and also he was good with his mouth, and later on we ended up doing all the press, because none of the rest of them wanted to do it.

The first ever front cover we got, on *Melody Maker*, was me and Bez with our hoods up. We didn't know they were going to use that photograph, but in order to see ourselves in the papers, we had to go into the newsagents, who thought we were coming in to rob off them as usual, but we were actually going in because we knew we were on the front cover, and we could say, 'See this, fucker? That's who we are, you cunt!' So, we go in, we get *Melody Maker*, and we've got our hoods up so you couldn't even really tell it was us, and after that me and him ended up doing all of the press, because the rest of them – y'know, do you really wanna get Mark Day talking about what strings he uses? Or our kid talking about bass amps, trying to be all smart and clever? Whereas me and Bez would just talk bollocks, and just be ourselves.

I suppose it was a bit like Johnny Rotten getting Sid into the Sex Pistols, to have his mate in the band – a similar thing. We all started originally as mates. We all enjoyed music, and we were like a little gang, and I brought in Bez because he looked good. I knew that videos were becoming really important, and I knew that he would look good in ours. We didn't even call it dancing, it was just 'being Bez', and yeah, he was like my version of Sid.

Shaun's mum, Linda, who was a nursery nurse and a great cook, used to feed me fairly often. Sometimes she'd wash all my clothes, and they'd come back along with these butties she'd make – corned beef and tomato, still one of my favourite sandwiches to this day. One Christmas in those early days, she knew I was on my own in the flat in Eccles, so she sent Shaun over with some turkey dinner for me.

That flat was where we had the first acid parties, because everyone then in and around the Mondays was in the acid and amphetamine stage of life - the cheapest drugs around. I was still getting all these black microdots, and after a night at the Hacienda we'd all pile back to mine, where one of the features was a two-deck tape player. We found out that you could hit both play buttons and they'd both start to play at the same time.

One night, we had Penguin Cafe Orchestra on one deck and Frank Zappa on the other, neither of whom are exactly easy listening on their own. You'd think it would be nightmarish, but not when you're on acid, and every now and then there'd be a magic moment where they came together and made this fucking unbelievably perfect sound. If you were on microdots, the two together made sense and morphed into one beautiful, mind-blowing tune. It definitely brightened Frank Zappa up a bit, anyway.

After that, we started to get a bit more ambitious, with a drum machine going off at the same time – mad shit like that on acid, and then Horse, aka Paul Ryder, would plug his bass into this sound system we had, and play over the top. We were off our heads like that, *every* weekend, like we were living our own version of the rock 'n' roll dream.

After I first joined the band, I used to go down every day to the Boardwalk where we practised, and just sit in the room with a load of whizz while the others wrote and rehearsed. My contribution was the energy, both onstage and off.

Nobody ever came in and said, 'Hey, listen, I've got a song, here it is!' It never worked like that with us, it always came from live jams. Maybe Horse had a bassline he'd stolen from an old northern soul or funk record – he was a great borrower of people's basslines! Or maybe Mark Day would come up with a guitar riff, and everyone used to jam on that until a song emerged out of it, and Shaun would join in lyrically, and they'd created something. Sometimes it came out in five minutes, sometimes they might jam all day and get nothing. Every song was written like that, without any idea of where it was gonna go. Everyone just got together and worked it out. Forty years later we're still playing the songs, so we must've been doing something right.

We'd be in the Boardwalk all day and all night sometimes, watching a gig upstairs, or just rehearsing and knocking about if there was nothing on. We spent a lot of time down there. A Certain Ratio also had a space across the room from us, and The Jazz Defektors were in next door. All the Manchester bands used to rehearse there. It was a great place to socialise, play pool and cop off with the young groupies of the era. It was like a little community going on, and it all led to what became the Hacienda scene, when it finally took off in earnest.

At that stage in 84/85, the Hacienda was just like an arty gig venue, with a cool postmodern interior. Now I was part of the clique with Factory, I was getting into everything for free, seeing all of these amazing live bands there and in the process reconnecting with music after my enforced lay-off. One of my favourite gigs was Gil Scott-Heron, the jazzy black fella who did 'What's the word, Johannesburg'.

Arthur Lee was another memorable one. In Manchester, Love had a massive following, and he got blown away by the reception he got. He had the whole crowd singing, 'Arthur Lee, Arthur Lee!' He couldn't believe it.

In there and at the Boardwalk, we've seen countless great local bands, too, because Manchester was a real hotbed coming out of the post-punk days with New Order, The Smiths and The Fall. Everybody we knew was in a band. There were that many of them, it now suddenly felt like it wasn't actually anything special to be in one. It seemed like the whole of Manchester was getting signed to somebody or other.

You had bands like Stockholm Monsters, who were also signed to Factory, playing more like 60s-influenced post-punk indie-pop. From another point of view, though, they were very much like us - working-class Manchester lads grappling with making music, trying to live the dream. Either you wanted to be in a band or to be a footballer, that was your way out. In fact, we would actually play a lot of football against them and some of the other bands.

The great thing was, there was so much variety. The Jazz Defektors were another band who kind of fell between the cracks, but they were great. They were actually jazz, and they had dance routines. The drummer, Mikey Williams, was one of the best drummers I ever heard in my life. Even with a kit stripped right back to the basics – just a bass drum, a snare and a hi-hat – he played it like no other man. He almost literally made the drums sing.

There was a lot of very different music incubating in the Boardwalk. One thing I read said that what makes Manchester such a creative place is that there's a big powerful ley line which runs right through the city. I don't know if there's any truth in that, but I like to think that it contributed to our little slice of music history.

Our other hangout was Phil Saxe's place. Phil was the band's first manager, and the best manager we ever had, in my opinion. He was doing it for the love, Phil, and I really liked him a lot as a person. He loved his music and was a very funny guy. He'd take care of us: sometimes the only thing we'd eat for days was on a Sunday, when he'd turn up at the Boardwalk with salmon and cream-cheese bagels – a real Jewish thing. That was the first time I even knew what a bagel was.

Phil was useful for clothes, too! He had a jeans concession in the underground market at the Arndale Centre in the centre of Manchester, so we used to all go in there to get free clothes off him.

As young kids, we were all Perry Boys, a youth fashion culture that was regionally specific to the North-west – Liverpool and Manchester. We wore Kickers, Flickers, king cords, Lois jeans, Fred Perry shirts and even dungarees, all very specific to 1979 and the turn of the 80s.

For trainers in them days, we had to go to the underground market just across from Phil Saxe's place, where this kid had a telephone box-sized shop with no stock, just catalogues from Adidas and other brands. You skimmed through and ordered the pair you wanted, then you had to wait a couple of weeks for them to arrive from Germany. There weren't trainer shops like JD Sports nowadays where you just walk in and buy them. To get really cool trainers back then was a task, a real palaver. I got this great pair of Adidas XLs really early on from that kid and felt like I was one step ahead of the crowd.

But it was Phil Saxe who pretty much single-handedly started the flares revival that later became associated with acid house and 'Madchester'. He had all these flares left over from the early 70s, like old stock, and we started wearing them. Slowly but surely, they started getting wider and wider – we started off on semi-flares, but by the late 80s we'd moved on to the proper nine-inch-wide flappy hippie strides.

At the very beginning, he got the gig as manager because he was friends with Tony Wilson, and they all used to mither him for an 'in' with Factory. When the Mondays were scratching around for a record deal, the people at the various labels were saying they liked them, but they wanted to change the image to more of a cool, Velvet Underground look, with tight black pants, winkle-picker boots and leather jackets – kind of like Primal Scream were in 1985, that whole Creation Records thing. We didn't want that. We wanted to represent the boys, and the feeling that we *were* the boys and that's what we came from.

One of the main reasons we signed to Factory Records

apparently was because Tony Wilson could see what we actually were and what we represented. He saw the gap in the market, because there were no bands back then who were just like 'The Lads' - as in football terrace-style boys, and that's what we wanted to put over.

I think that's why it eventually got big. All our gigs were full of the lads who had grown up with the same things we had and saw us as what we were - just a drug-taking, one-of-the-boys, off-our-heads, up-for-the-party bunch of lads - maybe one of the first council-estate type bands. We often got asked to leave venues when we turned up, because they didn't believe we were actually the band. We didn't have that 'band' look about us. It always felt like there was an element of danger with us as well. We weren't exactly obeying the letter of the law - that sort of edgy, punky, hip-hop, street feel.

It was good camaraderie in the beginning. The only person who was a bit outside of it was Mark Day, because he was the guy trying to be sensible, but it didn't take too long for him to lose that capability and become fully rock 'n' roll like the rest of us.

The only friction in the band was between the Ryder brothers, not with anybody else. I very quickly learned not to get involved in a fight between Shaun and Paul, trying to break it up, because I tried it once and I nearly got my thumb bitten off. There are that many petty arguments between them, I've long since forgotten what it was about. It was Paul who sank his teeth into my opposable digit, thinking he was gnawing off Shaun's when actually it was mine. After that little altercation, I decided always just to leave them to settle it themselves.

For a short while, maybe six months, Shaun, Paul and I were sharing a flat in Boothstown. It was a second-floor apartment on a newish housing estate, like a starter flat for people buying onto the property ladder. It could be deemed quite posh, but it wasn't – London and Manchester ideas of posh are so different. It was pretty rotten, especially with the three of us in there, all off our heads. Sometimes the washing-up used to pile up that much that we'd have to soak the cups, plates and cutlery in the bathtub, to get all the dried-up food off them.

For me, after all my residential issues, it was a really special time living there. There were lots of girls passing through, and there was lots of abusive drug-taking behaviour going on, mostly amphetamine. So there were a lot of late nights and early mornings, with good music always spinning on the record player. There were seven-inch 45s like 'Rip It Up' by Orange Juice, and 'Papa's Got a Brand New Pigbag', which was a bit of a joke record for us, because we used to put it on every time Shaun's ex-wife came around. It was like her theme music – an inside joke on our part. We were also listening to a lot of disco twelve-inchers, like 'Juicy Fruit (Disco Freak)' by Isaac Hayes, and all the other floor-fillers of the day.

We partied hard there, with extra-lengthy hours, and I'm pretty sure that the flat was condemned after we left: they got the fumigators in to try and make it safe for human occupancy, but eventually they gave up and knocked the whole building down.

When we weren't distracted by the Ryders in wrestling mode, we all believed that we were one of the greatest bands ever to walk the planet. A band needs that belief in itself. We used to talk about how we were going to get a Porsche each, with FREAKY 1, FREAKY 2, FREAKY 3 on the number plates. We really thought we were going to smash it. Little did we realise how right we were, or how badly we'd then conspire to fuck it up.

We were really lucky right at the start, that we got to play with New Order up north a few times, and then we got to tour with Terry Hall's latest band, The Colourfield, all of which really helped with getting the Happy Mondays name out there. Terry Hall was one of our heroes as kids hitting our teens in the late 70s, and The Specials were the first national-level band I ever saw.

Those dates were in mid-winter, and we'd sit in the back of this Ford Transit van with all the equipment on these long, freezing drives, with only Shaun's mum's corned beef and tomato sandwiches and the cheapest lager you've ever tasted to cheer us up. We used to call them lager lollies, because they'd freeze in there it was so cold, and we got so used to consuming them that way that in later years we'd put them in the freezer compartment on the tour bus.

Otherwise, we pretty much lived on amphetamine, which kept the hunger pangs at bay. There was a lot of amphetamine. Really good days, really *long* days.

Money-wise, we had nothing and earned nothing. We didn't even earn enough to pay for the trip - for the van and the driver to get to the gig, to feed us all, and keep us in lager lollies - let alone to trouser a bunch of notes each at the end of the night.

When we played gigs on our own, it was little outposts of madness around the country like the Adelphi in Hull, which was basically just a terraced house that had narrowly escaped a Luftwaffe bomb in the Blitz and was still standing in a largely deserted neighbourhood.

Among the kids who started coming to our gigs were a lot of people who had never been to gigs before. Rather than college-indie types, we had all 'The Boys' following us - a hooligan crowd, really. Our first lot of fans who used to follow us around were part of the Leeds Service Crew - proper football hooligans, and that kind of became the norm for who we'd attract. In every town, all the football boys used to turn out for us, so we got this reputation as a hooligan band.

Even when we were playing our first gigs in London, we'd be sitting in venues with our skinheads, flares and Fila gear, and often a couple of heavy geezers would materialise suddenly to ask us to leave because the manager thought we must just be there for a fight or something. Now it's a common sight, but back then bands didn't dress like us.

For one of our first headlining gigs, we played King George's Hall in Blackburn. After a couple of songs, this kid jumped onstage, Sieg-Heiling and shouting 'Blackburn Youth!' - the name of their team's hooligan firm - so I smacked him one with my maracas and this whole riot started. It was kicking off all over the hall. Pint pots in the air, fists being thrown, a full-on punch-up that very quickly spilled out onto the street. For most people, it was probably nothing more than a bit of excitement, punk-rock style.

The police arrived pretty quick, and in the middle of this affray I got arrested and taken off the stage. As they were frogmarching me out of there, I was trying to explain to them that I was part of the band, and they weren't having it.

'And another thing,' I told this officer, 'I'm going to be sick!'

'Yeah, yeah, likely story,' he replied, shaking his head at what he thought was some pathetic effort to escape their clutches.

He simply wouldn't believe it, so I was sick all over him. After that, he obviously threw me in the back of the van, but the next minute, God knows how, I was back out of the van again and up there onstage. The show must go on . . .

*

Phil Saxe had this brainwave to get John Cale from The Velvet Underground to produce our first album. He'd already overseen debuts by The Stooges, The Modern Lovers and Patti Smith, so it would put us in this amazing lineage of bands. Phil got Bernard to suggest it to Tony Wilson, and then Tony said he'd had this brilliant idea for a producer! Most importantly, he also made it happen, and we couldn't believe we were actually going to be working with him. It was definitely a bit of a scoop.

Cale picked this studio in Kentish Town in north London which a mate of his ran, called Firehouse, and we were all put in a bedsit in Belsize Park, all in the same room, and we had to walk for half an hour every day across to the studio. It wasn't anything near glamorous, and we had so little money. According to Shaun, Factory dropped us off down there with sixty quid each for the whole stay, and me and him had spent ours in five minutes. Shaun was just starting to like a bit of heroin, but mostly we were just on speed, cheap and cheerful.

Cale, on the other hand, came in with a big crate of tangerines and all these packets of extra-strong mints, because he'd just got himself off drugs and was now on the wagon. We were all that in awe of him, we were just looking at the floor, unable to speak to him, starstruck by this legend. The Velvet Underground was one of the big musical influences of the time, and we loved the whole story behind the band, the whole cool look that came with it, the songs about street drugs while everyone else was all blissed-out and hippie. Not one of us managed to say a word to him until Phil Saxe came along and started asking him about the Velvets.

For Cale, it was probably just a quick earner – we were in for six days and I think he's done the album for six grand – a grand a day to get this album out. He must've been needing money fast!

As well as business-wise, at the beginning we didn't have much of a clue musically either. We were proper off our tits on whizz, and I was sat in the control booth with Cale while the band was running through the songs, and he kept turning around to me, shrugging his shoulders with his hands out wide, going, 'What the fuck is this?' I was thinking, 'Great, brilliant, the guy from The Velvet Underground thinks our music is boss! We're tripping him out with our mad bass change in "Kuff Dam"!'

Actually, what he couldn't believe was, we didn't even know about basic music timekeeping – you know, like counting in with 1-2-3-4, and playing in time – the first thing you learn in music! The basics! We'd start off slow, get a little bit faster, then go really fast, then slow down again, so the whole tune was played at varying speeds. He couldn't believe we didn't know about 1-2-3-4, so he was the one that taught the band that, and double-time, and not changing the speed of your song all the way through. Serious music lessons from John Cale!

When we got back to Manchester, I talked to Bernard Sumner and Factory's A&R scout-cum-studio wizard Mike Pickering, because they'd each produced one of the previous two singles, but they said they'd left us as we really were, because they enjoyed the innocence of it. They were aware of it, but they didn't want to change it. They saw it as a strength, a selling point. John Cale obviously saw his role differently, but the whole scenario would never happen these days, because everyone goes to music colleges and learns proper music and production techniques – there's lots of courses where someone teaches you all about this shit, before you ever get let loose in a studio. That's one reason, at least, why you'll never see a band like Happy Mondays happen ever again, making records that aren't actually in time.

I met John Cale again years later, at some awards thing. All the bigwigs were there – Jimmy Page, John Cale, Dr John . . . all the big names of rock 'n' roll. I really wanted to meet Dr John, but I saw John Cale so I went over and said, 'Aaah, how do, mate? We've worked with you a long time ago, back in the 80s,' but he couldn't remember. I made my excuses and went off to find Dr John, but he'd gone by the time I got to his table. On my way back, I ran into Cale again. He still couldn't remember us, then I mentioned the extra-strong mints and the tangerines, and it all came back to him, and he knew who we were – it must've been a very specific moment in his life!

The album was pretty gritty, but it opened a lot of doors for us, especially with the John Cale connection. The sleeve had this shagpile carpet look to it. The idea of it was like you were sitting there on acid, looking at the carpet with this horrible pattern. It said, *HAPPY MONDAYS SQUIRREL AND G-MAN TWENTY FOUR HOUR PARTY PEOPLE PLASTIC FACE CARNT SMILE (WHITE OUT)* in big black letters and everything had this gnarly zing, like when you're on acid.

We stepped up the gigging, and with all the excitement and bad behaviour, I ended up in a pretty bad way. I went to the doctor and he said, 'Fucking hell, has no one told you that you're yellow?' and after some tests I got rushed to Monsall Hospital, diagnosed with jaundice, pleurisy and hepatitis B.

When I got out of there, we flew straight off to New York City for our debut show across the pond, and my first ever transatlantic trip - another wild experience. New York was an incredible culture shock back then, exactly like it was in the films and on TV cop shows, with all the yellow taxis and smoke coming up through the vents in the street from the subway.

We were due to play this club, the Limelight, but me and Shaun disappeared with the club manager. She took us off and gave us our first taste of American cocaine, and she was really flirting with both of us, because she was quite old and we were pretty young. She proper led us astray around New York, to the point where we nearly missed our gig.

This was when crack was first making an appearance in New York, and we were keen to try it. The record company would only go so far with us, and left me and Shaun on our own to go deep into the ghetto, in Alphabet City, which was really tough, like you saw in the movies. We were spitting at this Puerto Rican gang, and we got battered and robbed. It was pretty fucking on top, back when New York was still wild, before Giuliani cleaned it all up.

The Limelight was in this big old church, and we were a total shambles that night. Tony was really embarrassed because he had bigged us up for this appearance as part of an industry bash called the New Music Seminar, and the gig was absolute shite. In those days, we were either good, or really, really shite, and that night was definitely the latter. More than shite, in fact.

SHAUN: When we landed in New York, crack hadn't hit over here, but it got the greatest publicity campaign you could ever have for a bunch of kids. The *Sun* and the *Mirror* were both going, 'There's this drug now, it takes you to fucking

Mars! It's called crack, it's the most addictive drug, you get so high on it . . .' A bunch of kids like us don't go, 'Ooooh, no, that's so scary!' We go, 'Fuck me, we want some!' It was the same later with the E: when everyone was reading scare stories about all the dangers of it, we were having it in Manchester, London and maybe Newcastle, then the rest of the country cottons on and the kids go, 'Let's go and find some!' because that's how you are when you're a kid.

When we got to New York, it was still rough, pretty much how it was in the 70s, and all we were concerned about – it wasn't that we were doing a gig at the Limelight club. We just got off the plane, and the person who was picking us up, we basically said to them, 'Take us to where we can get that drug!' Normally, they'd pick you up and say, 'Man, you want some weed? Or some coke?' but if you went, 'We want some heroin, and we want to score some crack,' it was like, 'Fucking heeeell!'

So I think we basically put our bags in the Chelsea Hotel, got the girl driver who worked for Factory in New York to drop us off on the edge of the hood, because she wouldn't go in any further, and then we fucked off to look for crack. You know, we were off our tits anyway from the flight, drinking and smoking and that, and when Bez is off his nut, he spits, like, 'Pah, wha-pah ya taking ab-pah, ya fuck-ah!' and all this gob comes out.

We're trying to find crack, and this guy who was a Vietnam vet saw us walking around, took us back to his crib, a basement-type place, showed us how to make crack, how to smoke it, how to build the pipes, what you need, and he was also selling us some. We stayed in there to smoke it with him, and I'm like, 'I'm going first!'

'What's it like, X, what's it like?!' Bez is going.

'Man, slow down!' the dealer guy says, and I'm holding in the smoke, like, 'Fu-ck-ing he-ellll . . . it really is, mate . . . You – go – to – fuck-iiing – Maaaars!'

Bez is, 'Gimmeeeee!'

Anyway, he has his go, and pffff, we stay there I don't know how long. It could have been anything from an hour to many, many hours, but eventually we leave this place, and while we're walking out, we decide that we definitely want some more, and right away! But then we can't find this guy's place again, where we've just walked out from, so we're walking deeper and deeper into the ghetto, and we meet this bunch of street-kid drug dealers, who all sound like that rapper DMX – they had the same accent before DMX even came out, like 'mother-fuuuck'!

Anyway, we're buying some more off these kids, and while we're trying to explain what we want, and how much, Bez keeps butting in, 'Sssplwah-pah-pah!' This fucking kid who I'm dealing with is wired out of his head – about sixteen, he was – he goes, 'Mother-*fuuuucker*, you just spat at me, you fucking dirty limey mother . . .!'

I know that it's not me spitting, so I just go, 'Sorry, mate, sorry,' because you can't go, 'It's not me, it's him!' You don't do that, it's not cool. Next thing, obviously, Bez does it again, spitting everywhere – 'mother-*fucker!*' Third time, the fucking gun comes out, he sticks it in my fucking eye socket, and he's gonna kill me because he has been spat at again.

By some miracle, the Vietnam vet appears from fucking nowhere, like in *Mr Benn*, and tells these kids to put the guns away and leave it, and somehow he gets us out of there, and we end up scoring more crack off him instead.

God's honest truth, though, there was no shaking and no signs of worry with us, because at the end of the day we were cracked up, and there's No Fear, but the next day when we woke up in the Chelsea Hotel, and we realised just how close to death we'd come – *then* we've got our head in our hands.

And of course that night's gig hadn't been up to much.

The first time I ever heard about E was in 1987, and I was imagining something which did exactly what it said on the tin - gave you ecstasy. Wouldn't it be great if it was something that actually made you feel that way, that put you in a sort of orgasmic state? I'd been lying awake at night for years pining for a drug that would create that perfect feeling of wellbeing, and lo and behold, that's exactly what E did. It was in every sense the drug of my dreams, and it was out there, waiting to be discovered!

What convinced me that it had indeed arrived and that I should try one, was running into a mate of mine that Christmas at the Hacienda. He told me he'd just done a pill and was obviously flying off his head in a most extraordinary way. He's normally quite a serious and reserved type of guy, and he possibly wasn't the best-looking kid you've ever set eyes on, but he was convinced that every woman in the club fancied him.

With that, he literally boogied down the stairs of the Hacienda, which was completely out of character for him, and hit the dancefloor like John Travolta. This was the first time I'd ever seen anybody on an E, and that was when I knew that they were good - very, very good.

'Right, I'm going to get myself one of them,' I thought, but it wasn't to be that night, as they cost twenty quid a pop and I didn't have that much on me. Once I'd got my first pill down me the following weekend, however, it was like a dream come true. I completely lost all inhibitions. I loved everybody in the room. It made me social above and beyond my usual gregariousness. The music sounded totally incredible, and I just danced my socks off all night long. It was a perfect tonic that left you feeling warm and fuzzy.

I almost couldn't believe how good it was, so I went back to the Hacienda the next night to make sure, and from then on in those early days you'd do it almost every night – maybe four or five nights a week. It became the new normal for most people I knew, and I managed to make a connection who got his supply from Amsterdam so I could score pills in unlimited numbers.

In my new flat in Fallowfield, which I shared with my girlfriend Debs, we had probably the first proper E parties in the country, with everyone on one, and loads of semi-naked girls dancing around with their tits out. It was like, 'Fucking hell, this is our idea of heaven!'

This was before it actually took off on any national scale, or even in Manchester. In spring 1988, I used to go down to London, to Paul Oakenfold's Spectrum night at Heaven, and take a load of Es down there for all the cockneys, because acid-house was hip down there and it was kicking off in a big way. We used to look at each other like we were dreaming, and say, 'Fucking hell, we're going to get it like this in Manchester one day!' Because we had the Es up there but we didn't have the scene, like the cockneys did, and we couldn't even get rid of them. Heaven was only small really, but it seemed massive to us back then, full of all these London people off their nuts, and it didn't take long for us to replicate it at the Hacienda.

How we did it was basically us giving away Es to everybody we knew for free. It was almost like a marketing strategy, because we knew that once people tried it, they'd be running back to us for more (and more). I'd be there handing them out at Mike Pickering's house night at the Hacienda, and in a matter of several weeks the dance scene took over the whole club. They still had other nights and gigs going on through the week, but the weekends became exclusively dedicated to house music.

It's incredible, the number of people who've come up to me over the years and told me that I gave them their first E. At the time, it felt like I'd converted half of Manchester to it, because I had all the Es. I don't know if it's a proud thing to lay claim to or not. I really hope I didn't bring any issues to anybody's life. You know, one man's dream is another man's nightmare, but for me they were great times.

Joining the Mondays was the best thing that ever happened to me, from the point of view of keeping me out of that criminal lifestyle, of breaking and entering, and regular periods behind bars, but obviously I was still involved to some extent, in this context. It didn't just go away overnight. Even in the very early days of the band, I got by through the drug culture we were all living in.

Now with the Es, I was working as a middleman because by now I knew everybody. I knew whole swathes of the city, and I was able to move about, and use that knowledge to my own advantage, and connect people up with what they wanted. I knew everyone who had everything, and the people who wanted it, and I was really good at putting the right people together.

The way I see it today, I was just heavily involved in the whole culture of music. A lot of times it was just acting as a middleman, shifting big amounts about, bringing people together from varying parts of the city. People may have some misconception that I was some kind of Mr Big, running the whole of Manchester, when really to be honest it was a bit more like Arthur Daley, ducking and diving in his own community.

It was a continuation of that lifestyle for quite a long time in the Mondays, even after the band split up, because I still had to make money to survive, if there wasn't anything coming through from royalties and gigs. I was mixing the two roles together, selling whizz, Es, acid, moving keys of draw, because we weren't making any money out of the band. That was my income, my living, and eventually the band was very good for business.

Going into 1988, everyone in Happy Mondays was still totally skint. Phil Saxe had put us on the Enterprise Allowance Scheme, which Margaret Thatcher's government had initiated to support young entrepreneurs into business, and to try and show that they were tackling employment. It was the first time we'd signed off the dole, and we got forty quid each a week, which sounds mad today, because you can't hardly get through a day with that these days. You only got that allowance for twelve months, so the clock was ticking on Happy Mondays actually getting anywhere.

To that end, we got a new young manager called Nathan McGough. Now I do like Nathan as a person, but as a manager he was terrible. At his first gig with us, he shagged this bird who was hanging around and in the morning when he woke up she'd done a runner and stolen the gig wages off him. I always felt that Nathan wasn't right for the job. We soon got these accountants who were possibly trustworthy, but I still felt like we got ripped off right along the way. I know through doing band business later on that there must've been a lot of money that we never saw. If we hadn't had a monthly wage, and we'd actually got paid per gig like we do nowadays, I for one would've made a whole heap more money than I ever did back then.

The pressure to make headway was mounting when we started recording our second album with Joy Division's producer, Martin Hannett. Factory had put us in this cheapo residential studio called the Slaughterhouse, a former abattoir intentionally located away from Manchester, across the Pennines in Driffield, East Yorkshire. The sessions for what became *Bummed* were every bit as mad as the stories that people always tell about it - probably more so.

The studio had a pub adjoining it, so we had our dinner laid on in there every day, and there was also a nightclub next door. Driffield was a funny old place. There wasn't a fuck of a lot going on there, I can tell you, but what there was, we were right in the middle of. We had all the lads down from Manchester with us, coming and going, and visiting this weird nightclub, which was otherwise populated by all these squaddies stationed with the British Army there - quite literally, they were the only other people in town.

Predictably, we were having a bit of conflict with them in this club next door to the studio, the only place you could go out in the town. Before very long, they wanted to kill us, and at one point I had this sergeant major screaming down my face - he couldn't understand why we weren't scared by them all. Instead, we very calmly fed them all these Es - banged some pills down their throats - and the mood changed totally! Next thing, we had half of the British Army off their heads, and then we invited them back to the studio, and had them dancing around to our newly recorded tunes.

We did vast amounts of drugs at that time, and there was never a shortage because we were friends with a lot of people who made sure that we were always well supplied.

Indeed, during those three weeks, I had to go back home for a court appearance, because I think I was the first person in the country to get nicked with ecstasy. Tony Wilson gave me a character reference and stood me the fine.

SHAUN: We were living off the ecstasy. The scene was only just starting, but we were still getting no money off Factory, so that's why we started getting hold of ecstasy, and we sold it to survive. We didn't really start seeing any dough from the band until the third album was a hit. We definitely weren't getting any when we were making *Bummed* in Yorkshire, but the upshot of us being out of town to record in Driffield was that there was no E in Manchester. It was all with us, so we constantly had to be making journeys back home, and we had all these mates hopping over to see us as well, because all these people needed sorting out.

With hindsight, the album we came away with was top. Martin Hannett did a great job on *Bummed*, but it was all old-school production. It didn't have the modern techniques that eventually helped us to cross over. That came in the months following *Bummed*'s release, when my buddy from London, Paul Oakenfold, brought his acid-house wizardry to remixes of 'Wrote for Luck' and 'Hallelujah'.

We always thought Happy Mondays was a dance band. Shaun thought of himself as a rapper, backed by this party band of some weird description. We'd grown up in Salford, where dance music was a massive part of our culture, with northern soul, and before that the early days of disco, which we'd absorbed in our local youth clubs. But me, the first thing I ever danced to was punk - pogoing, and flinging each other about - so that was dance music too.

To launch the album campaign, we shot a video for 'Wrote for Luck' in Legends, which was a famous jazz-funk club in Manchester, with all the fancy lighting around the place, and the disco floor that lit up - a proper John Travolta-style place. I first went there when I was sixteen, in the days when there was a dress code, and everyone had to wear a smart shirt, trousers and shoes to get in.

But that night in Legends was very different. It was right at the height of our ecstasy exposure, and it was probably the first video ever where everyone in it - including Shaun and all the revellers grooving around him beneath the strobe lights on that precious dancefloor - was off their nut on ecstasy.

At last, our moment was arriving.

Chapter 3

ON TOP

Being in the Mondays always felt like a smash 'n' grab mixed with a car crash. From start to finish, the journey was conducted in that spirit, with as reckless an attitude as you could possibly imagine - a feeding frenzy of grabbing and taking what you could when you could, because you were always aware that the lifespan of a band is only short. Most bands only have two or three years where it's really happening for them. That was always at the back of your mind, that it could end at any moment. When success finally came, it didn't bring a feeling of stability in your life, because you always felt you were on this rollercoaster that was gonna derail any second.

If I'd known then what I know now, I might've approached the whole thing of being in the band differently, to do all I could to stop the car crashing. It was 1985 that I joined, and we're in 2022 now - if we'd had any idea that we'd still be touring and making money out of reunions all these years later, I'm sure back then everyone would've taken a different attitude towards doing it, and towards each other. But we didn't have that foresight or knowledge. Everything was always acted out from a position of massive instability, and thus it was that the Mondays wrote the manual on fucking up.

Plenty of other bands have written the same book, how *not* to live the rock 'n' roll lifestyle. We certainly went the whole hog, from taking all the drugs imaginable, to being completely naive and not having a clue about the business side.

We used to watch all the classic films about rock stardom, and we were simply living the rock 'n' roll lifestyle as it was portrayed to us in those movies. That was the dream, to live it full-on, no-holds-barred, to the fucking maximum, like David Essex in *Stardust*, and The Rolling Stones in *Cocksucker Blues* and *Gimme Shelter*.

During the making of *Bummed*, we were obsessed with Donald Cammell's *Performance*, and it turned up quite a bit in Shaun's lyrics on that album. We used to quote dialogue at each other, between Mick Jagger's reclusive star and James Fox's gangster on the run hanging out with all the beatniks and hippies – particularly the scene where he drops acid for the first time, which was one of our favourite bits in the film. That was our perception of what it is to be rock 'n' roll, so that's how we set out to live, and we did, or at least our own version of it.

And that's how we left ourselves wide open to get ripped off. We were the archetypal hard-luck story, getting taken advantage of and thieved off, because when you're that age, in your early twenties, having the time of your life, you're just involved in that thing without really giving much thought to taking care of long-term finances. Right through our whole career, every cunt robbed from us and that's why none of us became millionaires while the going was good.

What our somewhat reckless passage through those 'glory years' also means is that, for me, they're all a bit of a blur. I honestly can't remember much about that time where we'd finally made it, and we were pop stars jetting all over the place. I've got so little recollection, it's actually quite worrying. I often get told stories about myself and I just don't believe them, but I can't present any evidence to the contrary, and very often I have no alternative reading of events. When it comes to 1989 to 1993, my mind's a blank, because when you're living that life, you're too busy to take notes, and a lot of it just gets forgotten.

I wasn't ever a musician, with technical reasons for staying on top of my game, so I was just in it and living it. Because I'd had such a lucky break to be where I was, I particularly always had a feeling that whatever day it was, it was going to be the last – even more than the others. So I lived like there was no tomorrow, and to hell with the consequences.

What really kickstarted our success was when Paul Oakenfold started doing remixes for us, on 'Wrote For Luck' and then 'Hallelujah' off the *Madchester/Rave On* EP, which we'd recorded at the Manor, the train fella Richard Branson's gaff in Oxfordshire.

Oakey was a mate of mine, who I'd known long before he started working on Happy Mondays tracks, through those early days of ecstasy at Spectrum in London. He's a very quiet guy, not extroverted in any way, but he was there on the house scene from the very beginning, and he's one of the first people I think of when I try to remember the start of it all. He actually mentions me in his book, how we all used to go down there from Manchester, bringing the Es with us – he was giving us the credit in return!

By the summer of 1988, he was one of the first DJs to look at moving into music-making, on the production side. His way in was to team up with Steve Osborne, who was more your old-school rock producer, working on the song arrangements, and then Oakenfold brought in the modern production techniques from Chicago house, with drum machines, samplers and computer programming.

The two of them together were a great combination, and I think they both recognised what we were trying to do. They could see that the bottom line with us was that we were a dance band, and they made us that, in the most contemporary way. With their remixes, that's when everything changed for us: club DJs wanted our tunes, and our fortunes picked up – and everything got called 'indie-dance' after that, or 'baggy', in honour of Phil Saxe's clothing rations.

They called that summer the 'Second Summer of Love', but to be honest we'd had ours the previous year. The E trade was exploding, though, and through those legendary pill-crazed warmer months there would be queues around the block to get into the Hacienda, and we'd just sail in past them to make our killing.

We made more money out of the initial ecstasy explosion than we'd ever had in our lives before. We had money coming out of our ears, it felt like. Some nights when the club finished, we had to leave four grand behind the bar, for them to look after for us till we picked it up in the morning.

The consumption escalated very quickly nationwide: we knew a fella down in London who shall remain nameless, who, for the purpose of moving his stock around, could get a thousand Es up his arse. I always wondered how he managed that – you would hope that he bagged them up first.

It was our time, because we were the first ones in Manchester with all the pills, and the whole explosion in the Hacienda was based around our little culture that we had going. With Mike Pickering having all the Chicago records for his Nude night, and us lot having all the ecstasy, it made the perfect combination. Pretty soon, we were at the Hacienda practically every night of the week. It was like our local. Like some people went out to the pub of an evening, we went to the club and got loved up. We used to sleep most of the day, get up at teatime, then go to the Hacienda about nine or ten o'clock until booting-out time. The only night it was closed at the height of it was a Monday night – our evening off!

As is always the way, once you're successful things start coming your way for free, and with all travel paid for we were suddenly jetting all over the place, including our first visit to Ibiza, where New Order had set up shop that summer for a few months to record *Technique*, and we settled in for a rollicking ten days' drinking and drug-taking.

I got Bernard to hire me a car – a Ford Fiesta, nothing fancy – and I wrote it off. Then I wrote off another one, both times falling down into ditches on the side of the road. We were going to all the clubs out there – the big open-air places like Pacha, Amnesia and Ku, with loads of Es. It was very different then to how it is today. They had the West End, with all the clubs, but it wasn't as overrun by the English as it is now. It was really special, like paradise.

Initially I didn't realise that the girls' toilets were the girls' toilets. I was in there slapping all the creams on me, having a right old time. It took me about a week before I found out that I'd been going into the ladies' all the time. I was really apologetic, but people were alright with me because I was that nice with everybody while I was in there. I'd be jumping up on podiums and taking over, robbing them from the dancers and raving away, completely oblivious to Ibizan culture. It was just that, arriving there as a freshman, you were blown away by what was going on.

The music there was different to Britain, too: it wasn't all house, more that less genre-specific Balearic style. It was where the whole movement started, and it really felt like the beginning of the revolution.

SHAUN: We were living off the ecstasy, because now the scene was happening, and we were still getting no money off Factory. We didn't start seeing any dough for another two or three years, so we were selling ecstasy to survive.

The time when New Order were recording *Technique* out in Ibiza, I didn't go, but Hooky has got this story he likes to tell where it's, 'Oh, Bez turns up with whizz in Ibiza, to try and sell whizz, and obviously the people there didn't want whizz, they were all into E.' I look at that and think, 'Are you off your fucking head?' It was our pals and us who brought the fucking E into the Hacienda in the first place! Bez got landed a load of whizz, and just decided to take it out there and knock it out as well, but seriously – it was our fucking firm that brought the E! Hooky's stories, man!

When we first started doing tours, we might have been Number Five in the indie chart, or even Number One in the indie chart later on, but that meant nothing. It meant you'd sold twenty records! So there was no money, and we weren't making anything from shows in them days. Everywhere we went, in all these towns in Germany and everywhere, we just robbed. If we saw anything open when we pulled up at a motorway service station, or at the garage – like it was open around the back where all the booze was stored – we'd park the van back there, lift all the booze in and drive off at high speed.

When we first went to Switzerland, we discovered that everyone took their coats off when they went into a restaurant and left them hanging by the door with their wallets still in the pockets. Once we'd cottoned on, that was it – we went to every restaurant, taking the wallets out, and if the coat was really smart, we'd take the coat *and* the wallet!

Then, at a safe distance, you'd get the wallet, take the money out and chuck it into what you thought was a canal, or wherever there was water. I suppose the thinking was, if you did that at home, you wouldn't see anything because the water would be murky. But the next day, you'd go back past where you were, and you could see all the wallets down at the bottom of the lake or whatever it was, because the water was that clean over there!

Through 1988/89, we were bringing the party to the people, wherever there was demand for it, and I guess we became notorious for bringing the lads with us. When we played the Pyramid Stage at Glastonbury, we forged all these backstage passes and got half of Manchester into Access All Areas.

Without need for such chicanery, our audiences were swelling month by month, and the band itself was tightening up and taking off, parallel to the world falling for the charms of MDMA. I remember it as a joyful time, but again it's blurry and unspecific.

Tony Wilson brokered a licensing deal for *Bummed* and subsequent albums to be released in the US by Elektra - once home to Love and The Doors, which was a mind-blowing thought - so then suddenly we were touring over there with our new label-mates, Pixies. You might think of them as quite straitlaced college kids, but their bass-player certainly wasn't.

We used to knock about with her quite a lot, because she was up for almost anything – drinking, drug-taking – but I never found out much about the rest of them. She was definitely the wild band member.

When the tour came through Cleveland, Ohio, we had another brush with the Grim Reaper on our usual mission to score drugs. We all wanted some weed, so Shaun, our tour manager Anthony 'Muzzer' Murray and I took this taxi deep into the ghetto, as we would normally do to get sorted out, and it came really on top. As we were rolling down this street on the search, we got out to talk to this dealer guy, and suddenly there were people coming out of everywhere. We hopped back in the cab – a brand-new minibus-type taxi – and the gang started attacking it, smashing all the windows with baseball bats, trying to yank the sliding door off and drag us out. Somehow the driver screeched off and dropped us back at the hotel. It was all good fun, all part of the journey – just what you did when you were younger!

Otherwise it's only random stuff that comes to mind from this breathless period, like the time we met the Guildford Four. They'd only just been released from sixteen years' wrongful imprisonment for the IRA's Guildford pub bombings in 1974. I'd gone up to Liverpool to watch Mick Jones from The Clash's band, Big Audio Dynamite, and we all met backstage afterwards, along with these Scouser mates of mine.

In the dressing room, this one geezer called Basher – a typical Scouse name, or what? – starts telling an IRA joke, and everyone's thinking, 'Fucking hell, we're sat with the Guildford Four just after they've got out – this is the last thing they want to hear!'

'Why did the IRA never bomb Liverpool?' he goes.

'Oh for fuck's sake, Basher!'

You could've cut the air with a knife.

'Because they loved The Beatles!'

It was such an unbelievably shit joke, and you had to be there to appreciate how wrong it was, but the punchline was such a relief, something quite innocent, and God how we laughed . . .

The big milestone for our band came when we headlined Manchester's Free Trade Hall, where famously the Sex Pistols played (twice) in 1976. This was in November 1989: it was a very big gig for us at that time, and we had that many in on the guest list - 700 people or something crazy - that it was rammed to the rafters, even after security on the door had ripped up the guestie and defended the entrance against a few rush-type situations.

To accommodate the crush, the venue had to open up these three upstairs tiers that had been closed down for years due to Health and Safety (or whatever it was called back then), and these dodgy balconies were all packed as well. You wouldn't believe how many people we had squeezed in there.

The atmosphere was unbelievable, everybody off their head on Es, and that was when you first noticed that things were really changing. I'd done a lot of acid that night - acid and Es - so in the photos and video footage from that night, I'm particularly wild-eyed in this blue-and-white-striped T-shirt. To be honest, that one was all too much, I'd done acid to excess, and I wasn't quite prepared for how many people would be in there. It almost overtook you, where you were overcome - like, wow, fucking hell! I didn't know whether to throw up or stomp around laughing my bollocks off. The gig was over in a flash, and it took me hours to come down again.

It was like we were on a rollercoaster. The numbers of

people who wanted to see us were multiplying exponentially every week, and we were already in negotiations to stage a mind-blowingly massive show to try and cope with the demand.

We'd talked to Simon Moran at SJM, the big promoters in Manchester at the time who'd been handling our promotions up to that point, about making the step up to G-Mex, the vast conference centre where we'd supported New Order a few months before. He thought we were insane, so we talked instead to Jimmy 'Muffin' at Night Time promotions, who were actually ticket touts and our mates, and we let him promote the gig for us instead.

Simon Moran was like, 'What the fuck are you doing letting ticket touts run the show? You haven't got no chance of selling out G-Mex!' and we went and sold out *two* nights there, so you could say it took the ticket touts to realise our potential more than professional promoters, and to take us to the next level.

The gigs were only four months after the Free Trade Hall. I'm pretty sure they were incredible, but I remember nothing, and the same goes for Wembley Arena a few nights later. All I know is that it was always variable back then, even when we were playing big venues, arenas and stadiums. You didn't know what you were going to get with the Mondays: it was either going to be really good or really shit.

After G-Mex, I had a conference room booked for an after-party at the five-star Midland Hotel. I had my own bar running in there, and was landed with a four-grand bill at the end of it. In anyone's book that's a heavy round. It had taken five years, but at last we must've been making some money. If you're asking where the money actually went, there's one answer at least.

*

I first met Rowetta Satchell in December 1989, when I went to watch a gig at the Ritz in Manchester – an On-U Sound Christmas party, featuring Gary Clail and Adrian Sherwood, and these two local bands, Vanilla Sound Corps and Part E Unknown, both of which she was singing with. I was milling about early doors and casually turned my attention to one of those acts, which was two girls doing modern hip-hop/R&B sort of music.

Suddenly I clocked Rowetta up there onstage, and I was absolutely mesmerised by her. In all honesty, I was struck down with pure lust. I thought I'd never seen anything so sexy in my life. Perhaps one factor that led me down that path was that I thought she had all these spiders' legs hanging out of her knickers. She still claims today that it wasn't a load of her pubes, but actually the frays off her shorts. Maybe that was the case, but in my mind's eye I saw something else . . .

Anyway, I thought, 'Fuck, this is the hottest woman I've ever seen in my life!' so I just had to dive backstage to go and meet her, because this girl had really blown my head off in a sexual way. Once we got chatting, she said she'd seen me around town, and she thought I was going out with another black girl called Leah, who knocked about with my missus Debs, so she blew me out.

It was only afterwards apparently that she realised I was in the Mondays, like, 'Oh my God, there's that kid with the wild eyes who was trying to get into my knickers after saying that all my pubes were hanging out of them!' I still tell her that was the biggest mistake of her life, refusing my advances.

Around that time, we were recording a cover version of John Kongos' hit from 1971, 'He's Gonna Step On You Again', for a compilation celebrating our American label Elektra's fiftieth anniversary, and with a certain synchronicity Rowetta got hired to perform the female vocals on it.

Of course, with Oakey turning it into a piano, house-infused monster, 'Step On' turned out way too good to chuck away on a compilation, so we recorded Johnny Kongos's other big hit 'Tokoloshe Man' for them, and released 'Step On' as a single of our own in March 1990, with a video bathed in late-afternoon sunshine that helped the single race into the top five of the pop charts. Everybody thought it was filmed in Los Angeles, because the big E of the hotel sign on the roof had a California look about it, but it was actually shot in Sitges, just outside of Barcelona.

Everyone in our camp knew Rowetta because she'd been in various bands in Manchester over the years. She'd always wanted to sing with a proper steady band, rather than a clubby DJ-producer's thing, and you know Rowetta - when she has set her heart on something, she's really hard to hold at bay.

With the club season in Ibiza opening up soon after the single's release, we were booked to play at Ku again, but we couldn't take Row along with us because we didn't have enough budget to pay her way out there. However, there was a competition on one of the Manchester radio stations, where the prize was two tickets to see the Happy Mondays play in Ibiza, with flights and accommodation included. Rowetta entered the competition and, being her, she obviously won it!

Everyone thought it was a fix, but she genuinely won the competition fair and square, because she wanted to come that much and join us onstage. Row has always been slightly mental, and there really was no stopping her. She joined us onstage out there, and she's been with us ever since.

*

SHAUN: We did a good few summers working in Ibiza. One year – I think it was the time we played Ku, the one with the swimming pool at the front, and no roof on it – there was a delay with us getting paid, so me and Muzzer had to hang around on the island for an extra couple of weeks to wait for the money. To pacify us, the chief of police gave us a key to this bar he had, like a gentlemen's club, and in that place was tons of booze, and a mountain of cocaine that you just cut yourself a line out of, so we just stayed around there, killing time, as you do.

These were great times, but I remember very little about, say, G-Mex. I only know that we played it, because I've seen it on film. I can't remember anything anyway because of how my memory is from birth, but especially mixing that with chemicals and drugs, my mind's a blank.

I do remember shooting the 'Step On' video, though, and Bez looked great in that, as I knew he would. Don't forget, he hadn't been home for two or three years before that. He'd basically been out partying since the end of 1986. We shot it on this hotel roof, like it was Miami or LA. A bit later, I remember watching the opening scenes of *Bad Boys* with Will Smith, and thinking, 'Hmm, that looks rather similar!'

Sitges is where all the people of Barcelona go to holiday for themselves. It's like their Blackpool, only it's a lot cleaner. It's also the gay capital of Spain, and we went to this club there, a bunch of Mancs steaming in, and I'm sat facing one way and for some reason all our lads are sat facing me. Behind them are all these gay guys that they can't see, all pulling their kecks down, swinging their dicks and wiggling their arses. It's only me that can see it, and I thought, 'I'd better not tell this fucking lot, or there could be trouble here.'

When Rowetta came in, it was pure business. She'd seen us around without having heard the music or having seen us do a gig, but she knew Nathan, and she'd said something to Nathan about wanting to sing with us. Next thing, she's doing the vocals on 'Step On', and pretty much from then on she joined the band.

No other girl would have fitted in. She can be very feminine and womanly, but at the same time she's one of the lads, and she's as mad as all of us lot, and she just worked a dream with our chemistry.

Recording *Pills 'n' Thrills and Bellyaches* in Los Angeles that summer with Oakenfold, we were at our peak. That was the album that catapulted us right up there. Eight weeks in LA driving around in a big five-litre convertible - it was really the best of times.

Me and Oakey went to watch Afrika Bambaataa DJing, and it was meant to be the peace night between the rival gangs in the city - the Crips and the Bloods - but it didn't quite turn out that way. There were four people shot dead that night, and I've never seen a place empty as fast.

We'd done our first headline tour in America leading up to those sessions. Some Americans were really doing my head in on that trip. One day, I was sat on a wall with my eyes rolling back in my head, and this one guy knew exactly what I was thinking. I was sounding off about Americans in a couple of interviews, but I have to take that back now. You can't say they're all the same. It's a massive country, and I've met loads now who I really like. I did struggle to deal with some of them, but you can't tar everyone with the same brush, and the people who're good are *really* good.

I also really struggled with the food over there. It wasn't that clever for me and kept making me ill, all that mass-farmed shit. The battery-hatched eggs used to give me seriously bad stomachaches. I guess it was my body saying no to food that's pumped full of those kind of chemicals.

But we had eight great weeks out in LA. Again, just off our heads most of the time, driving around in big cars, living the LA rock 'n' roll lifestyle, going to parties. There's not too much of a story to tell. Well, I suppose there was the Julia Roberts incident . . .

SHAUN: We had just toured America, gone all over the place there, then the plan was that at the end we'd decamp to LA and make *Pills 'n' Thrills*. When we got to LA, before we started the album we should've played a gig, but then we found out that Soul II Soul was playing, so we sacked off our gig and we all went to see Soul II Soul instead, then the next day we headed off to Capitol Studios, the iconic place where Frank Sinatra recorded.

I can't remember where we flew in from, maybe San Francisco or New York, and when we landed at LAX, we had to hire some cars, which were really for the tour manager and the manager, the people that looked after the band, but somehow Bez blagged his way into taking a hire car. I knew as soon as he got hold of the keys that this wasn't going to end well. You know, he'd be driving around Manchester, we'd be going to the

Hacienda, and he'd smash into a car at the bottom of Oxford Road, and me and him would get out pretending to be injured, and then run off leaving the car right there, all smashed up.

That was in the UK, uninsured, so any car that you totalled you could just run away from. I just knew that it was utter madness giving him one out there, though, because any car that he's driving isn't going to last long, but he managed to wangle these car keys off Nathan and off he went.

Within five minutes of him getting behind the wheel, he'd stuck it up the arse of another car, which we then had to pay off. The thing is out there, as soon as they hear the English accent, they're like, 'We're gonna sue your ass off!' With these fuckers, if you have an accident, someone who breaks a fingernail is going to come after you for $5 million. So the guy he crashed into tried to do that, and it probably would've wiped us out financially, but we managed to get out of it – we bought the kid off, and it didn't turn into the legal caper that it could have.

For those few weeks, we were all plotted up at Oakwood apartments. Also staying there, we had Mick Hucknall, and Brian Tilsley from *Coronation Street*, whose real name was Chris Quinten. We knew Mick to say hi to, because we all used to rehearse in the same place. In fact, when Simply Red had their first hit with 'Money's Too Tight to Mention', they left their room in the Boardwalk, and we took it over from them. They were that skint back in the day, they would be putting plastic coffee cups in the pockets of the pool table, so they didn't have to keep paying 20p when the game had ended. But then they had their big hit, and they were out of there the next morning.

In LA, we always used to laugh because Hucknall played a lot of tennis with our drummer, Gaz. They both had the long hair going on and all that, but Mick would go out on the court and he'd have his shorts pulled up to his tits – like Simon Cowell but in tennis shorts. Mick was one of the lads, though, he was funny. Brian Tilsley, on the other hand, or should I say Chris Quinten – we've all seen him on *Corrie*, and we were like, 'Alright, mate!' He's looked at us and heard our accents, and he obviously just thought we were a bunch of scallies, he had no idea we were a band or anything, and he was quite rude to us – wouldn't even say hello or anything – so every time we saw him from then on it would be, 'Knobhead!' or, 'How tall is he, four-foot-seven?'

On that visit, I was still into my opium, heroin and ecstasy. When we got to LA, there was a Grateful Dead gig on, a couple of hours' drive outside, and this Mexican guy and girl that we had scoring for us went there and managed to acquire for me a really nice big cricket-ball-sized lump of opium. Otherwise we were just on the E, and the American equivalent of our skunk weed. Before skunk came in during the late 90s, we always got rather shit weed in England, just your regular bog-standard grass. The weed you got in LA, it was like the chronic – *potent*. But mainly I was on the opium and brown-tar heroin.

It was a great time. The thing is, when you're young, everything that comes along you sort of expect. You don't go, 'Oh, wow!' You just take it for granted. We might've been in the back of a shitty van somewhere five minutes ago, but then suddenly we were in LA hanging about with Johnny Depp, and we never went 'Wow!' It was just, 'Well, this is what's happening now, and it just rolls on and on from here.' We just took it all as normal.

It's not till years later when you start straightening up and you start thinking it over, that you can possibly get bashed with post-traumatic stress about it all. But as a kid, no matter how many guns you've had pointed at your head, and how many dangerous scenes you've been through where you nearly lost your life, like Cleveland and that first time in New York, it just doesn't register. That time in Cleveland, the taxi driver's door almost got ripped clean off his car, all his wheels and his tyres, too, the driver's crying, his windscreen and windows are all smashed in, and us lot are just *blasé*. 'Fucking hell, you've got to feel sorry for that cunt . . . Anyway, let's get off!' Next thing, here we go again, guns out, nearly getting killed.

And then there was Julia Roberts coming on to Bez. At that moment, she was the hot new female star in Hollywood. The big movie that brought her worldwide attention and made her into the 'Julia Roberts' that she is today was *Pretty Woman*, and we'd watched it on the plane over, because it had only just come out.

One night we were out at some bar in LA, and Bez is talking to someone, then he comes over to me.

'Who's Julia Roberts, X?'

'She's the film star from that movie we watched on the plane coming over, B.'

'Oh right, her, yeah! Well, she's just told me that she's got a bodyguard called Evil, but she's asking me to go back to her place after the club.'

'Dude, go on, go on!'

But the thing was, Bez already had about three girls on his case that night, all 'hot chicks'. He'd be going to one of them, chatting to her, then going to another, chatting to her, then going off to another . . . He was basically just sussing out which one was going to give him the best shag – like, 'Who looks the dirtiest of these three?' – and he couldn't make his mind up.

I was like, 'Look, mate – just go with Julia Roberts!'

She was speaking to him for a while, she invited him back to her place – she fancied him! When you look at the guy who became her husband soon after, Lyle Lovett, you can see a sort of resemblance between him and Bez, in a Frankenstein sort of way! She was right on him, but he didn't go for it.

Even with all the magazine cover stories, TV shows and crowds going mad for us, I never got any big ideas about myself. Since everything always felt very temporary and transient in the Mondays, I never considered myself to have acquired any kind of lasting fame. I went from being homeless between the ages of sixteen and twenty-two to headlining Wembley and G-Mex, but I always considered myself one of the boys, know what I mean? Everyone who knew me, knew me before *and* during. It wasn't about social climbing.

Because of all the Es flying around, people wrote about me as the Pied Piper leading the Chemical Generation out to an artificially induced state of euphoria, but I never read any of that shit, and I certainly never gave it much thought on that level. I just saw it as a means to an end. It was something I was using for financial gain, to finance my own party lifestyle, to put food on the table and keep the lantern burning. It meant that I didn't have to engage in a nine-to-five job, and that I could keep living the life I wanted.

The last thing I ever wanted was to become a slave to the mundane. It never occurred to me to fit in to normal society. I always liked living on the fringes of it. To become normalised on that level didn't appeal to me. All of that, I think, is why our band connected with kids our age at the time, and why there's still popular demand for the antics our band gets up to, with reunions and arena tours right up to the present day.

Back then, we were all living for the moment, because we'd all wanted to grow up in the 60s and experience that brilliant thing of the drug culture fusing with the music. That scene was our dream: to become part of creating a new culture based around music and drugs was what we wanted the most in life. So, now that it was a reality, with us right in the epicentre, we threw ourselves wholeheartedly into the whole thing. We basked in it.

Once *Pills 'n' Thrills* came out, it went into the top five, and soon after that was when the money started arriving. What did I spend it on? All the usual shit! Everything I'd still spend it on today: cars, motorbikes, going out, fast living, clothes, everything your heart may desire as a young man with money. I was always out, living the life. We liked to do everything to the maximum, partying, going out for meals . . .

That was something we used to do: all the lads going out on the town together, a fucking massive gang, going into top restaurants. These days, a lot of restaurants in Manchester won't let more than four people in together on one table without a prior booking, but we used to go in mob-handed, and we'd totally run the waiters ragged, with copious drinks orders and general piss-taking. That was the life that we'd always dreamed of living, constantly partying, nice cars, motorbikes – the sort of things that any lad would want, we had them.

It was my dream come true because I'd gone from starving, living under bushes, fresh out of jail, wondering where my next meal was gonna come from, suddenly to *not* having to worry about anything, and feeling like I was never going to run out of money ever again. I had the lot, I thought, and I could live a life of exuberance and extravagance, with no real appreciation or concern for the value of money. It was all about living the fast life, and in my new-found position, I expected that of myself.

Because I was never a musician, though, I did question my own worthiness sometimes, whether I should be there or not. I felt like I got a lot of love, but I couldn't really understand why I was getting this fucking admiration, because I didn't really think I deserved it. I was riding on the coattails of other people's success. I just happened to be in the right place at the right time. I sometimes felt like a bit of a fraud, taking the glory without having much talent.

What I did contribute was giving the band a bit of street credibility, because I'd lived the street life that Shaun was often spouting about.

Also, this was what I decided in the end: usually, people go and watch bands, and they have these heroes, like your guitar heroes and your great singers, and they're like, 'Aw, I wish I could do that!' With me, it was different: everyone used to look up and think, 'I could do that!' I think that was what endeared me to the wider public, that everybody knew they could do what I did, and that was a good thing, an inspiring thing for them. That's what I've boiled it down to. I don't know if there's any truth in it, but everybody knew they could get up onstage and have a good time dancing about. I was just the guy who actually did it.

Almost as quickly as it had materialised, however, the happy vibe of 1988/89 started to turn sour on many levels. For a while ecstasy had changed things in football culture, because everyone was too loved up to get violent. For a moment it brought peace among people who would normally be opposing each other, but it didn't last long, and Manchester gang culture and football hooligan culture soon reared their ugly heads again. Suddenly, there were heavy contingents who wanted to take control of the clubs, and 'Madchester' became rechristened as 'Gunchester', as rival gangs battled for domination in the illicit drugs market.

I wasn't involved in that sort of scene – it wasn't for me – but I did have a few scary moments. One night, some gang or other came in to get me at the Hacienda. They formed a big circle around me, but when they grabbed me and tried to carry me out, I'd been dancing and sweating that much, I was like a wet slippery fish they couldn't keep hold of, and I managed to wriggle away from their grasp.

Inside the Happy Mondays itself, inevitably, after a certain point, there was a lot of ego shit going down, because we'd got to that point where we were a big band. We had reached our peak, and then everyone could just see it all falling away. That feeling that it could be over at any moment was stronger than ever.

What I didn't really know at the time, and couldn't have foreseen, was that it would be quite a slow process getting accepted by the rest of the band, for what I contributed to the success we enjoyed. It felt like I was accepted at the time, because we were all partying together and getting high, but little did I know that a resentment was festering about my role, which wouldn't really surface until the shit finally hit the fan, and everything started to unravel. My acceptance by the others wouldn't kick in until the Mondays had died and been reborn again.

*

Our experience of the high life reached its zenith in January 1991, when we flew to Brazil to perform at Rock In Rio II in the Maracana Stadium - another amazing trip with the Happy Mondays. We'd originally only been booked to stay out there for three days, but we ended up staying a week because our instruments didn't turn up off the plane when we landed at the terminal, so we had to wait around in central Rio de Janeiro for them to materialise.

You could say that our reputation had preceded us. A lot of the bands playing at the festival had arrived at the airport around the same time, ready for press conferences on site, but then when we were all getting transported to our accommodation, it transpired that all the others were getting put up in the same hotel on Copacabana beach, except for us and Guns N' Roses - the two bands they perceived as being the most disruptive. They'd given us our own place, the International Hotel, six miles up the coast, out of harm's way.

Still, it was a bit of a crazed time, and we managed to cause absolute chaos. We were originally supposed to have gone onstage as main support to George Michael, but because of the delay with the equipment we were shuffled over onto the day with Norwegian synthpop pin-ups A-ha, which ended up breaking the world record for attendance at a ticketed gig - 198,000 crazed Brazilians, who had all read the front-page headline of the main paper out there - 'Happy Mondays will throw 1000 Es into the audience!'

The gig itself was incredible. We didn't think many people really knew who we were, so we weren't sure how we'd go down, but that side of things went pretty well all things considered, and we got really good write-ups in the Brazilian papers. After drawing such a massive crowd, A-ha felt that it was the biggest achievement of their career, but that we'd got all the press for it.

After a day or two out there, Piers Morgan, who was showbiz correspondent at the *Sun* back then and who'd obviously come over on some press junket or other, took us out to introduce us to the Great Train Robber, Ronnie Biggs, so they could get a front-page cover story, with photographs of us lot all together. The band always got on well with Piers. He always jokingly says that when we were having our barbecue with Ronnie, I stuck something in his burger, like I had spiked him and he was off his head. That's one of the stories he likes to tell, but I can't say that there's any truth in it.

That day, we also met this fella who was a former quartermaster for the IRA - another most-wanted man on the run in Brazil. He scored us humongous amounts of cocaine, so I had a mountain two-feet high on the table in my hotel room, which we proceeded to work through over the course of our stay. One night, we went to this club called Help, which was full of Brazilian prostitutes, and we had a few of them back afterwards. This one bird kept looking at the mountain of coke almost in disbelief, like she'd never seen so much in one place, and she wouldn't leave. In the end, I had to borrow $50 off Rowetta to get rid of her. Row's a good friend like that.

On the last night, we were back at Help, which was still packed full of Brazilian prostitutes, so you can imagine what the lads were like. One of them - and it had to be Paul Ryder - had this brass back, and he decided to give her some methadone. She fell asleep and wasn't to be woken, so he went in her purse, stole his money back off her, packed his bag and left the room! Instead of the prostitutes robbing us, they ended up getting robbed themselves, and this woman caused mayhem - the police were running about, all this commotion throughout the hotel, bedlam going on.

Luckily it was our last day, and we were off to the airport, but I'd still got about an ounce of this coke to get through. I ended up sniffing it all on the plane in First Class all the way home. I was fidgeting and licking my lips that much, I had a big rash right around my mouth. These were the times when the Happy Mondays were outrageous.

At one point, I noticed that there was an empty aisle seat in a prime spot with extra legroom, and I was jumping over all these other seats to get to it. After much kerfuffle, I'd made it and I flopped down, and everyone was laughing because Piers Morgan was in the next seat - it was free because nobody else wanted to sit next to him! So it was me and one of the lads from the band, who was sat the other side by the window, both with blankets over our heads, as we sniffed and licked all the way home.

Poor old Piers was shitting himself, pretending he was asleep through the whole of this twelve-hour flight. He totally knew who we were, but with us both snorting away, he was just trying to make out that he didn't.

We gigged intensively through the first half of that year, but already, after only a few months since the last album release, Factory were talking with increasing urgency about us recording the next one. The main issue was that Factory was in financial trouble, and they needed our album as quick as possible - to save their arse, kind of thing. Given how well *Pills 'n' Thrills* had turned out - it was the dream ticket, people of all music tastes just loved it - everyone wanted another Oakenfold–Osborne mix.

There was a problem, though, because those two were now much in demand and their diary was full. At our end, meanwhile, time was tight, so we ended up with Chris Frantz and Tina Weymouth from Talking Heads, more heroes from our youth. Because Chris and Tina had a home in the Caribbean, instead of various places we'd scouted out in Manchester, Amsterdam, Jamaica and Miami, in January 1992 we eventually took up residence in Eddy Grant's Blue Wave Studio in Saint Philip, Barbados, to record the album which became . . . *Yes Please!*

While we were out there, Shaun and I went down the same road as the first New York visit, toking on that highly more-ish smokable form of cocaine, and it turned into a crazy few months. We all had our own hire vehicles out there, and I'd found all the short cuts from where we were recording to the local village. I was cutting down through all the sugarcane fields, on these off-road tracks that I'd discovered.

One time I was off getting rum and coke for the team, and in my enthusiasm I managed to turn the vehicle over, and that's when I've done my arm in. But I didn't break a single bottle of rum, which was good - and I got back with the coke, too.

To be truthful, my perception of Barbados back then was coloured by my need to satisfy certain cravings I was feeling, morning, noon and night. When I went there for a holiday years later with my missus, it was fucking great, nothing like I remembered it. I'd missed out on a whole load of shit on that first visit because I was all caught up in the Persians, and that was our life.

*

SHAUN: Out in Barbados, we would go scoring crack in these cars. The hire firm we were dealing with had about fifteen vehicles, and we smashed them all up. They had no cars left by the end. What we used to do, once we'd smashed the car up, we took the car battery out because we could get a quarter of an ounce of stone for that.

Just one rock over there – we'd never seen them this size before. You'd pay twenty quid for a tiny pea in England; over there, you'd get a rock the size of a conker for twenty pence, and you could get ounces of the shit, and eighths and quarters at various knock-down prices, so we would take a car battery and get a quarter of stone for it – literally! We had a good trade going in car batteries with the local dealers.

We were racing about in these cars, scoring, but you just knew from looking at the potholes in the grass that you didn't drive on those bits. I remember looking out from Eddy Grant's place, and spotting Bez driving back one day. It was obviously his turn to go and score, but he'd used this short cut to come back, across what looked like a field.

I'm watching him whizzing along in one of the cars that we've hired, an open-top four-by-four, and then I see it go – bump! – up in the air, then down, and it just disappeared in this giant crater. Next thing, you could see him walking towards you, and he's dragging his leg, and his arm is just dangling down to the ground, out of its socket. So that's when he ended up with all the pins in his arm, and that contraption on the outside holding it together.

*

Before we went out to Saint Philip, I'd started taking my mate Kermit, aka Paul Leveridge, to band rehearsals. I first met him in the Hacienda days and I started hanging about with him at the Kitchen, an illegal party that was going on in Hulme Crescent. It was basically a squat made up of four flats that had been knocked into each other, to create one big nightclub. It was all part of that rave culture in the days when you still had 'blues', and unlicensed clubs. In Manchester there was the old Dunlop building, an old warehouse space, and there was the Kitchen, which was our preferred hang-out.

He's a fucking genius, Kermit, from Moss Side. His family are really nice church-going Jamaican types, but very strict and old-fashioned, so he rebelled with a bit of a rude-boy attitude, this 'tough from the hood' thing. That's totally what he was, but he's also a naturally gifted musician who won a scholarship to Manchester School of Music on the violin! He's literally a musical genius, and a brilliant writer, and he definitely caught everyone's attention in Manchester in his early days in the Ruthless Rap Assassins.

Kermit really wanted to do something with Shaun, so it was his idea rather than mine, but I was like, 'Okay, I'll take you down to some practices, and let's see if we can get something going.' I actually introduced him to the band before Shaun, getting him involved with us slowly but surely.

Fast-forward to the sessions in Barbados, which were pretty ragged, and there was a load of arguing. We definitely didn't come away with a finished album. Some more recording went on when we got home again, and the obvious thing to help fill out the remainder of the album was for Shaun to cut a collaboration with Kermit, which was how 'Cut 'Em Loose Bruce' came about.

At that stage, it didn't really help the album. I think Chris and Tina did a really good job, using their old-school analogue style from Tom Tom Club in the early 80s, but what we really should've been doing was looking for the next contemporary sound. Right from the start, . . . *Yes Please!* got slagged by the British press for the simple reason that it wasn't like *Pills 'n' Thrills*.

Suddenly everything was falling apart. The rest of the band – Gaz, Horse and Paul Davis, but less so Mark Day because he never got involved in anything political – were all moaning about how much money me and Shaun were spending out of our budget, to pay for all our drug-taking antics. They used to get extremely upset with me, because somehow in the money stakes I always seemed to come second after Shaun in getting the most out of management, but that's because I was in the office every day demanding it off Nathan McGough, and they weren't.

The bickering had escalated so quickly that everyone, even Nathan, thought the end was nigh. He was trying to sign off a deal with EMI, so he could get his last 20 per cent and bail out.

SHAUN: Our kid Paul and Gaz Whelan got very jealous of me and Bez, because all those years ago we'd decided to do the press since they didn't want to do it. Me and Bez did it, with our personalities, and that's what built the band and got us known. Then when the door started being held open for me and Bez at *Top of the Pops*, because we've got all the front covers because we did the press, and the door was let go once we'd gone through because they didn't know who the fuck the others were, that really started to rankle, and that's when the whole band started to break down – out of jealousy.

Me and Bez became the heads of the Mondays, and everyone wanted to speak to us. Even when we stepped back and said, 'Well, how about you journalists go and speak to those guys instead?' they didn't want to speak to them because they were fucking boring, or they were trying to be something that they weren't – like my brother trying to sound like an intellectual. Me and Bez were just how we are, which was actually pretty much the same as how they were, but they decided that they had to be 'serious musicians', which they weren't.

That's why they got on so well with Chris and Tina, because those two really knew where to tickle their belly, by saying things like, 'You guys are great musicians, you do this and that . . .' They really liked that, but at the end of the day, they're self-taught. Nobody could read music apart from Mark Day, it was only him who knew what an A chord was, so everybody looked to him to find out what key a song was in. Then those guys started to pretend they were real musos, and that's when the war started, and everything me and Bez said was a lie, and everything they said was fact. It was very petty.

The first sign of criticism for the Happy Mondays was . . . *Yes Please!* We always got great reviews – on 'Freaky Dancing', on 'Delightful', on *Bummed*. The criticism only came in when we did . . . *Yes Please!* and it was basically because we didn't have Oakenfold and Osborne and had gone with Chris and Tina instead – and that was *their idea*.

If something isn't fucking broke, then don't fuck with it, right? I was willing to wait for Oakenfold and Osborne. Their attitude was, 'We made them, so it doesn't matter that they're busy doing remixes for U2, and actually earning money and getting the respect that's due to them from *Pills 'n' Thrills.*' They thought Oakey and Steve should drop everything to do our next album, and they saw it as a diss when they asked us to just wait a few months, and they went and got Chris and Tina. That was all their idea.

Chris and Tina are brilliant producers, and they did brilliant things with Tom Tom Club, but they weren't right for Happy Mondays. The only thing about . . . *Yes Please!* which made it different was my lyrics, and the way that I sing. Otherwise you would've had a pretty static thing there.

It wasn't broke, what we had going with Oakenfold. They gave us our first major crossover pop album. *Bummed* was very indie, really cool, but to really break us, and go to *Top of the Pops* and become a big group, *Pills 'n' Thrills* was the commercial album we needed. To follow it up, we just needed another one, which meant waiting for Oakenfold and Osborne.

When those dickheads' big idea misfired and . . . *Yes Please!* wasn't as big a hit and Factory started going bust, suddenly me and Bez were blamed for taking drugs and ruining it. 'But guys, we've been taking drugs since day fucking one!'

The politics of why the band fell apart was because the others were sick of me and Shaun. Us two fought tooth and nail to keep the band together. There was a massive run of events, both sides were there at this meeting to sign the deal with EMI, but Shaun just walked off, saying, 'I'm off to get a Kentucky!' because we knew that the deal wasn't particularly good, and that me and him were being sold up the river.

It could've all worked out so much differently. We were on the cusp of Shaun and Kermit's relationship building after 'Cut 'Em Loose Bruce'. That was the stepping stone to the future. Me and Shaun were convinced that there was good stuff to come because anyone could see that their writing partnership would grow into something amazing, the way they just fed off each other. That's where the whole direction of the band should've been heading, but the rest of them just couldn't see beyond what was happening with the money at that particular moment, which was really sad.

The others basically lost patience, and decided to walk and form their own band called Delicious, with our security man Everton as the singer. I'm not exactly sure what was going on in their heads, but we knew they were making a very big mistake, and it didn't work out for them. They thought they could go on without me and Shaun, but they didn't factor in that you're only as good as your frontman and songwriter-singer. Once you've lost that, you're just back to struggling with everybody else.

Through our whole career up to that point, we never had massive money. Right through the Mondays, we were victims - a textbook case of how *not* to do it. We were ripped off and stolen from by absolutely everybody. There's not one man through our history who's not had his fingers in the pot. We suffered from poor management, and from not being business-savvy.

But we can't go back and change shit, and I'm forever grateful for being in Happy Mondays, because I'm fifty-eight now, and I'm *still* making a living from the band itself, and from that connection. It has enabled me to live a life I could never have dreamed of living, so I'm not voicing any of the regrets with too much bitterness - just that it would've been great to have had the hindsight in advance.

Chapter 4

NOT STRAIGHT, BUT GREAT

After the Happy Mondays fell apart, Shaun wanted so badly to come right back with something new before the trail went cold on him that he got us properly fucked over by the business. Shaun and I have always been friends, ever since we met. There's never any problem between us, but this was the period which tested our friendship the hardest.

All musicians are the same: they'll put up with anything to pursue their dream, and to keep that dream alive. They want to do what they love doing that much, everything else becomes irrelevant. The problem is: that way you set yourself up to become a victim. Your need to succeed blinds you to everything else that's going on around you.

In our minds, the whole process of forming Black Grape was about proving everyone wrong. We knew that the collaboration with my mate Kermit during the making of . . . *Yes Please!* pointed the way forwards. Kermit is such a great character, totally over the top. He's got this amazing bubbling energy, so full of life and ideas, and he's really fun to be around. I'd been bringing him along to rehearsals because I could see that him and Shaun would create magic together. Shaun and Kermit was the future.

During that period of transition between the two bands, which was probably only a few weeks, I fell back into low-level criminality - selling weed, kilos of the shit, like I was before the Mondays. That was the beginning of a road that led to me getting kidnapped three or four years later, and only thereafter would I try to put crime behind me once and for all. But at this point, I was making quite a bit of cash out of it – probably more than I was out of music in the final days of the Mondays, when we were supposedly huge rock stars.

With that money I paid for a trip to LA, to sort a deal with this label, Radioactive, because, as we quickly found out, they never paid for anything. I stumped up the air fares to go over there to keep Shaun company, to be a mate, and make sure everything went sweet for him.

It turned out that the guy behind the label, Gary Kurfirst, was a total gangster. Shaun ended up signing this shit deal with him that's known in the business as a 'New York contract', which basically ends up with you getting shafted every step of the way.

Right from the beginning, I was telling Shaun not to sign on the dotted line.

'You can't do it, X!'

'I don't give a fuck, I'm doing it!'

He just wanted to get back so badly, he was willing to sacrifice everything. After the Mondays had fallen apart in such a daft and avoidable way, Shaun was utterly determined to get something positive going, and very quickly he started working on Black Grape with people we knew from around Manchester. The first guitarist he got in to work on it was Martin Wright from Intastella, who might have played a part in writing some of the first songs, but it actually took a while to build the right band up.

Shaun brought in Wags, aka Paul Wagstaff out of Paris Angels, and with Kermit came Ged Lynch from Ruthless Rap Assassins, a great drummer, and a really talented young kid called Martin Slattery on keyboards and saxophone. It was a funny old mix of people, because Shaun, Wags and Kermit - and myself, of course! - were all way out there, totally flying the whole time and living life on the edge, and then the backbone of the band, Ged and Martin, were completely straight. We might have corrupted Martin a little bit along the way, but I don't think those two quite knew how to cope with this indoctrination into the hardcore party lifestyle.

Everything started out fine, because we got hooked up with this young rap producer from LA called Danny Saber. The problem with . . . *Yes Please!* had been that people wanted us to move forward with that modern acid-house production we'd had with Paul Oakenfold and Steve Osborne in charge, and they thought that what we'd done out in Barbados was a step back - which I thought was unfair. We made the best album we could in the circumstances, but we got really panned for it.

Having Danny Saber produce Black Grape was about recapturing that modern production vibe, and having Kermit rapping on there made it double-new and fresh again. We did most of the album at Rockfield, this legendary residential studio in Monmouth, South Wales. Kermit and Shaun were really good writing partners - the only collaboration Shaun ever had like that. They worked well together, bouncing off each other for lyrics and vibes.

But the whole business side of the band was set up so badly for us. I always knew we were getting ripped off, before even the first note was played at Rockfield. I was paying for everything, paying for the band's costs day by day. Up in Manchester, I was running about in the car, picking up all the band members from their respective homes for rehearsals, and I never even got a quid towards my petrol. When it came to getting down to the recording studio in South Wales, I was acting like a tour manager, running everyone down there – and because the Mondays had broken up and Shaun had signed this dodgy deal with zero advance, I'd gone from a Golf GTI to a fucking tatty £500 Escort – I used to drive it full-throttle like it was still my GTI, but it wasn't.

Still, overall it was good times, and there was a lot of hope going into the sessions that we'd all be rolling in it not too much further down the track.

The funny thing about Rockfield is that nobody can actually remember very much of what went on. Like it says in the song 'Tramazi Parti', there was a lot of temazepam being taken. We were getting high on absolutely everything that was at our disposal – that was just the way we were rolling back then, and it was a significant part of how we went about making music.

It turned out that the Stone Roses were just down the road at this other studio, Monnow Valley, finally finishing off their *Second Coming* album. Even though the press were always going out of their way to build up some perceived 'Madchester' rivalry and hatred between us and the Roses, there never was any of that. Mani was from the same area of Salford as me, so we've always been good mates, and it's the same with all of the Roses, because we came up together as young bands working the scene. Once we realised we were both recording within spitting distance of each other, we were each listening to each other's record while we were making our own one, and I'm pretty sure that at least a couple of them came down to join our little Temazi celebrations – probably!

For our part, we knew we were making a really good album, doing something amazing musically, and when it came

out in 1995, *It's Great When You're Straight . . . Yeah* was actually very well received and became the biggest-selling record
that we've ever had. We all got platinum discs. We went to
Number One for two weeks in the album charts, and great
times were had touring the album.

Things were moving. Shaun was going out with one of
Donovan's daughters, Oriole, and there was a feeling after the
end of the Mondays that things were back on track. Loads of
journalists had relished saying that me and Shaun were finished.
It was like, 'So who's fucking dead now?' That was the whole
vibe of the time. It felt like we were going to be bigger and
better than ever, and we'd proved everybody who'd written us
off wrong.

SHAUN: Here's one of the mad things, right? As soon as it
was out there that the Mondays had split up, literally within
a matter of hours I got a call off this guy Gary Kurfirst, who'd
managed Blondie, the Ramones, Talking Heads, Jane's
Addiction – he even went back as far as bands like The
Doors in the 60s. Kurfirst had his own label, Radioactive,
which he licensed out of MCA. He calls me and says he
wants me to be a solo artist, and within a couple of days I
was on a flight with a pal of mine who used to do security
called Pat Ward – he's now doing thirty-five years in prison,
by the way – and I got signed up with Kurfirst.

But nobody knew back in Manchester, so when I've
come home, I had Tony Wilson and Alan Erasmus from
Factory knocking at my door, saying, 'You've fucked up
here, Shaun, you know!' Everyone's believing the Paul
Ryder, Gaz Whelan and Mark Day story: 'Oh, Shaun is
finished, he's on drugs, he's lost the plot.' Because they'd

got three people saying that thing, as against one person who's saying nothing, they believed the three people.

I wasn't about to start shouting out who I've got behind me now, but them three are all saying how they're going to do something else and they're going to be massive. They were telling all the press how another one of our security guys, who's an old pal of mine, had become their lead singer in the 'new Happy Mondays'.

In the meantime, I agreed to do this track with Intastella called 'Can You Fly Like You Mean It? (Gungadin)', and even they were swallowing all this hype as well, thinking that I really needed to do it. But I did it anyway, and then this bunch of fuckers – I got them their first proper front cover and everything, for this single – when I asked them to do something for me in my new thing, it was, 'I've got to go to the pictures with my girlfriend!' and 'I can't come out tonight because my girlfriend wants us to go to her mum's!' I'm thinking, 'With an attitude like that, we really know why you've not made it in the music business . . .'

None of these other bands have got any television work, but I go on *The Word* and I'm dancing with Zippy and Bungle from the ITV kids programme, *Rainbow*. People were saying, 'This is where Shaun Ryder's career is, dancing with Zippy and Bungle!' To me, I'm on telly, it's publicity, but I also know what I've got coming.

Gary Kurfirst wanted to sign me as a solo artist, but I wasn't ready to be a solo artist. I was still in the frame of mind like, 'I need a band around me. I want to be in a band situation.' As I grew up over time, I realised that the best way is *not* to be in a band situation! Use session guys! Do it all yourself! But at that stage I felt like I needed a group environment, so I got Black Grape together.

Bez came into it because to me that was so obviously where he should've been, where he had to be. What both of us appreciated was that we'd got our break in showbiz, entertainment, music, whatever you want to call it, and on no account were we throwing that away, or giving it up for fucking anything. We'd got an introduction into this world, this life, and that wasn't going anywhere or changing.

The rest of the Mondays did not see it like that. They were just flippant. They made statements like, 'We'd rather be on the dole than work with them two again!' Well, pretty quickly they went back on the fucking dole. Me and Bez didn't, but they did. They did nothing. None of them did anything. All the big bullshit they had of what they were going to do, it was just their egos. They took it for granted, being in that world. That opportunity which was handed to us fuck-ups – all of us, with our conditions, personality disorders or whatever you wanna call them – they threw it away. Their egos fucking spat it out, but us two weren't making that idiotic mistake.

So when it was time to form Black Grape, Bez had to be in it. This is another of Hooky's stories – I mean, I might have something wrong with me, and problems with memory, but he's not supposed to. He tells this story where I wanted Bez out of the band: I did nothing but make sure Bez stayed in. He was my mate! After the Mondays ended, me and Bez opened up Black Grape *together*! Fucking Hooky . . .

Kermit was the other obvious move. The Mondays had done a couple of shows with the Ruthless Rap Assassins, and me and Kermit were drug buddies. We were both heroin addicts, and Manchester at the end of the day is a village. London is huge, isn't it, but in Manchester you get off at the airport or the train station, and anywhere you wanna go you're there in ten minutes. Wigan? Ten minutes down the road. So it's a village, and everybody knows everybody, and if you're in the drug world, that's even smaller. With drug buddies, you've only really got the drug in common, but me and Kermit had music, movies and all sorts besides.

When we were coming back out of Barbados, I had to go to London to write more lyrics, and I decided I was bringing Kermit in to do some writing, and I actually think we had his vocals on a few tracks on the quiet. When the Mondays ended, me and Kermit were together all the time, scoring H, and it was obvious for him to come into Black Grape. But going to record the album at Rockfield, the big thing we were into was Temazis because we had a really good source. We had a friend who knew a nurse with a coke habit, so we were able to get thousands and thousands of them. They came in these little green eggs of twenty or forty mil, and it became an everyday thing to neck four hundred mil. We were gobbling them like toffees.

If ever there was a drug you were going to die on, however, it's that lot – not just because of the drug itself, but because of the situations that the drug gets you into. If you ask around in Scotland, right, where it's unusually popular, anybody who has ever been on the Temazis has either got half a nose, one eye missing, or their throat has been cut, because of the trouble that drug will get you into, especially when mixed with alcohol. Even without, you get very excited. It's possible that you might nod off, because they can do that to you as well, but in the time when you're not nodding off, you do very extrovert things, and it can be extremely funny.

The great thing about getting on them eggs is that you can't remember what you've done, or where you've been. I mean, I've woken up in the basement of restaurants, where I've gone into this place to eat, pulled the girl who was either the manager or the owner, gone into the basement with the girl, spent the night there after the restaurant has closed, shagged her and then woken up like, 'Where the fuck am I? Who is that?' You just don't know. It's like it says in the 'Tramazi Parti' lyrics, 'Oh yeah, I've got my boots on the back of my head, there's a bucket full of jellies in the double bed, and no one knows what no one said'. It really is like that!

So we were doing a ton of them down at Rockfield during recording, and we got that album out of it, so it must've been a productive drug. At the end of the day, it puts you in a very happy-funny-party mood, and you have all these adventures that afterwards you're racking your brain to try and remember. Don't ask what actually happened down there, but the whole album has a very tickly-belly laughy feeling to it, so it was clearly a very funny, happy *Carry On Temazi Party* kind of album to make.

Once we were done, we knew we'd got this great fucking album here, with one of the biggest guys in the music business behind us, but people were still swallowing the whole 'Shaun has lost the plot – oh, he's on drugs' story. Everyone was still believing all this shit, so it was really sweet for me when the album comes out and I go to Number One. Then you had all the Intastella mugs saying, 'Well, I play guitar on that, I want some money!' It wasn't like we were ever not going to pay them for what they've done, but it was like pulling teeth getting these fuckers to do anything at the time, just to give me a few hours, because they were having dinner with the future father-in-law, so they went out of the picture as quickly as they came in.

When the album went to Number fucking One, boy, did they jump out of the woodwork, saying, 'I want this much for that guitar riff, and I want paying for this!' Back then, they all thought they were super-big, so I got revenge on all of them in the end, because unluckily for them they didn't get to enjoy the ride with us.

We all understood that we were creating something new and thrilling, like an indie hip-hop hybrid album, which nobody had really done before, at least not very well or convincingly. There was excitement in the band about the magic formula of Shaun and Kermit. Everyone was playing above and beyond their normal game, certainly by comparison with anything the other musicians had ever done before. We knew it was going to be an explosive comeback.

To be very charitable, maybe Radioactive weren't expecting the euphoric response that greeted the album, but the label together with management soon killed off all the positivity and destroyed something really special. If everyone had been treated right, and paid right, instead of them looking at the whole thing as a quick cash-in for themselves, it could've gone on to become something lasting. But no, they soon ripped the heart out of the band, and caused arguments and fall-outs and upsets that still reverberate through to this day. They snuffed out that magical writing partnership to the point where Shaun and Kermit didn't speak for almost twenty years. It was so sad.

It started off so ace, but very slowly the realisation of what was happening to us was dawning - we were getting carved out of the money that was rightfully ours, and it became like a nightmare. We were all so fucking skint, it was unbelievable. Through the whole recording of the album, we never got anything. Then we sold over a million albums worldwide, reached the top of the charts in the UK, got voted Number One in loads of end-of-year polls, and had tunes on fifteen different movie soundtracks, and still none of us had any cash in our pockets. It got to 600,000 sales in Britain and we hadn't even had a tenner out of them.

Even now, not one of us has had a penny off Radioactive. All I earned that year after the album release was £18,000 from a monthly wage. What's more, I was still basically funding the whole operation, paying for the band out of the money I was getting from selling drugs. It was crazy: I was on *Top of the Pops* and doing TV shows, but still having to make my living off the streets.

It's in my nature that I'm often trying to be the peacemaker, and in that situation where I felt that I was basically supporting everyone financially while we were getting shafted, I started to act like a trade unionist, trying to resolve the situation more in our favour.

One time when we were on *Top of the Pops*, it all finally came to a crisis point. For myself, I had money - my own money, not loads, but I was the only one in the band who had other income from the shit I was doing. I was dressed smart, I still had all my clobber. While we were at *TOTP*, I saw this exec from EMI floating about - Radioactive was just a subsidiary of EMI over here in Britain - so I took this geezer aside.

'Fucking hell, mate, this is beyond a joke,' I said, 'we're on *Top of the Pops* and we all look like a bag of shit, like we're fucking skint - which we are! We're going on national TV here to promote our record for you, can't you sort us some dough out for a bit of new wardrobe?'

The guy gave me a puzzled look.

'We just sent your management £10,000 to give to the band,' he replies.

'What? You gave them ten grand and none of us have had a penny of it?'

I started having a go at him for taking the piss out of us, but everyone later told me I was being highly diplomatic, trying to act as a trade unionist, and very reasonably threatening to arrange walkouts and stage protests to get our money. I just wanted some reward for the band, really, more for them than for me. I was standing up for everyone, trying to get everyone paid, but the rest of the band just left me on my own there, and I felt like I was getting hung out to dry.

It all came back to the fact that they were being taken advantage of, because they still believed in the dream of being in a band, at any cost. They were having the piss taken out of them, because they were too scared to put their head above the parapet.

Someone had to act, I thought. I decided I was going to batter one of our management team, so I blazed over to their office, and I totally lost it with this guy. I just started smashing him all over the place, giving him the biggest smack he has ever had in his life, across the whole side of his face. The mad thing about it: years later, I met a girl who was in the room when it was all kicking off, and she was hiding under a desk, totally petrified, too frightened to come out. Job done, I just walked off and left them to it.

In the days that followed, I had a falling out with Shaun, because I didn't think that he'd stood up for the band, or himself.

I was so angry about the whole situation, because I'd known what was gonna happen right from the off, and I'd sat there saying to Shaun that I smelled a rat. The only sound advice he was getting was off me, and he was having none of it. After the mess we'd made of the financial situation in the Mondays, it was like my worst nightmare, happening all over again.

The penny had finally dropped for me that the whole project wasn't going to turn out well, and with a heavy heart I told Shaun I was leaving the band, because I refused to get ripped off like that. It would've been so soul-destroying to carry on working for these bastards, knowing they were never gonna pay us a penny.

SHAUN: Bez was in Black Grape at first, because of course he had to come along and be in it. He couldn't not be, and it was important to get him back for the image, and how he looked in videos and photos, and for his presence onstage. But all of a sudden, on the side, he'd started to get a lot of work as a DJ.

Another factor was that he was spending far too much money. In the new arrangement with this band, we were trying to keep an eye on budgets, and not have ludicrous outgoings like before – you know, when you're off your head and you've got to buy 100 Es every night, so you never actually turn a profit and have money to live on. This is how the conversation went:

'What do you need, Bez?'

'I need a hundred Es.'

'Er, okay! I mean, there are ten gigs – can't you just have twenty Es?'

'Yeah, but if I get a hundred, I'll give ninety of them away to friends and fans, and I'll have ten for myself!'

The idea with Black Grape was that we were a bit older and wiser, and we weren't gonna let it go like the Mondays went. We were at the stage where we'd have two tour buses, one for the crew and the caterers, and one for the band, keeping things organised and sensible. Muzzer, the tour manager, and I were clamping down on a lot of things that in the cold light of day we saw as a waste, but because Bez was still in his full-blown adolescent party mode, and not thinking like a businessman, it caused problems. Bez was still Bez, but I didn't want it to go the same way as the Mondays went, throwing money down the toilet.

So there were little bits of a fall-out going on, also with marriages and things. I didn't exactly have the hump with him. We did the Black Grape tour, and then Bez went off to do his DJing, and not do Black Grape.

The good thing was that his profile had gone right up again, and the DJing and the other things he was doing were earning him really good money, so he didn't need to be getting paid for going onstage with us so much. He was generating his own work and being successful in his own right. He was becoming his own industry.

Looking back today, I can't believe I stayed around as long as I did, knowing before a note was played that we were getting stitched up, telling Shaun it was happening, trying to stop it but not getting listened to. Shaun was like, 'Radioactive's the biggest independent label in America, B, look at Gary Kurfirst's track record of artists, blah blah blah.' He'd been sold the dream, so he turned a blind eye to all the wrongs that were going on, because all he cared about was the comeback.

What really pissed me off after I left, was that Shaun and everyone else were trying to pretend that I was still in Black Grape. It was the biggest scam ever! The next single that came out, they had me in the video as if nothing had changed – even more untoward shit going on – and from the outside it probably looked like everything was hunky-dory.

When I made my first proper bit of money out of Happy Mondays, after *Pills 'n' Thrills* took off, I got a mortgage and bought a place in Glossop, Derbyshire. It was just a mid-terrace house in a three-row plot in a semi-rural district, right on the edge of civilisation. Once you went past my pad, that was pretty much the end of Manchester. From there on, it was the moors, and the next stop was Sheffield.

It wasn't particularly posh or glamourous, not like a big mansion of anything – just a nice working-class stone cottage with a Victorian fireplace and a shared back garden. A family home for me and my partner Debs to bring up our kids in, and the first house that I ever owned.

While it had that feeling of remoteness, it wasn't really like moving away, because the centre of Manchester was still only a twenty-minute drive away – jump in the car and you were back in the thick of it all in no time. I actually really loved it around there, being in the countryside and doing a lot of bike riding. I found it a really calming place to live, and a welcome break finally from the urban madness I'd grown up with.

The main reason I chose Glossop over Salford was because I didn't want my two sons growing up in an inner-city environment and maybe going through all the criminal shit that I went through. Arlo and Jack had been born in 1991 and 1992 respectively, at the height of the Mondays, and I wanted to

Me and Shaun performing at the London Astoria back in 1989.

Early Happy Mondays in a Transit van on the way to a gig in 1987.

Hanging out in London with Shaun, 1987.

Happy Mondays in 1990. From left to right: Paul Ryder, me, Gary Whelan, Mark Day, Shaun Ryder, Paul Davis.

Performing at Pinkpop festival in the Netherlands, 1991.

Me and Rowetta performing at the BRIT Awards in 1991.

Shaking my maracas during the video shoot for 'Kinky Afro' in 1990.

Kermit, me and Shaun. Black Grape in 1995.

Performing with Happy Mondays at Utilita Arena in Birmingham, 2021.

DJing at the Pretty Green store in Manchester with my son Arlo.

With Firouzeh and our two dogs, Yoko and Snoop.

With my youngest son, Leo.

With Firouzeh at Glastonbury, enjoying the music in Gaz Mayall's Rocket Lounge.

Shaking my maracas while wing walking to raise money for Tonic Music for Mental Health, as part of Barry Ashworth's Flying Circus.

Me and my family on a fishing trip in Cornwall. From left to right: my wife Firouzeh, my sons Jack and Leo, my grandson Luca and my son Arlo.

Me and Firouzeh at Camp Bestival after our debut performance of 'Flying Bus', the track we co-wrote with Doorly.

Action shot from my first boxing match, against Clayton Blackmore.

Barman Bez serving beer in The Shack, my self-made bar in the garden, where some of the best parties happen.

My first catch! As a child, I would go fishing with my grandad.

Posing with my bees as I harvest honey from a hive on the roof of The Printworks in Manchester.

At Barton Moss, protesting against fracking.

Me and Firouzeh doing our 'bed in' as part of the Reality Party campaign.

Chef Stephen Terry giving me some cooking lessons ahead of my appearance on BBC's *Celebrity MasterChef*.

Mid-routine on ITV's *Dancing on Ice*, with my partner, Angela Egan.

take them away from all that gang nonsense and bring them up in the 01457 zone, which foolishly I thought was a nice respectable area.

It's like any neighbourhood, though: kids are kids, and they'll get up to whatever they choose to get up to. It doesn't really matter where you take them, they'll find trouble if they really want to, but all their friends were really nice kids who weren't into crime, and that was my main concern. I didn't want them growing up with anyone influencing them to get involved in that side of life.

These days, the way the media works, kids are socially conditioned to believe that to be bad is to be cool. They're force-fed ideas and images and news stories where they end up believing in some way or another that the badder you are the cooler you are. That's not the direction I wanted for my kids. I didn't want them growing up with gang culture, thinking they had to get involved in stealing, stabbing and all the shit that goes on in the inner city. I wanted them not to experience that first-hand, and to have a chance of growing up differently, with better prospects, without those pitfalls.

As it happened, a lot of friends followed me out to our little corner of Glossop, including the Mondays' old security guy Pat Ward, who lived across the road, so I had a little community going on there – Mancunian expats moving out of the city – and it became a very happy place for me.

When I landed up back there after walking out on Black Grape, however, I was in terrible shape emotionally. Splitting up from a band is like divorcing your missus. Seriously, that's the only thing I can compare it to, a heart-breaking feeling, and although I probably wasn't admitting it to myself yet, leaving Black Grape had been really traumatic for me.

One night, I was sat at home in Glossop, and there was a knock at the door. I opened up, and there on my doorstep was Joe Strummer, with his wife Luce and his stepdaughter Eliza.

We'd become friendly with Joe, because he'd been turning up to Mondays and Black Grape gigs every now and then, to the point where in 1996, we teamed up with him to make an alternative anthem for our international football team for Euro 96, called 'England's Irie'. The track was great, too, but it certainly wasn't like the official theme tune. I don't think the FA would've gone for 'pull the trigger and fire like this' as their singalong chorus - that wouldn't have gone down well with the authorities. We had a load of fun making it, because Keith Allen was involved, too, and he definitely liked a party.

I'd hung out with Joe and his family at a couple of festivals that summer and got to know him a bit better. He'd obviously been a really massive influence from his days in The Clash, but now he was becoming like a mentor to me. That night, he turned up at my house with some DMT and a few cassettes of Colombian cumbia - a drug I'd never taken before, and a type of party music I'd not yet investigated - and we became even better friends after that.

Joe knew that I was in a fucking bad way, and it was like he was the only person in the world who understood the pain I was in. What I didn't realise until later was how bad of a patch Joe was in at the time himself - he'd had many dark days in the aftermath of The Clash, and it would be another two or three years before he put together the Mescaleros and made his big comeback.

He was a great character, and he lived the rock 'n' roll life-style so well. Joe was very warm, a real people person, and he was an inspiration to me in how to treat others and conduct yourself as a publicly known person. Like myself, he loved having a drink and socialising. He was at his best in those kind of settings, and after his darker days he was just getting back into exploring that side of himself. I identified with that, and Joe became like a role model to me.

It's so amazing when I think back to it today: this absolute fucking legend of punk rock had come to my rescue. Joe Strummer was tuned in to me. We were two injured souls, and so he took me under his wing, sorted my head out and showed me the way forward.

Another reason I was struggling was, now that I'd had my two kids with Debs and I was actually back home more, I was having to face up to the responsibilities of fatherhood. A lot of what we talked about that night in Glossop, on top of how to cope after quitting a band you loved, was Joe showing me how to incorporate your family into a rock 'n' roll lifestyle. You shouldn't view them as separate and incompatible entities. He showed me a lot of things – and, as we'll see later, many avenues and ideas that have been really helpful and inspirational in my life came through him.

SHAUN: I wasn't really privy to Bez's Strummer relationship because each of us was off doing their own thing at that time. Joe entered the picture on the scene in London in the mid-90s. We hung out quite a bit with the Primal Scream lot, and Strummer would be at the same parties. Primal Scream had this roadie guy called Fatty, aka Stephen Molloy, and he had a place called Fatty's Bar & Grill, like an unlicensed drinking den, and that was where we'd meet a lot of people like Joe.

Then at some point I actually hung around with Joe in LA. He was doing stuff for Walt Disney at the time, and he'd got me to come into the studio to work on some tracks for one of these Disney movies. It had totally gone out of my head until recently when someone produced some photographs, but me and Strummer actually drove down to Mexico together on this fucking beatnik adventure. But I didn't go and hang out with Joe at his house, and I didn't go on any holidays with Joe, or go on these fucking communal retreats to Buddha-land – that was Bez.

Another of his mates around that time was Johnny Depp. Johnny was going out with Kate Moss, and Bez was knocking about with Kate's PA-cum-best friend, Jess, who he'd met on the London party scene, so Bez, Johnny, Kate and this Jess were always going out for meals and hanging out around each other. I got to know them to say hi to, but Bez had the friendship.

We were spending a lot of time in London, doing covers for *Loaded* and all sorts of other things. Manchester might have been the hub in the late 80s, where people from London were coming up north to sign bands, but by the time we were into 1994, '95, '96, most of the work was in London. In 1995, I moved into a place in Hampstead, and Muzzer actually had the flat below, so when Bez came down from Glossop to London, he'd stay with us there.

Black Grape was still rolling along, and we were doing these exotic videos with Don Letts, because Gary Kurfirst had managed Big Audio Dynamite, and was now managing Don. It was Don's idea to shoot one in Jamaica, and obviously with the crack situation on that island, there were parts of Jamaica that were just as dangerous as the dodgy parts of New York. But obviously we'd got addicts in our band, and we still had to go out and score.

One time a gun battle went off around me and Kermit, but we just took it as how it was. Again, I was on heroin, so nothing really gets through – nothing frightens you, does it? 'Oh, that happened,' and you don't really think about it. Years later, whatever you can remember, you sort of go, 'Wow . . .' You know, in the Chelsea Hotel the day after that first incident in New York, you sort of went, 'Fucking hell, that was life-threatening!' But that was probably the first and last time for years and years where you thought twice about something kicking off. After that, it just became the norm.

Behind the scenes in Black Grape, everything was going pear-shaped: Kermit was suffering with addiction, and nearly died from septicaemia after injecting himself with Spanish tap water for a fix. It got that bad for him that he had to have a pig's valve implanted in his heart. I was turning up at the hospital before the op, and I was really worried for a fucking friend there - I really thought I was going to lose one to junk.

After all that, Kermit quit to go solo, leaving Shaun on his own to make their second album, *Stupid Stupid Stupid*, which never did as well as the first one - as I always say, that's because I'd left the band!

At that point, I had to step in on Shaun's behalf, because he had no money and he was obviously getting ripped off. I paid my own way out to America again to try and look after Shaun, and get a meeting with this New York gangster guy, Gary Kurfirst.

The thing was, it wasn't me that was signed to his label, it was Shaun, so it was me as an outsider coming in again like a

Scouse trade unionist, trying to rectify all these wrongs that I knew were going on and make sure that my mate was treated right. Again, I spent all my own money on the flights, and I certainly didn't get anything off the label to cover those costs. I just knew Shaun was getting taken to the cleaners. I was trying to be like a voice of reason, but he still wasn't having any of it.

You could say my mission was doomed to failure from the start. We very much went down the Barbados route again while we were in LA. As soon as we arrived, we were buying crack among other things, and we both got totally off our heads. Shaun, however, was pretty fucking out there, to new heights, where even I, who has lived a relatively debauched lifestyle, was going to myself, 'Fucking hell, this has got too mad!'

On the way home, he was coming down that much from all the crack we'd been doing, that we scored just before we headed out to the airport. We somehow got through the transatlantic leg of the journey to London, ready for the last domestic flight back up to Manchester, but Shaun was *rattling*. He'd bought about twenty packs of codeine and paracetamol, and he was sitting in the middle of the airport, really off his nut, in front of the whole world, with this pint glass of water, half full but frothing all over the top with this codeine as it dissolved.

We actually got barred from getting on the plane because Shaun was coming down that badly. He was sat in the departure lounge rolling around in pain, and popping this codeine into water so it frothed like a volcano. We missed a second connection back home to Manchester, and we were having proper arguments right there in the airport. We were fucked and jetlagged, we were at each other's throats, and it obviously took fucking forever to get home. It was possibly the first and only time I ever argued publicly with Shaun, over that whole experience, because even I was struggling to cope with his excesses.

The meeting, of course, had been a disaster. I was deemed a troublemaker, and Kurfirst, this big fat gangster, got me banned from America, so I could never get a visa to go back. He knew that I'd been nicked in a drug-free zone in Staten Island and given six months' probation, and I'd never actually done the probation. I was thus classed as a non-reformed character, and Kurfirst obviously tipped off the authorities, so I couldn't intervene any more to disrupt his crooked plan.

Radioactive was the dodgiest firm imaginable.

Either way, though, we're pretty good at fucking things up ourselves.

SHAUN: Black Grape had given Kermit attention: we'd gone on *Top of the Pops*, had a Number One album, and by the time we were ready to make the second album, Kermit had got all these people in his ear, going, 'You don't need the white guy! You're big now, you need to be on your own, doing *your* thing!' So that's what happened: Black Grape ended, Kermit's career didn't take off, and we had a fall-out, me and him, for a long time.

Kermit is a brilliant writer and singer, but he's as mad as a big box of frogs. Look, I am right on with UFOs and aliens, but I'm not right on with the flat earth, right? Kermit is right on with the flat earth and a lot of other things that I regard as bollocks. He's way out there, but he's also the perfect partner for me to write with.

After Black Grape split up, Shaun was at an all-time low. We'd had this major falling out, but I was still his mate. It was his birthday, and you know the saying, rats leaving a sinking ship. All these fucking people who'd been hanging on had all disappeared - gone! - and he was on his own in this shitty flat on what should've been his special day of annual celebration, with all his nearest and dearest around him.

I thought, 'Fuck, it's my mate's birthday, I'm gonna go and see him!'

I took a couple of bottles of champagne and went around to catch up, and I was so shocked by his circumstances. Everyone had abandoned him, the rats had jumped ship. He was at death's door, the worst I've ever seen him in his addiction. All the messing about with crack was over and done with - he was just totally gone on heroin and prescription drugs. He'd completely lost control of his whole body, he was just shaking - so fucking hardcore, it was scary. I really and truly thought that he'd reached the end of the line.

I've always been really fortunate, because even though I've been on some of these same journeys too, I genuinely don't believe that I've ever had an addiction. As I said in an earlier chapter, I've always been able to walk away from anything like that, whenever I wanted to. I've never had that monkey on my back, or been on the vicious downhill slope of addiction, where I suddenly found I was unable to claw my way up again.

For me, with heroin, it's often been more about the experience of having done it, than actually doing it, if you know what I mean. I've never really got deep into it. I've always been able to walk away, because I never really wanted that commitment for myself. Even though I obviously enjoy the party vibe and getting off my head, on Monday morning I'm quite happy to go back to normality. Partying has always been more of a social or recreational thing for me, rather than a full-time occupation. More like going to the pub for a pint!

For Shaun, it was part of his rock 'n' roll journey. He chose that life, to live the dream to its obvious conclusion like David Essex in *Stardust*. He actually used to watch that movie while he was ginking out on his couch! That for Shaun was heroic. He bought into that whole package, the tortured-artist genius thing, and he'd gone down that path as far as you can go, before the Reaper starts taking an interest.

Everyone was hanging on him through the Mondays and Black Grape, and then when they all thought he was finished, all those people were gone. There was only us two left. He wasn't with Oriole any more, all the yes-men had vanished and he was in his worst ever state. After the journey we had been through together, I wasn't going to be one of them rats jumping off the sinking ship. Even though we had fallen out over things, like an old husband and wife having a big row and a bust-up, I had to go back to him. You find out who your friends are, when the chips are down.

I knew I just had to get him out of his present situation, so I moved him up to Glossop, to a house across the back garden from me where I could keep an eye on him and get him off all that shit. There began a long road of getting him straightened out, which eventually wound up with him going out to stay with a cousin for six months in Perth, Australia, where he wrote pretty much the entirety of his debut solo album, *Amateur Night in the Big Top*. That whole journey was him basically turning his life back round again.

Through all of this, he was with another girl called Felicia, who was there for him in that whole period of withdrawal. It must have been really difficult for her, but they actually had a son together. The funny thing was, Shaun could never say her name properly. He told me that it was pronounced 'Faleesha', so all the way through I called her that, and it wasn't till years later after they'd split up that I found out that you were meant to say it 'Fer-liss-ia' - more like Felicity. I'd been mispronouncing it because Shaun, her other half, couldn't say it properly.

The important thing was, he was back.

Chapter 5

THE NEW NORMAL:
JUST BEING BEZ

Anyone looking to script *Bez: The Movie* for the big screen might consider starting right here: I'm on my knees in the front room of a derelict house, while a kid in a balaclava holds a gun at my head. I've chosen this derelict cottage on the outskirts of central Manchester as a quiet location for a weed deal that is now going horribly wrong. Aside from the lad pointing the revolver's barrel at my temple, there's another guy nearby waving a machete about, and way too many more behind them for me to consider any kind of heroic, two-fisted escape.

It's about 1997/98, and as I kneel there trying not think about how this precarious situation will unfold, it starts to dawn on me that my career choices in adult life are finally catching up with me.

Because of the lifestyle we all led before our so-called music career took off, I had plenty of connections in the drugs trade in Manchester, so as the Mondays fell apart and Black Grape failed to bring in the requisite finances that Shaun and I deserved, it was the easiest and most obvious move to go back into what I was doing before – that whole high-tension, easy-money lifestyle of shifting around prescribed substances.

To be clear, my thing was always about acting as a middleman, passing things on between people, shifting around large amounts of hash and grass to different people, all over the country, but not actually buying and selling and dealing it myself. I never had my hand in any of the parcels. I had someone else take them for me, and I'd act as a middleman does, never actually making the transaction myself, just acting as the point of contact and moving the gear along.

It would be about two and a half grand per kilo, and I was making £50 per kilo. That was my price for moving it on - I would just put fifty quid on to each kilo, as my competitive middleman's wages for shouldering that part of the risk.

I had no way of knowing, but this particular deal was a set-up. My contact was a kid I knew really well: we were good friends as he used to knock about quite a bit around the Mondays. It turned out he had been threatened by certain people, and they coerced him into setting me up for this deal.

They told him they wanted twenty kilos off me, so I fixed up the handover at this house I was using as the location. They'd actually asked if I could get more than twenty - one of the usual things they put you through in that situation where they're going to stiff you, because obviously they know they're not going to be paying you, so they might as well hit you for as much as possible - but unfortunately, I hadn't twigged that at the time. On the plus side, I couldn't lay my hands on any more than twenty.

Driving over there, I could see that one car was following us, which I assumed was them - because I'd driven quite errat- ically to make sure I wasn't being followed by anyone else. I didn't see the rest of the cars they had backing them up, so fuck knows how they got there, but as me and my mate piled out of our car, there were loads of them, and they all pulled out weapons, and forced us into the house.

They got me and the other guy down on the ground, started pistol-whipping us, and threatened to cut us with machetes. As I say, the house was outside the city centre, and remote enough that nobody could hear you scream . . . or the gunfire.

There was this one kid with the big machete, and the one with a .45 in my face, and I know for a fact that they'd been ordered to put one in me, because the kid who ordered the kidnap hated me for some reason. I never worked out exactly why, but it's a reasonable assumption that he didn't like the way I rolled at the time. I'd been on *Top of the Pops* and loads of other TV shows, and it was never exactly a secret that my job as a maraca shaker and dancer was intertwined with a more nefarious line of business.

Everyone in the trade knew that from touring with the band I had connections all over the country - more connections than your average 'man'. I had something that they all wanted, so I was more than useful to the majority of Mr Big type people, but there were two sides to the coin because I was also an obvious target for people with a grudge or a chip on their shoulder.

So there I am, held hostage in this house, looking at this cunt with the gun in my face, thinking, 'I could fucking knock you out!' and I'm really considering doing it. I'm trying to show no fear, just staring him down, trying to float him out, and I'm really starting to think I could deck him in one move if I hit him right. The only thing stopping me is the other kid with the machete. He'd cut me down in half a second.

There's no two ways about it: I'm fucked here, and I'm beginning to face up to the realisation that I may be approaching my final curtain, and a rather unglamorous and anonymous one in a knackered old farmhouse.

We're in there for the best part of a day – twelve hours, probably more – and relentlessly I'm getting pistol-whipped, and knocked about, and threatened with getting my hands cut off, while the other kid shivers nervously in the corner. This 'mate' and I aren't ever tied up, just constantly surrounded by heavy armoury, getting harangued for more weed and more money, while I take the punishment in heavy blows and every threat you can think of.

The worst thing about it? The humiliation, the lowest of the low, a terrible feeling I would never want to revisit, and a sickening dread that my end may be nigh.

Here's what saves my life: the kid who set me up starts screaming in the corner – proper squealing like a stuck pig because he's scared out of his wits, even though it's actually me who's getting pistol-whipped, punched, kicked and threatened with being chopped up.

In the middle of my battery, still at gun- and knifepoint, I decide that it really is this kid's turn to get a smacking, and without really thinking of the consequences I run over and boot him in the head as hard as I can. Cue more squealing and snivelling, echoing around the bare four walls.

My luck must be in tonight, because the tension in the room eases fractionally as the balaclava kids all fall about laughing, roaring away at the sight and sound of this kid being pathetic.

There must be something about the way I'm hoofing his head in that gets me off the hook, because while my so-called 'mate' is bawling away on the floor, the kidnappers can't contain their mirth and suddenly just tell me to get the fuck out of there.

I don't exactly hang around to check they're for serious. I bolt for the door, get to my motor, spark up the engine and screech away from that sorry scene at maximum velocity before they have time to change their minds.

Looking back on it today, it doesn't make much sense: those people definitely wanted to finish me off. For obvious reasons, I can't say too much more about them, because as far as I know they're still active as full-time career criminals, and still very, very violent. And I certainly don't want to make heroes of them people by naming them. The one thing I can add is that they took the twenty keys of weed off me, needless to say without giving me the cash, which was a nightmare in the short term as it took me fucking forever to pay back my source.

Even worse than that, the hardest thing to come through was the humiliation. In the long run, however, once I'd got past the immediate problem of scraping together that money, there was a seismic upside to the whole incident. It was a turning point, a life-changing moment for me, which actually ended up putting me on the straight and narrow. It made me reassess my whole life, and think, 'There's got to be another way to earn myself a crust without selling drugs.'

I started putting all my energy into other things, operating in a more honest way and having a belief in myself as a person. From that moment on, I decided that if I couldn't make a living out of being me, Bez, then I may as well fucking give up. I had the opportunity to make the most of what I had, rather than trying to be something I wasn't any more.

People may call me crazy for saying this, but getting kidnapped and done over by those scumbags was the best thing that ever happened to me.

*

That period in the late 90s, luckily, was when I found myself some nice little earners on a more law-abiding tip - fringe benefits, if you like, of having been a prominent member in a couple of notorious rock 'n' roll bands.

For a while there, DJing became my bread-and-butter. I'd roam all across the UK, playing classic indie music, getting on the mic and luring people up onstage to dance - bringing the party to wherever they'd book me, often in small towns where no big-name entertainer had appeared for months. I'd usually put a bit of acid house in the set, too, and sometimes I'd get jobs where they wanted house all the way. It was just a matter of what people wanted, I was ready to accommodate.

I soon found out that the fee for going up there for an hour or two playing other people's records can get fairly inflated. I was going around, telling all the lads, like, 'Fucking hell, I can't believe it! I just found a top way of making money!' That got all of them into doing it as well - people like Mani and Shaun.

At that point it was a matter of getting the word out about this new line of business, so the diary wasn't always full. I had to sign on for a bit, which I didn't want to do, but I had this mortgage-protection thing on my house, and they'd only pay it if I was signed on.

Part of the deal was, the dole office were supposed to find you a job like the one you'd just come out of, and you had to say how much work you'd done and how much you got paid. I used to say, 'I've done an hour's work and I got paid 600 quid!' which is what I was earning as a DJ, so they wouldn't pay my dole, but I got my mortgage paid. I wrote on the form, 'I won't work for less than £600 an hour!' and they were looking at me like I was mad.

This was all the stuff I had to do to make ends meet. Another one, as I mentioned at the beginning of this book, was writing a column for the lads magazine *Front*. It was my first writing job, and all I had to do was scribble out 700 words a month at a pound a word – what a fucking amazing job! I loved it! It went on for two or three years, and very genuinely it opened up whole new worlds for me. As well as giving me a painful and near-fatal introduction to high-speed motorbikes, another thing I got to do was snowboarding, which has gone on to become one of my life's passions.

Going to the mountain snowboarding – we never did that stuff as kids. We never even dreamed of doing it. It was a bit of a middle-class thing to do, if you know what I mean. I was around thirty-five years of age when I finally got introduced to the mountains, and it was a real game-changer for me, like a portal into a new adventure.

My first experience, which I wrote about for *Front*, was in Andorra, the Iberian microstate in the eastern Pyrenees mountains. For this incredible blag, I took a pal of mine called Dermot Mitchell, who is great company and a good friend, but who never leaves the bar, and in that sense he was a bad choice of partner to take with me. Off the slopes, he is the greatest company, you couldn't wish for any better, but he just sat there the whole week at the bottom of the mountain, laughing at me, while I was trying to learn how to do it.

Where I was dead lucky was that *Front* fixed me up with this Cornish legend called Kelvin, who taught me to snowboard for a week that first time. He's a proper Cornishman, absolutely nuts, and is still a close friend of mine to this day.

I discovered that, once you've got the basics, snowboarding is easy. You just have to make sure to bend your knees, put your weight through your front foot, flatten the board between each edge, and use the edges to steer - basically, wherever you look, you go. Just getting them basics learned, mind, there's a lot of pain involved. I spent a lot of time going down, and I found it was actually my arms that ached the most, from picking myself up off the floor. By the end of the week I could do it - not very well, but I was hooked. By the journey home I'd bought a board and all the kit.

I guess someone must've read my enthusiastic report from Andorra because after that I got involved in DJing at Snowbombing, an annual festival in the Austrian ski resort of Mayrhofen, which launched around that time. I was present and correct for the first few years, and that tied it all together for me because it was combining the two things I love - going out boarding on the mountains in the day, and partying at night. You don't get a tastier combination than that! The idea of a rave on a mountain, it works well, you know what I mean?

We kept getting asked back to Andorra as well, and one year I got given the keys to the territory's domed city. I can't remember the exact details because we got that fucking lea-thered, but everything was on Andorra - food, booze, you name it - and there were a few of us that went out there. Obviously, if I was getting the keys of the city, I was going to take a few mates with me.

Honest to God, it was the biggest mistake I've ever made going mob-handed, because our damages bill at the end of the week was unbelievable - we may as well have just bought our own drinks and food, and paid for everything ourselves. We caused absolute chaos. We wrote off cars, we smashed enor-mous plate-glass windows, ripped doors off their hinges. We smashed up the door frames on a couple of the hotel rooms.

We were so paralytically drunk, we broke almost everything we touched.

God knows what chaos we must have caused around the bars of Andorra town. One night I dimly remember standing there unsteadily, and the barman goes, 'Do you know that's your fifty-sixth large brandy and coke?' Just in one bar we'd had fifty-six double brandies. We took it beyond expectation. They don't anticipate that you'll rinse them dry. By the end of it we must have almost bankrupted Andorra. We never got asked back again, anyway. That was our final trip there.

I managed to source plenty of other destinations, however, who were more than happy to accommodate us - to begin with, at least - and I've remained very good mates with Kelvin, visiting him often in Cornwall with my family.

Kelvin's a little bit younger than me, and is an unbelievable kid. He has always managed bars, so he was running bars while teaching snowboarding out there in Andorra. He does festivals, too, and runs the Masked Ball down that way in Helston, and has a hand in a few other festivals. He never stops.

What I love about him is, he's been doing this Masked Ball for fifteen years, and when we went down there this last year, he was over the moon because it was the first year he had ever made a profit on it - after fifteen years! He doesn't do it for money, he does it because he loves it.

He does food festivals as well, and he's an all-round extreme sportsman. He's taken us surfing over the years, and he knows all the tides, proper Cornwall. One year he showed us this place called the Devil's Frying Pan and he did a swallow dive off the cliff face - I swear it was bigger than any Olympic dive. A few of the Cornish kids he brought along jumped it as well, and they were skinning their feet, had water blasting up their arse, and were practically giving themselves vasectomies. At the last moment, I shit out. I was too scared, it was that fucking high. But Kelvin was swallow-diving off there, like a full-on James Bond manoeuvre.

He really is extreme in every way, and one of my best mates. I ended up buying a fishing boat with him there, so we go down regularly each year. The kids love him, and so does my grandson now. Kelvin is the hero of the day!

All this excitement and adventure came from that snowboarding assignment for *Front* magazine in the late 90s. Back then, I always knew I was into fast living, from zipping around on motorbikes on the slagheaps as a kid, through to my scrapes behind the wheel as a young adult. You could say I was a reckless driver. In them days, me and my mates would get hold of these hot motors with no insurance and no MOT, and bomb around in them until they broke down. Then we'd leave them where they were on the street, and buy another one for fifty quid, or a hundred tops, and use that one until it was undrivable. This was the days before there were cameras everywhere to catch road-users doing illegal things.

When the money was good I had a BMW, an orange one with the round headlights in the back, but it didn't last very long before the gearbox went. It was one of them 'should never have bought it' cars. I got suckered in by the romance of the brand.

What I was learning, though, as my world opened up, was that all these areas in which I like to live fast and wild add up to an overall personal profile for yours truly: I'm by nature an adrenaline junkie, and drugs are merely one outlet for that lust for danger which is a driving force inside me.

*

Writing my first autobiography, *Freaky Dancin'*, was another way for me to bring cash through the till in 1997/98. I only did it because I was desperate to make a bit of money, and a memoir was my only solution at that moment.

I tried to do it all colloquially in a Mancunian accent, like Irvine Welsh was doing with Scottish vernacular at the time. It was all about getting to the magic total of 95,000 words, because that was how much we were contracted to come up with. I'd write the stories down, then Debs would get a thesaurus dictionary out and turn fifteen words into fifty, one line into a paragraph, obviously checking my spelling as she went - not my strong point.

It took us forever, because we didn't start straight away, only once we were skint, and you can tell we were rushing it at the end - it gets a bit sketchy partly because we were running out of time, and also because we'd almost reached 95,000 words. Job done!

The amazing thing that happened with that book was that Tony Wilson came out with me on a talking tour around Britain to promote it, just to help me sell the thing. The Mondays had long since split up by then so he really didn't have to do it. He had no vested interest, he was getting nothing out of it whatsoever: he just wanted to assist and support me.

That's the type of fella he was, a really fucking great man, which is why I always really liked him as a person. He was someone we all looked up to. At the beginning, he had the record label that the band wanted to sign for, but once we'd done that, he was really supportive of us as people and as a band.

A lot of outsiders wanted to dislike him because of who he was, with his own telly programme on ITV, and because he said controversial things. But he genuinely loved music, otherwise he would never have done all the things he did – starting Factory, running it in such an unbusinesslike way, and then sinking loads of the profits into the Hacienda. It was all because he loved it. Like Kelvin, he wasn't in it to make money.

Like me, he espoused a lot of old-fashioned socialist values. I used to have long chats with him about current affairs, but I used to laugh at him, because he never signed a deal with anyone, he ran everything on a handshake, and his word was his bond – madness, really, when you think about how successful and iconic Factory became.

Of course, that's also why, after all that struggle with the label teetering on the brink of bankruptcy in the early 90s, he died poor. It cost him dearly in the end, probably to the tune of millions of pounds, because Factory went bust, New Order went off to London Records, we imploded, and he missed out on all his rewards. He lived by his beliefs, which not many people do. He was a remarkable man.

In a way, from the point of view of his legacy, one of the best things that ever happened to the Hacienda was it getting closed down, because it gave it that iconic status. After all, it could have died a slow and ugly death, but this way it became a place of legend. This kid I sofa-surfed with when I was homeless has still got my original Hacienda membership card – apparently worth loads of money now!

To this day, I still get royalties paid for my contribution to the original Mondays records, and that's all thanks to Tony, because that was all settled for me on a handshake, and it all still holds good. I think he might have put Shaun up at one point, when he was down on his luck and needed somewhere to kip for the night.

Because the Happy Mondays had disbanded while massively in the red financially, we didn't start getting those royalties until all the debts had been recouped, which took another six or seven years of our albums selling and us not getting a penny from it.

When the band fell apart in 1993, a lot of the arguments were about money. At that point, an audit was carried out on the whole financial side of the operation, to try and identify where it was all disappearing to. Once our star was on the rise and there was more cash landing in the group's coffers, the idea had been that we would split it equally among the original six members.

The findings were, however, that Shaun was taking the most out of the business, closely followed by yours truly. I was constantly going into the manager's office, getting extra money every week wherever I could. With Nathan, I always knew I could, well, not intimidate him, but basically walk in that room and walk out again with a decent wad of notes in my pocket. I used to do that a lot! Well, I *thought* I did it a lot, but obviously Shaun managed to do it even more than I did.

So, when the accountants came in, everyone was fuming to see that I had the second most out of everybody - I'd managed to blag more money than the people who were writing the actual music. Perhaps understandably, that caused arguments, even though I did have royalty rights, and I was doing a lot of the interviews and everything else. They were pretty pissed off with Shaun as well, knowing that so much of what they'd worked hard for was basically getting frittered away on heroin.

Because of this whole kick-off about me getting more money than them, I thought the musician contingent in the band all fucking hated me as one, and would never forgive me for taking the glory for what they saw as all their hard work from the beginning (though I never asked for the glory to be given).

When we first got back together under the Happy Mondays name, though, it was only Shaun, me, Gaz Whelan and (initially) Paul Ryder aboard – the rift with the others was still too wide to patch up. The partial reunions began in spring 1999, when we played a bunch of enormodomes like Manchester Arena and a ton of festivals. A couple of the gigs in that first run have gone down in Mondays legend. This was when Shaun was still deep in his addiction, and to be fair both of us were pretty out of control.

One particularly mad one was at Slane Castle in Dublin, where we were opening for him out of Take That, Robbie Williams, which has to go down as one of our most chaotic gigs ever. Shaun turned up on the bus with three tarts and a madam, so you can imagine what was going on there from the moment we set off, but then we had this other girl who had jumped onstage naked with us at Glastonbury – she was on the bus, too. We had a few of the Scousers with us, and one of my friends who had just got out of jail.

When we arrived, one of the lads jumped off the bus, dressed up in all this brass's lacey gear and suspenders, and he was running around this horse track whipping himself. These really heavy fellas from Dublin came along and told us that if we didn't get on the bus and sort ourselves out, they were going to put us back on the ferry and send us home again.

On the bus, the craziness continued as this insane girl from Glastonbury was putting chocolate fingers up her bottom.

There was all sorts going on, but then in the melee Rowetta and Shaun had a massive fall-out, and I ended up not going onstage because I was defending Rowetta.

The other mad one that year was the night we opened the new season at Manumission in Ibiza. I'd been over to that orgiastic destination so many times I'd lost count since we first joined New Order out there in summer '88 and played Ku club ourselves the following year. It's mostly just partying off your head, when you're in Ibiza, going to the various different clubs, and I can't usually remember much, to be truthful.

Manumission, however, was debauchery taken to the next level, and the times spent there were so unbelievable that it would take some doing to *not* remember them. I also sometimes don't like telling debauched stories because it could actually get me into trouble, but at that place anything went and nobody cared who knew about it.

As we'd been invited to play at the opening party that year, we were all put up in the Manumission Hotel for a few nights, and it was the most extreme place I've ever had the pleasure to spend my time. I had a beautiful room with a sunken bath in it, and it was all going on in there, in a Manumission type way - a lot of sex, drug-taking, partying - a lot of women, and a lot of shenanigans. It depends on what your idea of sleaze is, but I suppose most people would have to say it was pretty sleazy.

On that trip, we spent quite a lot of time with Howard Marks. He was a lovely bloke, and he always had a top piece of hash on him. He was never without a quality piece of weed, either. I loved hanging about with Howard. He walked the walk, and he had done shit that most people only talk or dream about, but he was an intellect, too. I really liked him as a person, and indeed we had a similar set of friends.

Around that time, he was writing a book called *The Howard Marks Book of Dope Stories*, and he actually used one of my tales in there; what's more, in 2010, when they made a movie of his autobiography, *Mr Nice*, starring Rhys Ifans, he asked me to sit next to him at the premiere and watch it - because he really was Mr Nice, a genuine fella. Every time I'd go to Leeds where he lived, I'd call him up and go and hang out with him.

Back at Manumission in '99, it was amply clear that Mike and Claire, who owned and masterminded the whole nightclub-hotel complex, led from the front when it came to sex, drugs and rock 'n' roll. We used to call Mike 'Upside Down Head', because he had the bald head and the big beard, and they really were the sweetest hosts. The club itself was just as wild as the hotel, like there wasn't any distinction between what went on in that public space and in the privacy of a hotel room. There'd be strippers there, beautiful women from all over the world, dwarves . . . It all went on!

I don't remember too much of our actual gig, but I do know that Mike and Claire were shagging each other onstage in full view of everybody while we were playing. We became firm friends obviously after that.

So this was one of those occasions where you'd say that we were pushing the boat out. Chris Frantz and Tina Weymouth probably summed us up the best: they said, 'We've met a lot of bands who lived on the edge, but that lot didn't know where the edge was!' You could equally argue that we didn't know where to draw the line either.

SHAUN: We spent a lot of time at Manumission. I wonder why! I saw this photograph from there on the internet, or maybe Rowetta posted it. It's a guy in chains with an earring in, and these three black guys are pulling him along on a big thick chain, and in the background there's this sex-party thing going on. I was looking at this picture, and I thought, 'God, that guy even looks a bit like me!' He's all trussed up and being dragged along on all fours, with all these blokes around him – and women, I might add! And they're all going at it! And then I thought, 'Fucking hell, it *is* me!'

To start with I thought, 'Yeah, but it can't be, because I haven't had an earring in since I was fifteen!' but this was a thing to promote Manumission, and I'd totally forgotten that we did it. It was a picture shoot, but it was a shoot that was real, if you know what I mean – it was all for the photographs, but everything that was happening was *happening*. There were a lot of parties like that at Manumission.

Through those mid-90s years, Bez and I had had our fallouts but we were back on track now that the Mondays was happening again, just like we'd always been. That winter [1999/2000], there was a big scare that we were going to lose him, and this is where you find out who he really is.

I was working abroad when I started getting these phone calls: 'Bez has had a motorbike accident, it has turned into some sort of superbug infection, and he's getting his last rites!' So I had to come back from wherever I was, fly back and get on a train to Scotland as fast as I could, to go and see him before he breathed his last.

I get into the hospital, and the first thing he says to me, all faint and slurred: 'X, the nurse just gave me a blow job!'

I thought, 'You fucking can't be having your last rites that much, can you?'

The thing with Bez is this: you throw him out of a jumbo jet at 50,000 feet, and he'll land on a mattress and walk away.

149

That is just him. He's like a cross between Tigger, Stretch Armstrong and Captain Pugwash – if Captain Pug washed!

There was another time, many years later, where we were doing a shoot with the superbike racer Carl 'Foggy' Fogarty, for *The Face* or one of those magazines. Carl takes us around on these bikes for a while. Then we stop and he starts going off somewhere else, and he says, 'Now don't follow me, or try and keep up with me!' Of course, me and the others don't, we stay – but, you guessed it, Bez *does* try to keep up on his motorbike, because that is just how he is, and a couple of minutes later he crashes and he's got his arms and legs done in again.

Being that we're so different in some regards, it goes without saying that we do piss each other off, but we don't argue, me and him. Something will happen, and we'll be silent for ten minutes, then it's forgotten about. Whenever I've had problems in my life and I've not had anywhere to live, I've ended up at Bez's, and whenever he was going through something similar and needed somewhere, he has ended up at mine.

One useful thing we have in common is that we've both got blocked-up noses. My nose has been permanently blocked – fucking hell, since I was a baby. We've both not got the best sense of smell, and that means we can't smell each other's socks. When we used to live in a flat together, it was that fucking messed up, we had to do our washing up in the bath – all the plates and cups and cutlery in the tub – but neither of us were picking up the aromas for weeks.

So we just got on. I mean, Bez's character traits: he's obviously incredibly easy-going in so many ways, but only once you accept that Bez looks after Bez. He will look after his mates, too, but Bez looks after Bez. When we lived together, it really was 'first up, best dressed'. One time, I had my Burberry jacket hung up all nice and clean ready to go with my Adidas Gazelle trainers and my jumbo cords, but he woke up before me, so I wasn't going to be fucking wearing them that day – he was. First up, best dressed.

Having said all that, Bez is very, very loyal. The way he sees things is extremely simple: you are his mate, and he will fight to the death for you. It doesn't matter about anything else – 'I've got your back, X, right?' – and he means it. It's that straightforward and clear-cut. It doesn't matter whether he was first up, best dressed, he's got your back – just as you have got his back, but with him it's all or nothing, and it's earnestly stated.

I've said it a million times before: it's like a sexless marriage between him and me.

He probably wants more out of it.

I don't.

In the movie 24 *Hour Party People*, Shaun and I were apparently portrayed as cartoons of our real selves. I've never been able to speak about it, though, because I've never actually watched the movie and you can't pass judgement on a film that you've not seen. Or at least, I can't.

I really like a lot of the other stuff that Steve Coogan has done, and I heard that he was really committed in his portrayal of Tony Wilson, but I guess all his parts are like caricatures of the people he's playing.

I had no involvement in the making of it. I was a bit upset at the time, because the producers offered me one pound to use me as a character. I said, 'Fucking hell, you could at least have offered me enough to get half a pint!' They offer you this token amount. I can laugh about it now, and I kind of regret the angry stance I took, but you should at least be able to get half a pint, if not actually a whole one!

However, I did go down to the night they put on where they'd recreated the Hacienda. It was uncannily accurate to the point of being pretty scary. Barney, Hooky and everyone were there, too, and we were all agreed: for a film set it was like, 'Wow, unbelievable!' It was an exact replica, and we all had a really great night. I actually thought that they should've got a licence for it and kept it open for a month afterwards, and done a few nights in there. It would've been a massive hit with the whole city.

But I'm still waiting for the right time to watch the movie itself. I've got a copy on DVD somewhere. I'm looking forward to the day when it feels like the right moment to stick it in the player. I'm going to choose the time well, probably on my death bed, like watching your life flash before your eyes.

Playing all the big festivals again with the Mondays, some seriously mad and unfathomable shit has happened to me personally. At Glastonbury in 2000, I was just cutting through the backstage area, and this geezer shouted at me, 'Alright, Bez?' *and it was David Bowie!* I nearly dropped dead! It was a shock to the system – like, Bowie knows who I am! Another time at an awards thing, I got told that Jimmy Page had asked to meet me. Like, 'Fuck off, no he hasn't!' I couldn't believe it.

I first went to Glastonbury in the early 80s – back when there weren't any fences, and we actually went a couple of weeks early. A few weeks before, we'd just set off in the van, and we ended up in Wales for a bit. It was the days when they were closing Stonehenge down, so we got involved in trying to save Stonehenge free festival as well. When we first jumped out of the van at Pilton, because we were all skinheads, they thought we were the army - or maybe some skinhead mercenary kids from Salford!

These days, it's become much more corporatised, with everyone constantly looking at their phone. It's different, but it's still really great.

What I liked about Glastonbury in the old days, which you don't get any more, was that you'd go there with all your mates, but within half an hour you'd've all lost each other - you'd not see them again all weekend, but you'd make all these new friends. You'd just have to get on with it and have the maddest adventure that you'd still be figuring out when you turned up the following year.

That stuff always happened to everybody: you'd go up to the stone circle on the first night and there'd be all these lost souls up there shouting their mate's names. Like, 'Steeeeeve!' or 'Aaaaaaaaannnne!' It reminded me of sheep bleating, going, 'Baaaaaah!' in search of their flock. Each one of them would do that for twenty minutes, but then all these lost souls would meet up with new people and spend their Glastonbury with a completely different crowd.

Of course, them days are gone: nobody gets hopelessly lost and is forced to find something else for themselves. They just get their phone out and find their mates again in ten seconds.

In the late 90s, when it started getting bigger, hipper and more mental, I was there pretty much every year. I think of that whole time as when I started pursuing my own life outside of the band, and again I owe a big part of that to Joe Strummer's openness and camaraderie. At Glastonbury, we'd

153

all hang out around Strummer's campfire, with friends of his like Chrissie Hynde, Keith Allen and Damien Hirst. He had a huge vintage Buick parked alongside it, with a huge Jamaican flag flying over the top.

At Glastonbury 1998, I got arrested by undercover police 'on suspicion of intent to supply drugs'. They said I was selling E, but I actually only had one pill on me, so I got nicked for that – one E. That morning, someone had given me a drink called 'The Future', and everybody who drank one ended up doing some pretty crazy shit. When they tried to arrest me, I went a bit insane on this stuff and had a big fight with the police – it took thirty of them to contain me. Believe me, there's definitely no future in that shit.

I duly got taken off the site to a custody unit in Yeovil and went to court the next morning, where among other things I was told I wasn't allowed back into Glastonbury. Damien Hirst's wife, Maia, came and picked me up after the hearing, and she just happened to have this Mexican costume in the car. So, with a big sombrero and a false moustache, which she affixed onto my lip with sticky tape, I reinvented myself as a Mexican, illegally crossing the border into Glastonbury – like Mexicans do, apparently. No way was I getting banned from Glastonbury, and the disguise only really convinced the people it was meant to fool – the Old Bill.

Back then, Strummer was consciously trying to get this whole campfire thing going on an ever-grander scale, sat around at Glastonbury and other little festivals. He liked the idea of the fires of Avalon, carrying on an ancient ritual, and Glastonbury was like an archetype that we gradually started to replicate elsewhere and take to the next level, with great commitment and enthusiasm.

At that point, he was living in a place in the countryside near Hook in Hampshire and we were constantly down there burning fires outdoors, gathering people together and partying.

I've got photographs of the very first campfire down there. It was actually my middle son Jack's fourth birthday. He's thirty now, and he's grown up with a lot of the other kids who were around that weekend, and we're all still close friends, like a big extended family.

That was what Joe meant by 'integrating your family into the rock 'n' roll lifestyle' - you take your family with you, you don't just leave them at home while you're out living the good life - and that's what I'd started doing. I've got great pictures of Jack and Arlo at four and five years old at festivals in Japan, out there with Joe and his family. For the kids today, it's some of their happiest life memories, so I'm glad I did it for them. In Australia on the Big Day Out touring festival, we'd take them to all the skate parks in the daytime, then do the gig at night. One night when Limp Bizkit were playing, the only people allowed onstage were the band and my kids.

Thus it was that Joe and I became really good mates. We were with each other more or less every weekend, having these mad five-day benders around the campfire. Some of his nearest and dearest told me that he was really made up when he met me, because obviously, Joe being Joe, he'd needed a kindred spirit who liked hanging around campfires for days on end without anything else to do apart from talking shit and listening to music.

I fitted the bill perfectly, and I think it really helped him as much as me, to get out of the doldrums and be creative again, because after a summer or two of living that way he started to write what he called his 'tunes from the woodshed', which was songs like 'Yalla Yalla' and all the early Mescaleros stuff that he'd come up with in the outhouse at the bottom of his garden. Some of my favourite songs of his are on that first album, maybe because I can identify with where they were coming from, like 'Johnny Appleseed', which almost foretold my life to come – planting apple trees and looking after the bees!

When Joe passed away in December 2002, it obviously affected the whole family – my sons, and their mum Debs, everybody was pretty distraught. He died at fifty, which is too young. He was twelve years older than me, and I used to say to him back then, 'C'mon, Joe, aren't you a bit old now for all this carrying on?' It's funny because now I'm fifty-eight, my sons say the same thing to me, and you probably don't like to own up to it. I know how he felt, though, because I feel like I'm a youth and haven't lived much life, and still have a lot left to live. Joe went so young.

A few weeks after his passing, we planted a load of trees near his home in Somerset and called it Rebel Wood, and that vintage Buick is in a big clearing in the middle of the wood. I was back there a year or two ago, and I couldn't believe how quickly this wood has grown up. When we planted it, it was just whips, and now it's actual woodland. We went back there to coppice it all, thin it out and give the trees room to move.

Now that I live in the country myself, I've decided that I want my own woodland, and it's my dream to plant one. Apart from anything else, it gives a good supply of branches and kindling for the campfires, so we can keep them burning in Joe's memory.

Chapter 6

ROCKIN' THE HOUSE

By January 2005, I was in desperate financial trouble. I'd been served with this huge tax bill which I wasn't expecting and didn't understand. The tax office had been sending me letters, but I never used to open letters from anybody. I sort of knew it was all happening but because I hadn't been responding, they eventually had to come and doorstep me.

As things stood, I certainly couldn't pay them what I supposedly owed, so Her Majesty's Revenue & Customs froze all my bank accounts, and I was threatened with having the house in Glossop repossessed, along with all the contents, and anything else they could find in my legal ownership.

It was a lot to have hanging over you suddenly, and I was obviously going through a lot of stress, worrying about losing the home where my family lived, and where my kids could walk to school every day. I certainly didn't want to have to give it up this way.

It was starting to look extremely bleak, like I was about to get everything taken off me, when out of the blue *Celebrity Big Brother* called. It turned out that the third series of the ratings-topping reality show was due to start in three days' time, but they had a last-minute vacancy to fill because someone had bailed out at next to no notice.

After a short explanatory conversation, they popped the question:

'So, Bez, will you do it?'

'Maybe – how much do you get?'

'Fifty grand just for turning up, then there's another fifty grand in prize money if you win.'

'Fucking right I'll do it!'

With timing like that, it was one of those things that was just meant to be.

My saving grace was that I'd never watched the programme, so I had no idea what I was letting myself in for. I had no fixed perception of how you should behave, or what they might put you through. I was going on there in ignorant bliss, which definitely played in my favour, because if I went on there now knowing what the show was about, I don't think I'd be able to cope with it as well.

I went into the house and just was me. I was right off my head when I went in, and I managed to keep that up right through the whole three weeks I was in there.

It started in early January, and I'd been out all through New Year with my mates, all completely off our nuts. By the time I knew I was doing *Celebrity Big Brother*, I was on a mighty roll, and there was no stopping me. The night before the first broadcasting date, we had a wild party at some posh hotel in London. We had all the lads down from Manchester, some of the maddest kids you might ever meet, and these girls who I was seeing, and we had a total fucking bender.

Still in a lively state of mind, I barrelled into the house with little or no idea of what lay ahead. After I disappeared inside, I don't know quite what happened because I wasn't there, but all my mates got barred and weren't allowed back in the studio.

In the house, I'd wake up every morning with the sheets soaking with sweat, then have to go out into the garden in the daytime to dry them out and try to make it look like it was normal. I was up for fucking days, I can't remember how many, and during the daylight hours you weren't allowed to sleep. They used to make all these mad alarm noises over the Tannoy to prevent you from doing so, but I did actually finally fall asleep, and I slept for a full day – right through all these fucking sirens they let off to make sure you stay up. When I eventually awoke from this fucking coma I was in, nobody could believe that I hadn't heard a thing.

Even without that kind of challenge to your system, doing *Big Brother* is a test of endurance. There were a couple of games I wouldn't do because I thought they were fucking stupid – I hadn't watched the programme, so I didn't understand what they were about. I flat-out refused to participate once or twice. Like, I wouldn't dress as an Austrian. I sometimes used to sit there with a glass on the wall, so I could hear what was being said in the next room, and mad shit like that.

The first couple of weeks, I was getting put up for eviction every time, but I was surviving. Talking to the other contestants in there, none of them realised how big the Happy Mondays were. We were like a cult band, but that cult had grown, so they were wrong in thinking that the voting public wouldn't know or care who I was.

I'd gone up against some of the biggest characters in the house and survived the vote. That's when they realised I wasn't going to go, because it felt like I stopped getting nominated after that, because nobody wanted to come up against me in an eviction stand-off any more.

Probably the most controversial housemate was the ITV horse-racing commentator John McCririck. At first I wasn't really liking him. He was a larger-than-life character, and pretty outrageous, but he told some quite funny stories, so it was a bit of a love-hate relationship that I had with him initially. Then I kind of changed my mind because I realised that he was purposely taking on the role of a pantomime villain, the one that everyone booed at, as his game plan on the show. He talked about how he had a proper old-fashioned relationship with his wife – Booby, he used to call her. He'd come across as pretty chauvinistic, and the others would all ridicule him.

But I soon realised that at the end of the day he was one of the better characters in there, because he wasn't two-faced – at least with him you got what you saw. In *Big Brother*, you're allowed to take in one luxury of your own choice, and he took in a load of tea with his teapot, and I used to have a cup of tea with him every day, and he would tell me about the finer qualities of loose-leaf tea. Part of his appeal for me was that he loved his tea, and I actually got into good-quality loose-leaf tea because of him.

Also in there was the model Caprice Bourret, who I quite liked. I wasn't overly friendly with her, but at least she was one of the less antagonistic people – unlike Brigitte Nielsen, who was Sylvester Stallone's ex-wife and had a pretty huge Hollywood ego to match.

The one I really didn't get along with was Jeremy Edwards from *Hollyoaks* – I just didn't particularly like him. The only thing I really wanted to do in there was to beat him at chess. I actually learned how to play chess while I was in there, because I'd never really done it before. This fucker Jeremy said he'd been a chess champion in his public-school days, so I played him a lot, and eventually I ended up beating him – my finest moment in *Celebrity Big Brother*! A real punch-the-air moment!

Germaine Greer was in there, too. I liked her whole history as a kind of rock 'n' roll feminist journalist, and I supported her because I felt a bit sorry for her when she was feeling ostracised from the rest of the house. I felt drawn to take sides with her. You know, the whole thing could be described as a bit strange, and I ended up liking the misfit-type people in the house for some weird reason.

To boost the ratings, midway through they sent in Jackie Stallone – Sylvester's mother – obviously hoping to create a scene with her former daughter-in-law Brigitte. When Jeremy Edwards started having a really bad go at her, to the point that I felt he was bullying and picking on her, I defended her. Because I'd had a bit of a thing with him and didn't really like him, it was my opportunity to jump in and take him down for picking on old ladies. To be honest, I could hardly wait for it. The chance came along when he was bullying old Jackie, and I was like, 'That's Rocky's mam, how fucking dare you speak to her like that? I'm not fucking having it!' I just stood up and kicked off on him and everyone else, and it was an argument where I knew I was on the right side of the line, where I could step in and most right-thinking people would agree with me.

One of the other main things I remember from the whole *Big Brother* experience is that I was always gagging for a beer. I was fucking begging for more booze, to take the edge off everything. At one point I had a look up on the roof. Everyone thought I was trying to do a runner, but I think I was just doing it for attention. I sat up there a while to cause a bit of a commotion, but what I was really thinking about was going to the pub. I was desperate to get myself more beer, to quench my thirst. Put it this way: I definitely had a few when I got out.

Along the way, I actually won twenty grand of the prize money in this surprise competition they threw in, so I was kind of on the road to winning anyway, but it was incredible each time to not get voted out, because I'd been having my own private party in there.

It got to the point where I was so exhausted by the whole experience that I couldn't even talk or formulate the words I was looking for.

By the final day, it was down to the last three in the house, which was me, this pop rapper called Kenzie, and Brigitte Nielsen. She was going on to me how Kenzie was going to win it, and really kind of putting me down. You should've seen her face when they announced that I'd won it! I think it was a big shock for all the other housemates, because I had no game plan. I was just being me, talking about things like wanting to smoke weed and what have you, and they probably thought to themselves, 'Ha, he hasn't got a prayer!'

To be truthful, I never thought I had a hope in hell of winning either and I didn't really give a fuck what people thought about me, so I just carried on the way I wanted to.

Apparently, I won 54 per cent of the vote. My theory is that the moment where I was sticking up for Jackie Stallone endeared me to the blue-rinse brigade, all the old women who sit watching telly of a January evening.

It goes without saying that I can't really remember much about exiting the house as winner. It was all a massive ordeal that stood between me and my first beer as a free man. Once I got out of the studio, me and my mates scarpered, and all the paparazzi and everybody were looking for me, trying to find out where I'd gone for my after-party. People usually go to the Ivy restaurant and places like that, but I'd hired this pub called

The Macbeth in Hoxton – and this was before that area had become all gentrified like it is now. Half of London had turned up at this boozer for our rave in the pub, and we had a leaving party there that went on for three days. It seemed like the only people who weren't there were the press. They were looking in all the wrong places.

How *Big Brother* changed my life was: after that, *everyone* recognised me, not just music fans, because I was that guy off the telly. When you go on there, you're probably putting yourself in three rooms in every household in the country. It ends up taking away your privacy, because you can't actually go anywhere without anyone knowing, and the paparazzi trailing you.

Obviously, at my level of stardom up to that point, I'd never had all that before, but I'd seen it with Johnny Depp and Kate Moss. I'd enjoyed getting to know them, and what surprised me was that they actually wanted to get to know me. I was being invited out by the royalty of show business – you didn't get much bigger than them two at the time. We'd go out for dinner at posh restaurants in London, and it's not for me to say what we got up to afterwards, but you can imagine!

I was a Z-lister moving with the A-listers or whatever you want to call them. They were perfectly normal people behind it all, but I was always shocked by the attention they used to have to put up with, being chased by photographers.

Coming out of *Big Brother* was like a crash course in how intrusive the media can be. I hated it, and my reaction was to turn down lots of TV work afterwards, so I could get my own life back.

What I quickly found out is that people's memories are brutally limited. When you're not on the telly for a few months, you're quickly forgotten and life goes on without you. It's a very short-lived emotion that people have for you, whether it's affection or disdain. You disappear off the screens, and it's like dying, basically, without any fanfare. You've just ceased to be, in that world.

I can't slag off television and people who work in it, because I'm guilty of using it to my advantage. I haven't got great power, but I'm lucky that everything I've done since the Mondays has always got media attention. Not through anything I ever planned, because I'm always a bit puzzled by it myself, how I get all this coverage.

Unfortunately, I'm not left with a lot of choices in life. I'm not very well educated, I grew up wasting my teenage years with petty crime, and my range of alternatives are pretty slim. I've got no apprenticeship, I've definitely never been a merchant banker like Jeremy fucking Edwards. I haven't got any alternative, or any great skills to fall back on. My thing is quite narrow. I'm not a big-time fucking anything. I'm just a con artist, really.

I made money off *Celebrity Big Brother* through the inevitable deluge of spin-offs, but since I'm very good at mismanaging myself, it never really did me that much good in the long run.

As soon as the hangover wore off from all the on-set tribulations, it was no surprise to find that the tax people were waiting for me, already laying claim to whatever money I might've earned out of it. They simply informed me that they were taking the lot. I wasn't bothered exactly, just glad and relieved that I finally had the money to pay them.

They somehow managed to make it that the sum total of everything I owed them was exactly the same as what I earned out of doing the show, which was £100,000 – fifty grand for doing it, and fifty grand for winning, twenty of which I'd already won in the little competition in the house halfway through. I felt like that twenty should've been a bonus really, particularly once the Revenue had nabbed the lot.

But I guess it all worked out well in the end, because it was perfectly timed to help me raise the cash to save my home, and I really couldn't have cut it any finer.

Wikipedia says I've been declared bankrupt twice, which is false information. I've *gone into liquidation for bankruptcy*, gone through all that bollocks on two occasions, and there is a difference. I've never actually been bankrupt, because I've always managed to stump up the money to pay my bills.

The only thing I'm guilty of is bad book-keeping. It was all because I never did tax returns. I never did any paperwork whatsoever because paperwork wasn't a very rock 'n' roll thing to do. It wasn't necessarily because I couldn't pay what I owed, it was just because I couldn't handle doing that shit. I didn't even think of getting someone to do it for me. It was only much later in life that I decided to get on top of stuff like that – the normal things that everyday normal people do. Back then I drifted along ignoring such mundane realities until they caught up with me and demanded some money.

It caused a lot of grief, though, and times were pretty fucking rough while I was struggling to pay up, immediately before *Big Brother* came calling. The Mondays reunion had been all off for a couple of years. DJ wages were enough to get by hand-to-mouth, but not sufficient to meet a hundred-grand tax bill. It was getting fucking close to the bone.

Debs and I had split up through that period while the Glossop house was in jeopardy, and in 2004, I'd actually moved down to London, to a flat in the corner of Hoxton Square. That estate pub where I had the after-party was one of my locals, so I was already integrating myself into the local community.

It was great there in that whole Hoxton-Shoreditch neighbourhood at the time, with loads of bars and clubs open into the wee hours in those early days of gentrification. There was a Scottish kid who'd turned his flat into an after-hours club off Kingsland Road called Gary's Place, and Pam Hogg, the mad Scottish punk designer, and all these people used to DJ in there – a great little scene going on – and there were loads of art galleries. Right across the road from my flat, we had Jay Jopling's White Cube showing all the Young British Artists of that era. Every two weeks there was the most amazing new exhibition in there, the best of what that world had to offer. I really enjoyed having that on my doorstep.

To be truthful, though, my life was pretty fucking chaotic in London. I was getting off my head every day in late bars, and flying by the seat of my pants for money.

Great opportunities, however, still had a habit of coming my way. That summer, I got invited onto the Gumball 3000 Rally, which was kind of like the film *The Cannonball Run*, but in real life. I loved it, but you'd have thought that some of the companies involved would've looked into my track record with motorised vehicles and refused to deal with me. That year Jaguar had lent the rally three cars for the run, and when the Jag people found out that I was getting one of them, they were going mad trying to get the car back off me.

As things turned out, I'm proud to say that, of the three drivers who went out in a Jag on that trip, I was the only one who brought theirs back in one piece. It was completely dirty, mind - black, like you wouldn't believe. They also probably wouldn't have been too happy if they'd known there were five of us zipping around in this two-seater motor, because as per usual I took all my mates with me, all staying together in my twin room as we went round.

It was great because we started off in the centre of London for the launch of the event, then we were taken out to a private airport where they were loading all the cars onto this Russian cargo plane. We had the choice of either flying out on the biggest one-of-a-kind cargo plane in the world, aka the Antonov An-225, or on the Russian version of Concorde. We opted for the former so we could scope out some of the other cars. They were unbelievable, the top end of every type of car you could think of, and you couldn't ever dream of having so much money as actually to own one of them.

After we landed in northern Spain, we spent the night in this top-end hotel in Bilbao, and then the following day we drove on through Brussels, Prague, Vienna, Budapest, Dubrovnik, Bari, Palermo, Rome, Florence and eventually wound up in Monte Carlo. Other people - the super-rich - were shelling out daft money to be part of this crazy dash across Europe. There was one Euro-toff who crashed his car, got a helicopter to pick him up and had a brand-new car waiting for him in a few hours in Cannes.

I was along as a guest so I didn't have to pay a penny for the whole trip. Goldie was another of the freeloaders, as well as the socialite Tara Palmer-Tomkinson - she got a Jag, but she ruined hers! Others on the rally included Johnny Knoxville off *Jackass*, Quentin Tarantino, Caprice (her again!), Jodie Kidd and Jamiroquai's Jay Kay, variously driving Ferraris, Porsches and Lamborghinis.

The great thing about it is that you were staying in these finest hotels right around Europe, and at meeting points you'd get your dinner and your tea thrown in for free in these really fancy hotels, which you'd never in a million years be able to afford to stay in on your own purse. Particularly memorable were this amazing suite in Sicily where part of *The Godfather* was filmed, and the best hotel in Rome right by the Colosseum. In Monte Carlo at the end, we partied on yachts – which really did make a welcome change from the *Big Brother* house.

It was funny, though: as we drove through Cannes, somebody screamed at us that we were yuppies. They obviously had no idea who was sat in the car! The last thing we ever were was yuppies, but it was nice to get mistaken for that kind of person.

I enjoyed the Gumball Rally so much that I got myself invited again a couple of years later, where we went through Germany to the Hockenheim Ring, but sadly the year after that it went to America, and because I'm barred from the US thanks to Gary Kurfirst I couldn't go.

A blagger's work is never done, but I wasn't indiscriminate in which junkets I accepted. On the strength of winning *Big Brother*, I also got invited to rub shoulders with the Windsors in the Royal Enclosure at Ascot. That one I had to turn down, because I wasn't about to be cast as the working-class joker in their pack of cards, know what I mean?

Part of my whole problem financially was that there hadn't been any Happy Mondays gigs in the early 2000s. Shaun and Paul Ryder had had one of their regular fraternal disagreements, which put an end to things for a while.

In those lean years, I started my own band, Domino Bones, and Shaun produced and sang on the first track for me, called 'Rattle My Head', which got released in Australia largely because he'd been out there straightening up and writing *Amateur Night in the Big Top* at the same time.

In my own band, I got to explore my musical abilities, and what I found was that I can strum a guitar really badly, but not with any style. I would certainly never go out and perform in public, because I'd describe myself as at proper beginner-amateur level!

From where I was standing, it was great news when a new Mondays line-up came together for shows at Get Loaded in the Park on Clapham Common, and Manchester Arena. For this incarnation, Horse was out, as was Rowetta, but Mark Day had come back in, along with an enthusiastic new fella called Kav Sandhu, who was part of this particular reunion.

It's hard to explain how the band has completely become my life. The name Happy Mondays has rarely dropped out of usage, and that's because it was all that me and Shaun had going for us, to make any money out of, and to keep ourselves alive with. That's why, come what may with fall-outs or whatever, it kept going and going and going, in whatever form or guise was possible at a given time. Me and him are like the Blues Brothers – 'When are we gettin' the band back together, maaan!'

With hindsight today, I think we both regret that, by carrying on and on in many different forms, with loads of different people coming in and out, we kind of cheapened the name of the Mondays.

With this line-up, we made the only Mondays album of this millennium, *Uncle Dysfunktional*, with Howie B and Sunny Levine producing. I really like it, particularly some of Shaun's lyrics on a few of the songs, but it wasn't the Happy Mondays, and it sort of took away from what the Mondays of old had done. If we'd done it differently, with foresight, and maybe not used the Mondays name, it might have been better for us.

Between tours, my own life just bumbled on in chaos as always, but things started going downhill when I got chased up for another tax bill to the tune of 98 grand – cue another Mondays tour to cover the cost. By now, I was living with a new girlfriend, Monica Ward, in one of Manchester's leafiest suburbs, Chorlton-cum-Hardy, and we had my third son, Leo, but these were otherwise not the happiest times of my life.

In 2010, Monica made a claim of domestic violence against me. I pleaded not guilty because it was something which I categorically didn't do. But they convicted me, and because it mattered so much to me to prove my innocence, I refused to do the community order they gave me. My feelings about this, then and now, were so strong that I'd rather lose my freedom than comply with an order that would mean an admission of guilt. So, because I stood my ground, the magistrate's court said they had no choice but to send me to prison. They sentenced me to four weeks in Strangeways – this time in the grown-up men's part of the prison.

After the magistrate's ruling, I was bailed by Howard's solicitors in Manchester and they willingly handled my appeal. I had wanted to conclusively prove that the charges laid against me were completely false, as I didn't give my side of the story as well as I should have. But the judge still upheld the conviction, and ultimately, I was only issued with a fine.

I was really disappointed at the result, as I had gone to great lengths to defend myself – even going to prison rather than accept the ruling – and launch the appeal just to clear my name, nothing more. I'd had confidence in Britain's judicial system to know what was and wasn't true, and they really let me down so badly by not believing me.

This whole verdict was perverse to me given the British justice system is built on people being innocent until found guilty beyond reasonable doubt. In this case, Monica had no injuries, there were no witnesses, no medical evidence and no photographs of any injuries; the only evidence they had was her statement. I still to this day cannot believe that I was found guilty on the basis of only her word against mine. However, I believe that people that know me – my fans, friends, and especially my family, know the real me and know that I am not an aggressive man by nature.

SHAUN: That last time he was in Strangeways, it was different because he was going in as a famous person, and a lot of prison guards go to gigs – so do cops, funnily enough! Sometimes they're actually fans of our band, so a lot of the guards totally knew who he was and loved him already and looked after him. He's a likeable guy, and he's not an egomaniac. He's not a nasty cunt. At the end of the day, he is happy-go-lucky. Of course he has another side to him, we all have, but essentially he's a likeable dude, so he didn't have any bother in there.

But then you get people who go, 'Oh, Bez, he's off his nut and he hasn't got a clue!'

Wrong!

Bez is one smart motherfucker! Anyone who thinks he's daft should think again. Dom Joly said something to me once, like, laughing, 'Oh, Bez, haha! I I'd leather him!' I was like, 'Are you having a fucking laugh? He would knock you over with his little finger!' People underestimate him.

*

After I got out of jail, I wrote a letter to Theresa May, who was home secretary at the time, keeping my letter short and sweet. I got my thesaurus dictionary out and spelled out very clearly on an A4 sheet of paper exactly why I was going off grid, and why I wasn't going to pay any taxes, and how they were never going to get another penny off me.

She actually wrote back to me fairly quickly, and it was the shortest letter I ever had in my life, just one sentence: 'You can get in trouble for that, Mr Berry'!

I was, however, deadly serious about opting out of mainstream life. I was so sickened by the state of the country, and what it had done to me, I was determined to fight my own one-man revolution against it and stand up for what I believed to be right.

The second time they came after me for unpaid taxes, I rustled up the money from playing Mondays gigs, and I started really to regret paying it after getting fucked over in court. I should've just gone bankrupt and spent all the money myself. You know, if I'm getting classified as bankrupt everywhere anyway, I should've just kept the cash I'd earned. But I didn't, I paid another £100,000 tax bill, playing by society's rules, and then a year or two later got sent to prison for something I didn't do.

I was absolutely fuming: I had just handed over every fucking penny I had to my name, then they went and treated me like a wanker. What I should've done is, I should've spent the fucking lot on having a good time, because that one left me broke, and it took me fucking years to recover again. I was trying to be an upstanding member of the community, paying my tax and doing everything else you're supposed to do, then I got treated like a cunt for it, and it made me extremely unhappy.

I'd always considered myself an anarchist, politically. I believe in total freedom, living your life how you want to, without governments getting in your way. If they have to be there, with judges and police forces and what have you, these institutions should at least look after and protect you when you've done nothing wrong.

I started to think about a conversation I had one Glastonbury just before Joe Strummer passed away. I was around Joe's campfire and I got chatting to these geezers from Wales. This guy called Godfrey started telling me about permaculture, the idea of living off the land in a sustainable and self-sufficient way, without ever having to engage with capitalism.

From what I can remember, I was pretty much laughing in his face at the time, because what he was saying seemed so mad. It was a bit too much for my relatively youthful brain to process and I was still pooh-poohing it for a while afterwards, but I must've filed it all away in the back of my mind, because as time went on those sort of ideas started to make more and more sense to me – like a more practical and thought-out version of my lifelong spirit of rebellion. Proper anarchism!

Back at the turn of the millennium, Godfrey had invited me to a gathering of what he called the 'Welsh tribes', and it must've been eight or ten years later when I called him to take him up on his offer. A few weeks later, I went down to visit him at his farm in South Wales – I can't be too specific about where exactly it was, but it was out in the country, not far from Swansea – and went to this meeting along with all his aristocratic land-owning Welsh hippie mates. There were groups of people there from permaculture communities talking about revolution through peaceful means.

It all made a massive amount of sense to me. We talked afterwards back at Godfrey's, about the ideas discussed at the meeting as well as my position in life. Being that I was single and at a loose end, I soon went down to live on Godfrey's land. These people are now all my friends, and after initially dismissing all their ideas as a bit shit, what a load of bollocks, I came to realise that they were actually really good, and adopted a lot of them for myself.

I was determined to join them in fighting the revolution against capitalism, and I actually gave up all ownership, because I was unshakeable in my resolve that I wasn't going to give them any more money.

Because what can you take off a man who has nothing?
Nothing.

So, I went completely off grid, and Godfrey's place was the perfect place to do so. It's an extreme path, effectively telling the world to fuck off. You have to burn every bridge, and completely extricate yourself, because once you're registered back on the computer system for any one thing, that's it, you're over with - everything is linked up and you'll get caught up in the net eventually. So, I didn't have bank accounts, cars, or anything official. Nothing was in my own name, and the great thing about shunning the system is that you stop getting letters. That was one of the best consequences of the whole thing for me: I never got a letter for years!

The funny thing about it was, I'd actually made no secret of it, I'd written to the home secretary clearly stating my intention, and I was actually easy to find. I was in Happy Mondays,

I wasn't exactly hiding. They just didn't know where I was living.

The way I see it, they forced me into a situation that I didn't necessarily intend to be in, where I was kind of self-compensating for them putting me in jail.

Through the early 2010s, I was basically living in a hippie commune on a fifteen-acre farm, surrounded by all these aristocratic types with their strange theories of revolution.

Once I'd decided I was going to fight it with them, I quickly came to understand that the fight was everywhere. I realised that we're getting poisoned daily through all this shit food that we're force-fed, the pesticides in the vegetables, all the chemicals they put in our drinking water. It's a fight about everything, against the whole system. I learned that modern diseases like Alzheimer's, dementia and diabetes were all a man-made creation, almost masterminded to make people ill and thus keep them scared and under control.

Everywhere I looked I could see that there was a battle on, over your health, wellbeing and freedom. It all infuriated me, so I started thinking about what I put in my body, and completely changed my diet. I got on the organic juicing every day (which I still do), as well as drinking apple cider for the digestion and distilling my water.

My landlord Godfrey has sadly since passed away, but he was quite a charismatic fella, and one of the things he turned me on to was keeping bees.

Ever since I was a very small kid, beekeeping was something I'd always wanted to have a go at. It was my grandad who turned me into a honey monster. After fighting Rommel in Africa, he spent the rest of the war in Italy, and when he came home all he had was four massive tins of honey, and I have very fond memories of honey being a big part of our family life. I used to love going to my nan and grandad's for that very reason, because you always got honey in your tea - honey with everything! - and it tasted really good. I always thought, 'That's what I want to do, so I can have access to an unlimited supply of honey!' It was quite literally those memories of my nan and grandad that drove the whole thing, although they never actually kept bees, and I'm the first beekeeping Berry that I know of, so you could say I've gone a step further.

My first hive, I actually bought for fifty quid off some local fella around where I was staying near Swansea. He had hundreds of hives, and he was downsizing, and mine was one of the ones he was getting rid of. We installed it at Godfrey's place, and called it Hive Number Seven, because it had a big '7' painted on the side.

Around that time, I told the *Daily Telegraph* that I was keeping bees and that the hive had only cost me £50, and this infuriated some woman reader beyond all reason. It can be a very expensive hobby if you go down the road of buying the dearest kit, but the fact that I'd bought this hive for fifty quid and a second-hand bee suit angered her, apparently because it made her think I was doing it on the cheap, or maybe dabbling without putting in the proper investment of time and money. Either that, or it was a middle-class reaction to a bloke like me getting involved.

In all fairness, I hadn't read up about it all in advance. Me being me, I obviously just jumped straight in there.

Now, I can recommend some great books on beekeeping, and I've found out that there are actually beekeeping courses, although I've never been on one. Other people who I've introduced to beekeeping have been on them, and I always admire how efficient they are, and how they teach you to use your tools properly. My first tip to anyone who is a complete novice would be either to go and get lessons, or to buy a really good book on the subject. Definitely find out what you're doing, or what you *should* do, before you actually do it. I think it's well worth doing, with hindsight, but I didn't realise that at the time.

For instance, I've got a great bit of film of my first attempt at harvesting honey from Hive Number Seven. I was basically going straight into it blind, and I got stung like fuck. I would never recommend anyone to approach it like I did, with no experience, and without finding out what you're doing from the manual.

So, I learned about it the hard way. One key pointer I read about was that you should never ever stand in front of the entrance to the hive, like I was always doing at the beginning, and I couldn't work out why I was getting attacked all the time. When you do that, you're blocking the entrance and the bees just want to get rid of you. You're a threat to the hive, and the bees think you're there to prevent them getting in and out.

On numerous occasions I had proper stingings. One time I went in with my jeans tucked into yellow polka-dot socks, and I couldn't understand why I got stung around my ankles too many times to count. By the time I'd escaped the painful scene, both ankles had swollen so much I looked like the Elephant Man. I later discovered that yellow polka-dots to a bee are like a red rag to a bull.

I had a particularly feisty hive as well, because my lot were native English black bees, which are quite aggressive and feisty, not like these poufy Italian bees that most people keep these days, which are quite soft and mild. These were proper hard English fuckers!

During my first honey harvest, I had everyone down there to enjoy the spoils, including my youngest son Leo, who was wrapped up in a net curtain and was sat right near the hive. How he stayed calm I don't know, because he got absolutely swarmed. He just sat there really still, wrapped up in his net curtain, till they all buzzed off.

Another time, I left my flies open, and I was stood in front of the hive. At the time, I didn't realise you weren't meant to stand there, and they all came in through my flies. There must've been about ten of them inside there, and obviously you start getting stung where you never wanted to get stung in your life. I was apparently screaming really high-pitched, running around the field trying not to hit myself too hard.

Over time, though, you become quite immune to bee stings: when you get stung, it's nothing like it used to be at the beginning, and it happens less often because you're wiser to some of the basic mistakes. Still, there are occasions where, say, I've asked my missus to do up my bee suit, she has done a half-hearted job on it, I've gone out and the next thing I've got all bees inside my bee suit - you know, on my face and stuff. That was a bit of an horrific turn of events. There's not a lot you can do when you've got four bees inside your hood with you, buzzing around your face.

I can see that the possibility of something like that happening might put many people off, but I've always been attracted to anything that has a perilous element to it, and I love the sense of danger that comes with beekeeping. For me, the whole purpose of doing it, the thing that makes it all worthwhile, has always been the bounty - the honey. I love it on harvest day because I'll shovel in spoonfuls of the stuff, eating as I go.

One of the things I learned about bees is that I have a lot in common with them. As I always say, they're buzzin'! As a kid growing up, I was always called Bez, which is quite similar to 'buzz', and my other nicknames were B, and Bumble. Bez – buzz – B – bee! We're on the same page.

Also, they do this thing called a waggle dance. When they return back to the hive with pollen, they let the next bee know where it came from, where the good pollen is, and they communicate with each other via this waggle dance. There was a researcher called Karl von Frisch who actually sat and observed them and worked out the language of the bees in this waggle dance – to me that is incredible, that somebody spent enough time studying bee behaviour to work out what they're saying. That guy's a genius, in my book – that's like Doctor Dolittle stuff, but of the insect world.

What's more, this guy actually wrote down what they're saying in a book, so if you're watching some bees, or keeping hives yourself, you can actually try and work out what they're saying. They do this waggle dance where they spin around, because they always use the sun as their guide, to point their way, and then they kind of describe where the pollen is, how far away, what sort of pollen. Fucking amazing!

Over time, through reading and experience, I've acquired sufficient knowledge to run my bee colonies properly. By good management of your hives, for instance, you can keep the population as high or as low as you want. The main objective in that is to prevent swarming, and that requires a certain amount of strategy. You have to kill off the queen cells in the hive, if you don't want the swarms and various other problems. It's all about good hive management.

Luckily, bees don't really sting you unless you're attacking the queen, because they're all swarming around the queen, to protect her. Once they land, you can capture them, and that's not too difficult once you know what you're doing. Sometimes you can knock the whole lot off in one fell swoop - they'll all fall into a box, and then you can lead them straight into a hive. It's amazing!

People often think bees are the same as wasps, but they're very different. Wasps are the terrorists of the insect world. Bees are a lot gentler, and they won't bother you if you don't bother them. If you're stood near their hive but not actually in the entrance, for example, they'll be cool with you being there and leave you alone. Wasps, on the other hand, turn into terrorists at certain times of year - especially at the end of the year, when they're busy trying to get as much sugar in as they possibly can. So if you're eating an apple, or you've got sweets lying around open, you may come under attack - or they may go after your beer, and they can become a right fucking pest. These tiny little winged things will terrorise a human being into giving up a sugary drink or an apple or a beer, and they'll converge and attack to get their own way. They're bastards!

Bees are much cooler. One of my favourite books on the subject is *The Shamanic Way of the Bee: Ancient Wisdom and Healing Practices of the Bee Masters* by Simon Buxton. I highly recommend reading it, because it goes into British shamanic history, which has been passed down over 4,000 years. I didn't really associate this country with having shamanism going on - in Britain's case it was more or less like paganism, or herbal witchcraft. Apparently, there are only four shamanic temples in the whole world, and one of them is here in the UK.

I found a great practical tip in there, and it's not the kind of thing you'll read in any of the Victorian beekeeping manuals:

you know the metal colander that you wash your veg in? You put a big metal nail in there, and you spin it around, and it makes this loud, clanky, rasping noise. I now totally love that metallic sound of the nail as it goes around, because the bees come out to investigate what's going on, and they sort of fly around this thing because they love the noise, buzzing like, 'Zzzzzzz!' and the book says you should start telling them psychically why you're there, what you're planning to do in the hive.

It's basically a way of spending some time starting a bit of a conversation with your bees by making a racket that they're inquisitive about. It's like you're breaking into their world and introducing yourself before you go into their hive - and, honest to God, the difference it has made to my whole beekeeping experience! For me, it has completely changed everything.

The book is also a must-read for anybody who wants to find out about any shamanic stuff going on in Britain. It talks about how one male and one female would be chosen from within these shamanic communities, and the male had to capture and kill a stag with his bare hands, cut off its ball sack and fill that with bee pollen and all sorts. Then he'd put it on the end of a stick and collect all these sticks along the way and keep them in this sack with the bee pollen inside, which they called the 'ancestral rig'. Once it was full, he'd have to pin it on his back so it was hanging off the back of his arse, and go off to some little island off the coast somewhere, and on the island he'd make this hallucinogenic honey.

The particular bees on the island would collect pollen off three different highly poisonous plants and only make a very small amount of honey every year, but it was strongly hallucinogenic, and the males would rub it on their bollocks.

This ritual has all been handed down verbally over 4,000 years, but it has always remained a secret exactly what was demanded of the females, who were known as the Melissae - a name linked with bees in Greek etymology - and where this mysterious island was.

I know a woman who lived on Godfrey's commune, and her daughter got cancer. This girl does all the healing-type shit, and she actually had her leg chopped off in the end, but she went to see Simon Buxton to do some healing work for him, and now she has got involved in the Melissae of his shamanic organisation.

I'd love to find out more about it all myself, this whole hallucinogenic journey. Part of the male's trip is: you get four bees, and you purposely sting yourself on each of your four meridian points - your dream circle. After that, you apparently go into a feverish two-week hallucinatory trip caused by the bee venom. The male flies around with a big hard-on, like a witch's broomstick that he's riding thanks to this hallucinogenic, virility-enhancing honey, with his ancestral rig hanging off his arse.

So yeah, to become a shaman of the bee is no easy task. You've got a real bunch of shit to go through to get there. I should clarify that as yet I'm not following any of it out of this book - I just took the tip about the colander!

Chapter 7

EVERY DAY IS LIKE MONDAY

Making it as a band is like trying to make it as a footballer: it's every kid's dream. It's not an easy task, but we actually managed to do it – *us*, the Happy Mondays, you know what I mean? What's different with us in later years is that everyone has this realisation now that we were a band at a certain time in music history, and how lucky we each are to have been part of it. We're all less inclined to be as ego-driven as we maybe were at the height of our popularity first time around, with all the individual battles for supremacy that typically went on.

What we found out through the 2000s was that a complete reunion of the original line-up would do a lot better than the various partial ones we'd had going, and it finally came to pass in 2012 that all the differences were put aside long enough to get all seven of us onstage together again – *just about* long enough, as PD, aka Paul Davis, only lasted for a year or two.

What I found out for myself was that the bad feeling I'd had after the audit in the early 90s, where it was calculated that I'd been draining the second-most money out of the band after Shaun, was unfounded. Nobody hated me at all. I almost felt like the rest of them bar Shaun wouldn't want me back, like I'd be a deal-breaker to them. But when I stopped to think about it, I'd always got on with everybody great. I'd never had problems with anybody, and – especially after a little more water had gone under the bridge – they'd all come to appreciate what I brought to the party.

So we are the Happy Mondays, and that's who I will always be – a Happy Monday.

This new lease of life commenced with a run of shows in South America – the unlikeliest territory to embrace our return, perhaps, given the carnage we'd wrought upon Rio de Janeiro twenty years previously with all the disgruntled hookers and mountains of cocaine.

We played Rio, Santiago, Mexico City, Buenos Aires and maybe a couple of other gigs, but we also got to travel deep into the rainforests of Panama to write a song together with the Emberá Drua people of the upper Chagres River. The track was called 'Ooo La La to Panama', and it was all filmed for UKTV's Watch channel. It was a great bonding experience for us hanging about for a few days there in the jungle – one of the best things we've done as a band. I was just in the middle of having my teeth fixed at the time, so you'll see a few gaps in my smile if you find the *Singing in the Rainforest* footage on YouTube.

Before we came back to Britain for our victory lap around the arenas, larger venues and summer festivals at home, I managed to squeeze in a shamanic journey with the local Emberá tribesmen. It was a proper three- or four-day trip on some kind of cactus they use for initiation ceremonies in their community, and I was totally gone hallucinating.

On that gear, you see all the spirits of the jungle, and I was actually speaking with them. I had little electric spirits, tree spirits, every fucking spirit you could ever hope to imagine, and I had full-blown conversations with them. There was a twelve-foot-tall woman mothering her young, and little tiny ones that wouldn't let me pick them up. People who saw me in the middle of this trip said that I'd have my arms around someone invisible, talking gobbledegook - but I was talking to spirits, man, and they were everywhere.

I got that bad, this SAS geezer who was with me actually tied me to my bed. I had to pretend to go to sleep - blag him that I'd finally come down and nodded off - to send him off to bed, so I could escape back outside. I went off to the toilet, this concrete khazi in the tribal village, and it was the only place that was devoid of spirit life. I got in there, and it was like, 'Aaaaaah, thank fuck it's all fucking stopped!' So I sat on the toilet a while in this dead concrete block, but then someone opened the door and they'd all been waiting for me to vacate the toilet - shit or get off the pot, mate!

By the early 2010s, Shaun was clean and sober. Personally, I just got on with doing what I do, both on- and offstage. After a few arguments about timekeeping, for example, I stopped travelling with the band, which works much better and more efficiently for everyone.

That whole separate travel thing came about because I like to go out after gigs and go to parties. I socialise. Under the old arrangement, I'd sometimes still be out partying at departure time and not ready to get on the bus to take us to the next gig. I got sick and tired of the bus leaving without me, and fed up of losing my temper about it. I threatened to do all sorts - pop the tyres, etc. - if it ever went without me again. I totally understand that the bus has a timetable to keep, and it has to get the band from A to B, so I eventually decided that the bus ain't for me any more. I go by my own clock and make my travel arrangements accordingly - and separately. I have my own driver, and I do my own thing, so that my tour goes exactly how *I* want it to.

It's been like that for a long time now. I even have my own changing room, because nobody in the band likes having a party before we go onstage. I like to have music, people in the room, tunes playing, building an atmosphere for myself. The rest of the band don't like that, so I have my changing room separate, so I can do what I want, and prepare for the gig in my own style.

I guess you could say that I just like doing things my own way, and rather than upsetting anybody and everybody, it's better for me to get on with doing my own thing, to my own timetable, in my own room, where I can have as many people backstage visiting me as I like. It works better for everybody.

Shaun and I have had our ups and downs, like any old married couple, as he likes to put it. We've had huge fall-outs. One time I've actually kicked his door in and gone in to batter him, but I couldn't do it because . . . you know, you just can't do it! But we have had some raging disagreements, that's for sure, and around the Black Grape time was probably the worst. Then I went rescuing him, when everything looked like it was falling to pieces. I moved him into my back garden so I could keep an eye on him.

It goes from one extreme to the other, and the same from his side. He looks after me in his way, by having me in the Mondays for so long. It's a life that you can only dream of, and I get that through our friendship. I don't think that has ever been in danger, not that I can remember, but he may possibly tell you different.

*

SHAUN: I've got to tell you this, right? Bez has got his idea of what happened, and I've got my *truth* of what happened. Even if we went somewhere last week, his story would be different to mine.

But look, I've now been diagnosed with ADHD. I've known I've been different all my life. I can't do things that others can. I've always forgotten things – later in life, people would say, 'Oh, it's because of all the drugs,' and all that lot. But me not learning – learning is all about remembering, and I have never remembered shit. Whatever was taught to me in the classroom, by the time I'd gone out of the door I had retained *none of it*. So I never really learned anything.

Everything I learned in education, I had learned before secondary school. One thing I didn't learn was my alphabet. That didn't come until I was twenty-something, not at infants or junior school. I've never been able to retain stuff like that, and the same goes for a lot of other things, because ADHD isn't 'one size fits all'. You might have someone with ADHD who has a great memory, or can do mathematics. I also have dyscalculia, which is the maths one – like dyslexia but with maths and numbers. I have that mixed in with my ADHD.

Because of my ADHD, I forget things, right? And so does Bez, but he won't have it. He's like, 'I'm not AD Double Diamond ABC! I'm not like that, X!'

I've known him for almost forty years, and if he hasn't got some condition, then my name is not Shaun Ryder. Even though he can't spell or remember stuff, and he's obviously got something very similar to me, he just won't believe it.

The thing is, even before I knew I was ADHD, I always knew that I'm different, and people like me attract each other, because normal people, if you keep getting into trouble and you do things that are a bit 'not right', they avoid you. So our kind of people end up hanging out – you attract each other because you're just a bit too wild for your normal straight members of society to be knocking about with.

This is before I was diagnosed, and before society knew what conditions were. I was put in the 'special' class at school, Set 4, which was for people who were . . . well, we didn't call them conditions then, the word for it was actually 'educationally subnormal', right? I now know that class had nothing to do with learning, it was about crowd control, and throwing all the disruptive kids in one room and shutting the door. I was in this class, so I know that and can see it as an adult, right?

As a kid you might think, 'Oh, we're all a bit mad, or a bit naughty,' but I also know for certain that everyone in that Set 4 class was either autistic, or ADD, or ADHD, or had some sort of condition.

I bump into the odd person from school in adult life, and one of the funny things about it is that some of us – not all, but quite a few people out of our special class – have become more successful than the ones in Sets 1, 2 and 3 who passed all their exams and behaved themselves, and who you thought would do well for themselves. There's a few from Set 4 that have their own businesses, who've gone into garages or got their own building companies. There's some criminals, too, but they're still more successful than the ones who passed their O levels.

When we started this band, we'd barely even crawled out the other side of that troubled education. I was eighteen, Mark Day was eighteen, my brother was sixteen, and Gaz Whelan and Paul Davis were still at school. We were babies! I mean, now, I'll even call someone who's thirty a kid, because I'm sixty! Like, 'Aw, you're still a kid to me . . .' But I think what we achieved for a bunch of kids from that unlikely background was remarkable, given how dysfunctional we were, yet we had this music thing going on, and we were doing something different.

These days, we can keep it together because we're not twenty-year-old kids any more. The sex and drugs have gone – now we're just left with the rock 'n' roll. All the pettiness and jealousy were just the bullshit that goes on in a young man's head. You look at things in a totally different way as a man, from your forties onwards. Where we are now, in our fifties and sixties – the things that meant a lot when we were eighteen or twenty-eight mean absolutely nothing.

Back then, the other guys in the band didn't quite see what I could see – about us having something lasting between us, or about Bez being the final piece of the puzzle, if you like, looking cool at the front – but now, everything looks very different.

And you know, if we were still the same as we were when we were eighteen or twenty-eight, the fucking guys with the yellow van really would be coming looking for us, wouldn't they . . .

When you see Shaun how he is in later life, he might not always look so well, but he is always as funny as fuck and he

189

has completely made a success of himself. It's a long journey we've all been on together.

Shaun is definitely still the leader. It's his band, really. He's the one who, if he doesn't want to write a song, there's no song written. He's the leading influence, but he's a non-interferer. He doesn't lay down the law in any way. There's no disputing that he's the lead singer and the frontman, but he doesn't do all that 'captain and crew' stuff - he's really good like that. The times he has dug his heels in, it has been for a reason, so I've got great respect for him and the way he handles himself.

He's had his moments, everyone's had those - even I've had my diva moments, where I've spat my dummy out. You'll have to ask other people about them. I've got a selective memory - I only remember things I want to remember.

What I always say is: thank God Rowetta isn't the leader of the band, because then we'd all be in trouble! Shaun has always been really good with Rowetta, too, and the three of us are all on a really good footing nowadays.

Row has been a really good friend to me over the years. She was very supportive during the craziness of the whole *Big Brother* experience. She's always been there for me, and I have supported her in her life and career, too. She has had huge fall-outs with Shaun, not very nice ones, and I had to be there for her. It hasn't always been easy for her being in the Mondays where she is often the only girl on the tour.

Shaun had a bit of a thing with her for a while back there, and I was once caught in the middle of it - in her bedroom with her, when she and Shaun were starting to get together. That wasn't a very pleasant experience. It was pushing the boundaries of friendship, you could say, not to mention professional conduct. I couldn't believe it, because everyone was waiting in the corridor outside the bedroom. It didn't really work out very well, and it did lead to a lot of bad feeling for a while.

On occasion, she can be a really big diva. I've learned to ignore her when she's going over the top with it but, having said that, when she has her meltdowns, I'm always the one who has to go and calm her down. I'll get the call, 'Bez, come quick, Rowetta's having a mental breakdown!' I have my own special way of sorting Rowetta out.

Just keeping the band on the road gets easier with time. Mark Day was always very mellow and easy-going and never said anything out of turn, but he's turned out to be one of the funniest members. Gaz Whelan, the drummer, has changed a lot. Back in the day, he was never happy, always moaning about the last performance, but he told me recently that he's going to stop being grumpy now and be more happy about what he's doing. I was laughing about it with him, and he now realises that's what he was like. You know, once you've performed and the show's over, it's done and dusted, and you can't have it lingering on, but that happened a lot with him – people blaming each other for missing bits and bobs of what the musicians were meant to be going through.

Gaz used to play to a click track, and once you've decided to go with that technique, you have to stay with it, but that meant he didn't have the room to jam things out and go away from the script. It's why I never liked the click track. I used to love Grateful Dead, because they used to trip out and jam off on these tangents, but then they'd remember what they were supposed to be doing and eventually they'd bring back the tune again. They had the room to do that because they weren't shackled by any kind of rhythm track. So I always thought this thing was a problem – since I'm not an actual

191

musician, I always think it would be cooler for the drummer to have freedom.

Probably the single factor that destabilises the band is that we've had brothers in it. Brotherly love can quickly turn into competitiveness – certainly in our context! It was the same thing for the Mondays as it was for Oasis. It's a love-hate relationship that develops very intensely in a band situation. Horse always felt badly treated by his brother, because obviously Shaun's the frontman getting all the attention, but Horse saw it as 'his band', and that he should be running things. There was always this batting backwards and forwards between the two of them, almost like a leadership battle, which often led to them getting into fights. After that time when I almost got my thumb bitten off, I vowed I would never intervene again.

This is why we've never made another record – Shaun didn't want to work with his brother, for one thing, or with the rest of the band, for another. I think he would work with Mark Day, because Moose has got that individual guitar sound.

What I always say to Shaun is, 'Why don't you get some songs together with a writer, and then take the album pre-written to the band and they record what you've written, to give it the Mondays flavour?' Because I always think we should bring some new stuff out. Nowadays it doesn't really matter what you do, you're not going to get any hits because of the way things are with the record business in the streaming age, but it would be nice to show people that there's life in the old dog, and still be writing some new music – like, say, Paul Weller does.

I think we should still be breathing life into the band, because we've got a following who would buy that music and be interested in hearing it. You know, you've always got to play your hits when you go on tour, but it would feel cool and exciting to us to drop some new ones in as well. It would keep the thing fresh for everybody.

So, while I'm an eternal optimist, I don't think we're ever going to write another album. However, I'm just thankful that we've grown up sufficiently that we all acknowledge and appreciate the fact that we're in the same boat together. When we go out, we consider ourselves to be really lucky to have been involved in a band like Happy Mondays, and still to have the opportunity to have an income that you can depend on every year.

What's changed? When we first set off as a band we dreamed of this rock 'n' roll lifestyle, or how we imagined the rock 'n' roll life to be, and we went out of our way to make it ours and live it as much as possible – and push the boundaries, too!

With time, plenty of reading, and some deep conversations around the campfire with the Strummer crew and at Godfrey's place in South Wales, I've started to question the validity of that lifestyle as any kind of alternative or rebellion against the establishment. It came as a really bad shock to me, after all these years when you thought you were rebelling by living that way, that you actually weren't at all.

In a book about 1960s counter-culture, I read about how the US government had a load of these cultural agents like Dr Timothy Leary effectively playing into the hands of a mind-control agenda concocted by the CIA. When I thought that one over, it kind of ruined the idea that you're doing anything radical or new or anti-establishment by taking drugs and partying hard. In fact, at the end of the day, you aren't actually rebelling – in a mad sort of way, you're conforming with this mind-control programme dating back over fifty years now and helping to promote this junkie drop-out culture which they use to neutralise dissent.

That's what puts me off bigging up the lifestyle now because I don't want to add to that agenda's effectiveness. Obviously, I don't believe there's anything wrong with enjoying yourself, but I personally started to get really confused about it all, and about speaking in favour of it, because I don't want to advocate something, even indirectly, that I don't believe in.

Don't get me wrong, though: I still love bringing the party to the people, and I have a constant stream of DJ bookings all the year round. I've played everywhere, every one-horse town in England – the places that other artists never go to. On any given weekend, I'll maybe play at the top of the Friday night in a big club for a couple of thousand people, then on the Saturday it could be for a hundred people in some tiny social club. I go from one extreme to the other. I never say no to any job. I always say you can never look a gift horse in the mouth.

Getting the audience to participate in the evening is what makes the night for me, getting them up onstage to dance and fool about and enjoy themselves.

In my younger days, I used to do my set, then when the club finished I'd go out partying afterwards, to random places like people's houses, after-hours drinking places, 'blues', wherever. Some of those have been quite entertaining over the years: one time, I rolled up to a night in Scotland, did my bit, went on to a few parties, then ended up going to a Celtic game in Glasgow the next morning, and actually stayed out drinking for a few days.

I try not to do that any more. A while back, my girlfriend started driving me everywhere, and she's quite good at making me behave. Generally speaking, I come home with my wages (or most of them at least!), without spending them all in the space of four minutes after my set's over.

I used to drag mates along with me to help behind the decks, but in the last few years I've started doing it with my son Arlo. He cues up the tunes, and I just get on the microphone and do what I do.

In 2010, I started up my own thing at Glastonbury, the Flying Bus stage. It was in the Unfairground which is the old New Age travellers' field. It's run by One-Eyed Sam, Joe Rush and all the Mutoid Waste crew. Mutoid Waste used to do all these crazy free parties around Europe, using scrap metal, power tools, motorbikes, all sorts of shit. People were never sure whether they were artists or thieves, but I always really liked them a lot. They're outside society.

I met them that very first time I ever went to Glastonbury, before I was even in the Mondays. I had just done a robbery, so we arrived in the van with loads of money, and we'd scored all this weed and acid. At that time, there was this whole traveller festival circuit, with the Elephant Fayre in Cornwall among others, and I've got to know all those people gradually over the years to the point where they've become good friends of mine. Some of them are in caravans near where I live right now, in fact. This lot have a punk-orientated band called NFA, aka No Fixed Abode.

The whole thing in the Unfairground was about doing acid house down there. When we started, it was me and Andy Barker from 808 State who were putting the nights together, and Andy was always the headliner, just playing total old-school acid, like early acid-house days.

Initially, it was like an experiment, and a total laugh. We had no idea it would take off like it did. It's a bit like the

Strummer campfire: that started as just Joe turning up with his family backstage, and it's taken on a life of its own where it has turned into a Strummerville stage. It's the same with the Flying Bus stage: it became a popular destination, because we always had the late licence, so it would be mobbed at two and three in the morning, and everyone would want to be there until 6am when the licence was up.

There's other places on the site where I enjoy drinking late at night, like Block9, and particularly Wally's Crew Bar, because they always have really nice mead and Somerset ciders. A lot of Glastonbury has become really corporate, for sure, but there are still bastions of the old Glastonbury out there if you know where to look. Hopefully, we're all keeping Joe's spirit alive.

ARLO: I must've been seventeen when I first started DJing with my dad, and that was before I could actually do it. He used to have a guy who manned the decks, but then one day he asked me to fill in.

'Arlo, I need you to DJ the music for me onstage.'

'But I can't DJ, Dad. I've never done it before.'

'Just use this mix CD for now and we'll blag it!'

So my first experiences of it with Dad were literally just pressing play on a mix CD, like the guy out of Sleaford Mods. My very first 'set' was in the Moulin Rouge in Paris, not just in some pub back room. We got that fucking pissed, we were struggling to pull it off. I couldn't even pretend to DJ. We ended up both raving at the front of the stage, with the mix CD rolling and not even any charade of doing it properly, and everyone loved it. The very first time, and it was a bit of a mad one.

After I turned eighteen, I actually learned to DJ properly at Manchester City College, where I also studied music technology. Because I wasn't doing anything at the time, Martin Moscrop from A Certain Ratio, who was seeing my mum Debs (he later became my stepdad) and was the head at the college, took me aside and said to me, 'Look, you're not doing anything, but you're DJing, come to college and get the rest of your skills up.'

Me and my brother Jack had a go at putting on a club night called Stepping Out in Manchester for a bit, but after we realised how difficult it was to maintain, we went back to being DJs instead. When Dad started the stage at Glastonbury in 2010, Jack became the head honcho of booking the acts and DJs for it.

It certainly was never the plan for either of us to go into music. We weren't coaxed into it. If anything, we were advised against it – not by Dad specifically, but by relatives and friends. Growing up around it, nobody had to tell me the pros and cons of that lifestyle. I watched all these people over the years in the industry, and there's only a very small percentage of them who come out the other side with much to show for it. You've got to work fucking hard to get anywhere.

Of course, we have had a bit of a strange upbringing but at the same time somehow it has been reasonably normal. We never went to private schools or anything like that.

From an early age, we'd go to the gatherings Joe Strummer would have down at Ivy Cottage. We'd hang out with Joe's posse, which consisted of Damien Hirst, Gaz Mayall, whose dad is the British blues guy John Mayall, members of The Clash, and Amanda and John, who aren't musicians but are part of that friendship circle. Their kids and Joe's daughter, Eliza, are some of my best friends to this day, and back then we'd be up all night doing this and that while the parents were partying. We didn't see it as them getting off their nut. They were all just having a good time, and us kids were doing the exact same thing, but in a kids' way. We knew that we pretty much had a pass to do anything we wanted. One night we decided to chop wood for the campfire, thinking we would help out, and I got an axe in the back of my head.

We used to go on holiday every year with Joe's lot down in San José, near Granada in southern Spain – the best holidays of our lives, growing up. Joe being Joe, he'd have all the kids on the roof of the hire car, driving down to the bar in the village. It was very rock 'n' roll, but we just saw it as a huge load of fun. A lot of Dad's friendship group – Fatneck, Dermot, Tommy Dunn – they were all down with us as well. Joe kind of took the Manc lot under his wing, didn't he? You wouldn't've put it down on paper as happening, it was just a really natural thing.

That whole social scene shaped the kind of music I liked from a young age. Joe and Gaz Mayall's brother Jason were massive on Colombian cumbia, so that was like the soundtrack to our childhood. Going to Fuji Rock Festival in Japan in 1999, and the Big Day Out touring festival in Australia in 2001, when the Mondays were on the bill as well, these were the first times I was discovering music through actually seeing people perform.

My dad loved turning me on to music. At home one time, I was upstairs in my bedroom listening to some rapper or other, and Dad goes downstairs, comes back up, and gives me a CD – Eminem's *Marshall Mathers* album. He goes, 'Have a listen to that, but don't tell your mum!' I must've been about ten years old.

He had always played us Black Eyed Peas, the really early stuff, and in Australia we were walking past all the portacabins backstage, and Dad goes, 'Look, it's Black Eyed Peas!' He grabbed me and Jack and took us over to say hello.

Limp Bizkit were on there as well, and me and Jack ended up being the only people who were allowed next to the stage to watch them. Obviously Dad must have fixed it with Fred Durst, and I would say that experience changed my life, because when I came back home, I wore my baseball cap on backwards, I'd got the three-quarter shorts on and I pulled my socks up a bit higher, trying to copy their style. I was already a skater, and that kind of sealed the deal.

Another one on at the Big Day Out was Roni Size – the first time I'd ever heard drum 'n' bass. The combination of cumbia, Black Eyed Peas, Eminem, Limp Bizkit and jungle kind of shaped who I became as a teenager, all through my dad opening our minds to different things.

As kids at school, probably the most difficult question people asked was this one:

'What does your dad do?'

'He's in a band.'

'What does he do in the band? Is he a singer?'

'Erm, well, no . . .'

'What does he do?'

It was the hardest thing to explain.

Like, 'He's the vibe giver, mate!'

I can look back now and see exactly what he was to that band, but as a kid it was hard to see through it. I suppose he was an MC, really. He was the host.

Even though we were seeing them perform from quite a young age, I didn't quite gauge how big the Happy Mondays were. In the early years, when I was four or five years old, people would be shouting down the street, like, 'Yes, Bez!' and 'How are you doing, Bez?' no matter where the fuck we were. I remember asking him, 'How do you know so many people?' I didn't understand it. Like, 'Why have you got people you know *everywhere* we go?'

Only going into early teenage years did I realise that he's actually quite famous, like when he won *Big Brother*. At that point, you started putting things together, and maybe you saw it as something a bit out of the ordinary because, as mad as it is, I've never ever seen anyone come up to him with anything negative to say. It's never like, 'Huh, fucking Bez!' or anything like that – ever. It's only ever positive stuff.

I think with him being who he is – being in a band, but doing what he did – that's almost what made him an iconic figure, because he wasn't just an ordinary band member. He was the face of a movement almost – part of that movement of drugs and partying and free living. He was a big part of that ecstasy thing in the late 1980s and 90s, and I think he allowed a lot of people to be who they wanted to be, in terms of going to a rave and getting off their nut and dancing like a knobhead and enjoying themselves.

Before the pandemic we did a DJ gig in Moscow, and by this point I obviously knew that everybody knows my dad internationally, but I did question Russia – are they really going to know him there? Surely the Manchester thing can't be big out there? We got to the venue and straight away, all these kids came over – we're talking young adults in their twenties, all with bucket hats on, and 'I wanna be adored' tattooed on their shoulders, and going nuts meeting him. I was like, 'Wow, you lot are the Russian Mancs – the Rancs!'

When we're doing a DJ gig together, I look after all the music, while Dad takes care of what he does best, which is to bounce around and give out a vibe and shout shit down the mic. His favourite thing to shout out is whatever the post code or area code is for the town we're playing in. Quite often he'll shout out the wrong town names, but it doesn't seem to upset people.

'Come on, Edinbuuuurgh!'

'Da-a-ad – *Glasgow*!'

He's dead clumsy, too, and I will actually look at the stages before the doors open. I'll see that the decks are a bit close to the front and he's only got a thin little space to walk along, and I'll say to the stage guy, 'He's just going to go over the front, and then the show's over – can we move these back a few feet, please?'

I'm sober for a lot of the gigs nowadays, because I often do the driving, then I do the DJing, get us paid and generally act as his minder. We'll arrive, everybody will swamp him for a photo, he'll get smashed onstage, and not long after we come off, I'll be like, 'Come on, Dad, we're going home now!'

He's like, 'No, no, no, we're staying here!'

By the end of the night, it's like the tables have turned. He's chatting to everyone, and *he* won't leave *them* alone.

He never wants to go home, still to this day, at the age of fifty-eight. I have to be pretty stern sometimes. 'Alright, I'm getting in the car, Dad – I'll see you in ten minutes!' I've had that role for a long time. I've got a little boy called Luca, who's ten now. I had him at twenty-one, and that brought a change of mentality for me at a young age. I'm the sensible one of the bunch, and that's even including my brother and everyone else.

We pretty much get one of three different crowds: it's either the old-school Indie-Madchester lot, or it's a completely mixed bag, young and old, including the ravers who've had their first E for ten years and want some acid house, or it's the students, who just want party anthems and maybe some newer bands like The Courteeners. Gigs range from little pubs around the back end of nowhere, to 30,000 people on a mocked-up warship at Bestival. We tend to do one or two nights a week, all year round, with occasional breaks when, say, the Mondays are touring. Sometimes I won't even bother looking at the calendar in advance, we'll turn up onstage, and it'll be, 'Fucking hell, it's a big one!'

Over the years, there've been some mad adventures. We were booked to play on Shiiine On Mini-Cruise, which went from Hull to Amsterdam and back. There was a party on the ferry over, then you got the gig in 'Dam and another big party on the homebound crossing, where we were DJing and Cast were playing live. Obviously, we got steaming in Amsterdam, but the crossing back was extremely choppy. We got pissed again, and we both started feeling really sick. I was like, 'I'm going to lie down for a bit,' but that didn't help because the boat was wobbling everywhere.

I came back down an hour later to find my dad drunk as a skunk, holding on to a pillar, with the boat swaying, and he'd been throwing up everywhere all around him, and everyone has seen him throwing up. He was holding on to this pillar, looking at me, going, 'Arlo, I'm cancelling the gig!' I was like, 'You can't fucking do that! You're stood right next to the stage now, and everyone can see you!'

After that, someone gave him a mix of port and brandy, an old sailor's trick to get rid of seasickness. He drank this mix and it was amazing – it totally brought him back. The gig was hilarious: John Power was on with us dancing, and the whole crowd was lurching from side to side – like a mosh pit, but actually just trying to stay stood up with the movement of the boat.

New Year's Eve with Howard Marks in Leeds was another funny one. We DJed for him, and he properly looked after us, taking us out for dinner beforehand at Azucar, his tapas bar. Afterwards he goes, 'Oooh, boys, I've got a little present for yous!' We were all thinking, 'Great – Howard's gonna pull out the weed!' Instead, he gave us this little bottle, after which he had to split and we didn't see him again.

We read the label, and it said it was an aphrodisiac-type thing, and to rub it on your skin. We all piled back onto the minibus with this bottle, and started splashing it all over, but it stank like shit. Even worse, it didn't do anything, and we were all going, 'Fucking Howard has had us over!'

We next saw him about a year later at Kendal Calling festival, so me and my dad went over, and said, 'Howard, what the fuck was that stuff you gave us in the little bottle? We were putting it on our skin, but it stank and it didn't do anything!' He starts pissing himself. He goes, 'Boys, you were supposed to drink it!' It was some ayahuasca-type hallucinogenic tincture, and he'd only put it in that bottle because it was the right size for the job. He had a good laugh at us about that.

Glastonbury has become a big thing for us. We've had Carl Cox DJing there, and 808 State, because their DJ, Andy Barker, was a driving force with the stage from the beginning. Dad has actually fallen off the stage a few times, but mid-set at Glastonbury one year it was nearly a bad one: he fell off to the left-hand side, grabbed the monitor as he was going down and took that down with him, which pretty much pulled all the decks off and stopped the music. Luckily, his coat got caught, which stopped him going all the way down to the ground beneath. The decks were still just about on the table, then he bounced back up and in about ten seconds the music started again and the crowd went, 'Yeeeeaaah!' like nothing had happened.

Another year, we had Noel Gallagher onstage with us – not at the front, just hanging around at the back. I was trying to manage people going on and off, and I felt somebody stood behind me, at my shoulder. In that situation you have a little look to see who it is, don't you? 'Fuck me, it's Noel Gallagher!' I'll never introduce myself to somebody like, 'Hello, I'm Arlo, Bez's son!' I think you sound a bit of a dick that way, but I did this time, and asked him if there was anything he needed.

He goes, 'Fucking Bez's son, no way!' He stopped and thought for a moment. 'Mate, I do need something – have you got an E?'

*

One Friday in 2013, one of my mates and I decided to go around the bars in the centre of Manchester – the usual pub crawl we've done so many times before without much to report. On this occasion, we were just walking past one place, kind of looking to see if it was worth diving in there, when a female friend of ours ran out to say hello and started bringing us over to the table where she was sat with her lot.

I took a seat, looked up and there was Firouzeh Razavi.

Our eyes met across the table, and that was it – love at first sight!

Frou had just turned thirty, so she's almost twenty years younger than me, but somehow I knew that she was the one. We nattered away in the bar for quite some time, and then later on in the evening we were in a car together, and she blew my socks off when she put the Grimethorpe Colliery Band on the stereo. She was the first person I ever met of my age or younger who genuinely loves brass bands, as I do.

Other than that, I can't really say how I *knew*. She's the one, because she just is, and we're still together now, on our ninth year. She's got me at my best age, when I've been at my most well-behaved ever, and not looking at the greener grass on the other side – a time of life when I've lost interest in the hunt and am happy to settle down.

We have many of the same issues to deal with. She's the singer in a melodic metal band called Control The Storm. You should check them out on YouTube or on tour, or at festivals like Download and Bloodstock. I'm really supportive of her and the band, and she looks after me when I need it on that level, too.

We get on extremely well, and we live a nice life together. The most important thing in the relationship is that I make her feel like a woman and she makes me feel like a man. We've got that old-fashioned type of relationship. It works for me, and it works for her as well.

So, this chapter really does end with a 'happily ever after': I'm in love, and it's for keeps!

Chapter 8

MARK BERRY MP . . .
WHO'S 'AVIN' IT?!

In March 2014, one of my permacultural mates took me to a fracking site in Salford on the Barton Moss Road. Outside, a bunch of protesters were camped, trying to get this company IGas to stop exploratory drilling there. Before that day, I'd barely even given a moment's thought to fracking - which is short for hydraulic fracturing, a process whereby shale gas is formed by breaking up bedrock formations underground with high-pressure blasts of toxic fluids.

I was shocked both by what I learned about what this company were actually doing to the environment there, and by how brutally the police were treating the people who were peacefully protesting against it. One of those brave people lent me a combat jacket saying on the back, 'Frack off, David Cameron!' - a clear message to the prime minister of the day, to which I was more than ready to lend my voice.

It was really obvious that these massive corporations will do anything for money, at any cost to the community and the health of the people who live there. And they're totally sneaky, doing it without making it clear to people what they're up to, and what the risks might be.

For instance, it was believed in some quarters that they were talking about using the fracking wells as a dumping ground for nuclear refuse. They've got all this uranium waste piled high at Sellafield in the Lake District. There's that much of it stacked outside the bloody power station that they just don't know how to dispose of it, so they were hoping that they could kill two birds with one stone and use it to fill in the void space left after fracking, which can otherwise cause landslip hazard and other environmental problems. If they just stuck it all down there, it would get into the aquifers and start poisoning all the water supplies. The fracking fluids they want to blast down there, like graphene oxide, would also badly contaminate the water.

The health risks to local residents are frankly horrifying. When corporate profit is being put before the welfare of the people, and nothing is allowed to get in the way of that, not even the elected government, I find it very concerning. These people think they don't have to answer to anyone.

In the case of Barton Moss, the government obviously sanctioned it, thinking they could get away with it in a deprived area (in what certain Tory parliamentarians have referred to as 'the desolate North'), but they didn't bank on the people of Manchester standing up to them. I just felt compelled to do something because the situation was so dire.

Thinking about it afterwards, I realised: it's not just fracking. It's the selling of all our public services, like what they did with Royal Mail, and the same is happening with the NHS. Our grandparents fought in two world wars so we could get the NHS, and now successive governments are dismantling it.

When I went out to Barton Moss, I didn't have any agenda whatsoever. I just wanted to investigate for myself something which certain friends were telling me was an eco-catastrophe about to unfold on my old doorstep, where many of my family still lived. I certainly didn't know I was going to commence my political career that day until I was actually at the site. It was just something I said off the top of my head because the whole situation infuriated me, and there were loads of newspapers there to listen.

'Fuck it,' I thought on the spur of the moment. 'I can't stand by and watch this going on - I'm gonna start a political party!'

Looking back now, I can see that my decision was driven by a bruised ego: I knew I had been wrongly convicted, that I had not done what she claimed. I wanted to bring down the fuckers who sent me to prison, and the whole system behind it. I felt really let down by the British judicial system for failing to see what was really happening with this accusation, and that drove me absolutely berserk.

I'll never reveal the true facts publicly, for my son Leo's sake. You never want to air your dirty washing in public. I could've made my defence in court and exposed the truth, and the truth wouldn't have done certain people any favours whatsoever. I decided that wasn't the way forward, because I was brought up never to be a grass. So I decided to keep certain things to myself, but at the end of the day I was hoping that the rule of law was all about sufficient evidence, and if there's any reasonable doubt then you have got to be found not guilty. There was no photographic evidence, no medical evidence, it was just hearsay, and I foolishly thought that would've been enough. Apparently not.

I suddenly saw fracking as my way in, legitimately, to cause as much trouble as I possibly could within the establishment ranks - government, police, corporations, all of them - as my revenge.

In the ensuing weeks, with the catchphrase 'Shake your maracas if you're against the frackers', I started looking at ways to disrupt these evil fracking multinationals.

One of the first things I did was to write an open letter to Prince Charles, because I thought that was sure to generate publicity, and because I genuinely thought, 'Yeah, he'll jump right on board! He lives this organic lifestyle in the Duchy of Cornwall, and he's always piping up about sustainability in building and shit like that!'

I wrote him a letter, pleading with him to consider the consequences of fracking. To wit: 'contamination of ground water, depletion of fresh water, contamination of the air, noise pollution, the migration of gases and hydraulic fracturing chemicals to the surface, surface contamination from spills and flow-back, and the possible health effects of these'.

I went on: 'As a respected proponent of permaculture, we are appealing to you to help us raise awareness of the risks to our environment due to fracking and would welcome a public statement supporting the necessity of protecting and maintaining our environment. We hope . . . that you will come to the aid of your people.'

In mid-April, the *Manchester Evening News* very kindly helped our cause by printing the letter word for word, and because I was beginning to imagine that me and him had similar ideas on this issue, I was hopeful of a positive response.

I like writing letters to these people. When I wrote to Theresa May, I thought I had kept my letter short, just one side of A4 paper; I got my thesaurus dictionary out, used some of the smartest words I've ever used, and I got a one-sentence reply.

In the instance of Prince Charles, I got about five sentences explaining that he doesn't get involved in politics, and I was really disappointed in him. He'll make the nice speeches, but he won't get involved in any of the stuff that really matters.

He talks really boldly and convincingly about how the future of the country could be, with organic farming and beautiful buildings, and he actually does it on his own estate in Cornwall. I'd recently seen him out promoting wild-flower meadows around that time, so I thought there was a good chance he'd give us his support. But was he interested in talking about the mineral rights? He wasn't. Within the Duchy of Cornwall, he'd invoked some ancient right to dig for the minerals under some poor villagers' homes, so he obviously doesn't give a fuck on that level.

He does all this organic shit and will live the good life for himself like Felicity Kendal and Richard Briers, yet there's a flipside to him, where he doesn't give a fuck about anyone or anywhere else. On one hand he's all green, and on the other he's like the fucking devil, happy to entertain the notion of ripping up the lands and taking the minerals out. I realised he was just like the rest of them: all he wants is to rape the country for as much dough as he can possibly take.

After a few months of campaigning on the fracking issue, to raise more awareness me and my partner Frou staged a bed-in for a week in a lovely five-star hotel called the Montcalm in central London. We had loads of press from all over the world coming down throughout the seven days - all the main UK newspapers, ITV, BBC, Russian TV news, all sorts of media from across the globe, they all came down to discuss the issue.

We didn't get out of bed for the entire week, and each night we broadcast a TV show live on the internet from our bed, with guests debating issues of our choosing. One visitor was Sean Lennon: his mum and dad, John and Yoko, obviously set the template for peaceful bed-ins in 1969, but Sean himself is a committed anti-fracker and it was good to talk about it all with him.

It was all good for us two as well, because the week ran through Valentine's Day 2015, so we got to spend the day under the covers together, while doing something constructive – and it took the hassle and expense out of working out what else to do for it. It was an all-expenses-paid week in bed, talking about something we passionately believe in, so what was not to like?

We had loads of support and help from everywhere, and I think we helped bring fracking to the notice of the wider world. The anti-fracking community was really starting to grow worldwide, because everyone was under attack from fracking, and it has never completely gone away. Our government suspended the fracking programme here indefinitely, but it has raised its ugly head again with 2022's new Cold War and Putin's threat of a worldwide gas shortage. We actually only get 5 per cent of our gas from Russia, so if Russia really does turn the taps off for Europe, it's like they'll just be using it as an excuse to start fracking again.

Another person involved in the anti-fracking community was Joe Corré, Malcolm McLaren and Vivienne Westwood's son, whom I'd met around the Strummer campfire at Glastonbury. He has become a really good friend over the years and, like the other Joe, an amazing influence on my life.

He's a modern legend, and what I love about him is that he uses his own money to fight huge corporations. He's got enough cash not to give a fuck – he's got a very good entrepreneurial mind.

Having made his millions selling up his ladies' underwear business, Agent Provocateur, he could easily kick back and happily live a luxurious life without having to get involved in the world's problems. He actively chooses to take on the fight, however, and I really admire him for that, because if I was sat back with close on to £100 million in the bank, would I give a fuck about what was going on with the rest of the world?

'No - I'm alright, Jack, you lot can fuck off!'

He could easily take that attitude, but he doesn't. He enjoys the struggle, and these corporations aren't expecting men like Joe to come along. They expect no challenges, because nobody can afford to take them on - you wouldn't dare, because it would break you financially inside half a day. But then here comes Joe, who's got enough money to drag them through the High Court, and he's putting his own money on the line to fight them and prevent them from riding completely rough-shod over us and taking the piss unchallenged. To me, that is fucking admirable.

The whole of politics now is run by lobbyist MPs, who are doing the dirty work for these corporations; they get funding and free hospitality and they lobby in their favour. Owen Paterson, the disgraced environment secretary, is accused of helping the genetically modified foods companies get into the country. But they're all at it, every single last one of them MPs, doing the bidding of these corporations for God knows what gains - a filthy business, and they're all bang at it, up to their necks in the filth.

It takes people like Joe, who has got the money, to challenge these cunts and I love him for that.

When I went down to the fracking site in Barton Moss, and it came out of my mouth that I was going to set up a political party, I hadn't thought it through at all. Joe Corré saw it all on

TV, however, and he called me up a day or two afterwards. I came down to London to have a meeting with him, mainly to talk about fracking specifically, but we joked about my saying I intended to enter politics, and I explained how one of my ideas for stopping fracking was actually to take over the whole country – to get into government and ban it forever!

'I'll take the North,' I said to him, 'and you take the South!' That was the plan.

What came out of that meeting instead was that Joe offered to back me financially and fund my political campaign to stand for Parliament as an MP. One of Tony Blair's old lackeys, Hazel Blears, had announced that she was vacating her seat in my old home constituency, Salford and Eccles, so with Joe Corré's investment I stumped up the deposit and put myself forward for the contest to become her successor in the general election of May 2015.

It was all driven purely by a bruised ego and probably an overactive imagination, but I was hoping that all the lads and people who never vote might see this as the chance to bring down the whole system that represented us. I knew I wasn't alone in having those kind of feelings of being let down by that system.

I decided to call myself The Reality Party, but the problem was that there's another party called The Realist Party, and so the same day that we were launching our billboard campaign in Salford, we were struck off by the Electoral Commission. They claimed the British public are not intelligent enough to know the difference between the two. That's like saying people might mistake Liberal for Labour, right? In my opinion, it was kind of insulting to voters' intelligence.

It was obvious they were just trying to stop me from standing, so, under the Freedom of Information Act, I wrote back to them asking why I had been struck off, and saying, 'I want everything – every phone call, every fucking bit of paper, everything you've got on me – I want to see it all.' By law, they had so many days to deliver it. There was a lot of the usual palaver you have with these government institutions, but in the end they wrote back saying that, rather than giving me the information I requested, we could resolve it by just changing our name to We Are the Reality Party, so that's what we did to get back on the electoral roll.

I stood as an anarchist. Obviously, I first heard about anarchy from punk music when I was growing up as an early teen, but in the intervening years the idea has never been completely fulfilled by anybody, I don't think, because we've been engineered and conditioned to behave and act in a certain way. It's really hard to see past all those layers that have been put upon us.

In the process, anarchy has been given a bad name. The connotations have been bastardised now to the point where it summons only thoughts of violence. People think it's a fiery uprising, with everyone going out on the street leathering everyone else – chaos in the worst sense – whereas to me anarchy is actually about freedom – freedom from the state, freedom from corporations, freedom from the banking system.

It's hard to imagine a life without money. People think you're mad if you talk to them about it, but that's what I stood for – free food, free everything, just like I'd read in Grogan's *Ringolevio* as a teenager. I think everything should be for free. The fastest revolution in history, we were calling it.

From the off, mad things were happening. I started out going into the Arndale Centre for 'Wake Up Manchester' meetings, and I was getting all these people coming in to confront me, but then I've had probation officers, solicitors and judges coming to me, asking for my help, to raise awareness of what damage the coalition government were doing by cutting the legal-aid system.

What I immediately found out was that in Manchester you are up against seventy-five years of Labour dominance. Up at Salford Town Hall, my banner said, 'The welfare of the people is the highest priority' - reminding Labour of their own fucking principles. I was getting socialists coming up to me - because I was calling them all commie cunts - going, 'Bez, I can't believe you're showing us what a let-down Labour are to the socialist ideal.'

I was giving it to everybody, the left-wing *and* right-wing, because as far as I could see there wasn't any difference between them. They were both the same to me, peddling untruth. I told the *Sun* that the first thing I would do if I got into power was, I'd get a lie-detector test, line up all the MPs and test them all.

'Are you taking bribes to lobby Parliament on behalf of huge multinational companies?'

'No!'

'Will you cut taxes like you say in your manifesto?'

'Yes!'

'Okay, you can stay.'

I was trying to explain to people the blame game that the two main parties play, how they have turns in taking the blame, but that they are all equally to blame.

David Cameron got asked on telly about the threat of the Reality Party, and he didn't even answer the question - he just laughed! But then not long after the election, Labour turned back into proper socialists - they voted in Corbyn as leader.

Through the fracking movement, I'd met Nigel Askew, a pub landlord from Ramsgate, who offered to stand for the Reality Party against Nigel Farage in the Kent constituency of South Thanet. It was really important to me to take a stand against UKIP and the far right in general, and to stop Farage's rise, because he really thought he was going to take Ramsgate. I had to play my part in stopping him in his tracks.

I'm really not into hate. It's just not my thing, so I went down campaigning in Ramsgate, the day after Farage had done a little tour of the pubs. He only did three pubs, though, whereas I did ten.

I tried to arrange a meeting with him. I went to his political headquarters and made a polite request, but I was informed that it wasn't happening, and he didn't turn up at the hustings, where he could be challenged or taken on. He definitely knew who I was and had his little firm of bodyguards there to meet us.

During the visit, I was getting death threats off his far-right cronies, so we walked into this boozer where I was getting all the death threats from, with my rosette on and all that, and one of them shouted, 'Fucking smack him one!' I ended up getting into a debate with these people who were literally threatening to kill me, and they were getting right in my face - right up close. They couldn't believe I'd just walked into their boozer.

The next morning we stood in the middle of Ramsgate with a massive open letter to Farage and the reaction we got was amazing. I compared his lot to the Blackshirts before the Second World War. It's the same agenda, blaming the immigrants who have no voice, and Farage gives some of the older generation a chance to be bigoted.

I was trying to give a counter-argument that people might understand: you can't turn against people who have come here

217

out of financial hardship, to look for a better life for themselves and their families, when we roam about the world taking it by the sword. How can you go on about immigration when we go around the world taking countries with violence?

It didn't always go down too well there, but I couldn't see what the upset was. If anything we are far worse than anybody else in the world, because of the way we occupy countries. We were never there merely to survive in the world, and to tolerate others, we were always there to dominate and rule. We just go in and take countries by force, whereas these people who come here are being forced out of their homelands through their own country's dire economy. They're coming here out of desperation, not necessarily because they want to be here. All they want is to make a living and send money home. If you asked them where they would rather be, they'd rather be in their own country looking after their families.

In short, they're here out of fucking desperation, not because they want to come to England because it's such a great place! If the same working opportunities were available in their own country for them to remain where they are, they wouldn't be travelling here in refugee boats to cloudy rainy fucking England.

No, the immigrants aren't to blame, it's the bankers. They've got away with massive fraud, scot-free. They're criminals. It's the bankers we need to take action against. They're the ones that have caused all the problems we're facing.

On the more positive side, I tried to drum up support from high-profile people of my acquaintance. What's he called from the Stones? That Ronnie Wood – I know him, sort of. I was at one of the rock 'n' roll awards, and I mentioned to someone that I was fighting the revolution, and they said, 'You've got to meet Ronnie – Ronnie is really into all that.' We chatted but nothing happened – he obviously didn't want to get involved with the likes of me!

But you know, I'd actually set up the political party and was trying to make the dream real. I was doing more than talking about it at posh dinners and in interviews; I was actually in the process of trying to make it happen.

I also wrote a letter to Russell Brand, asking him for his help and support. I'm never quite sure what to make of him, but he says some of the right things, and he understands about consciousness and all that crap. I thought he could help us out with it, but I didn't even get a reply off him.

Before the election itself, I was out every day in Manchester handing out flyers saying, 'I Am. You Are. WE ARE THE REALITY PARTY.' Our policies were listed as things like being 'committed to SAVING THE NHS', 'united in the fight to stop fracking', and 'actively working towards bringing an end to austerity measures, such as Bedroom Tax and Benefit Sanctions'.

I told people of my belief that Margaret Thatcher started the de-education of the working classes, and that they'd done an amazing job of it. I used to think I was thick at school, but you look at the standards in some of the schools now and it's diabolical. They've done a job on us like you wouldn't believe. The general population now don't want to engage with the political system.

The one thing I wished for was to be able to articulate myself better than I do. Some people have no problem waxing lyrical, but unfortunately I've never had that ability. I'm shit at getting my opinion across. One of my favourite speakers was always Tony Benn, a powerful passionate orator, to be sure, who first came into politics just after the war in the Attlee days. He was pretty left-wing, and a supporter of trade unions, and you could feel the conviction behind every word that he spoke. You don't get politicians like that any more, who speak from the heart with real feeling and commitment, and I really admired him all the more once I started trying to do it myself.

On my journey, I met some really talented public speakers. I met politicians and local councillors who got into politics for all the right reasons and urgently want to make change and do good for their community – mostly, little town councillors who nobody has really heard of. I think most people get into politics for the right reasons.

It was an interesting social experiment, me running for Parliament. In case you missed the election day TV special, the adult constituents of Salford and Eccles chose not to vote me in as their MP. Was it all worth doing? Well, I got 703 votes, and it was a funny journey. It took up a lot of time and effort, I had death threats off the far right and I had the socialists telling me how disappointed they were. I was an out-and-out anarchist, and I absolutely gave it to the lot of them. I wanted to end money and make everything free, but in the final analysis people just didn't get that point of view.

What drove me to set up the political party was my desire to become a thorn in the side of the government. On that level, I believe that I may have succeeded, because I must've cost them millions in the long run over the process of the fracking issue, as my little act of vengeance. I hope that, in a country that didn't know very much about fracking, I helped to bring it to the attention of more people, and played my small part in costing the corporations that were setting up these companies to do fracking on the sly – I hope I cost *them* millions, too.

The terrible thing is, though: fracking may yet be back, because it's only been suspended temporarily. It's not an outright ban, it could return at any moment, and with the so-called gas shortages around the world, that moment for it to become an option on the table again could be any time now. It'll raise its ugly head again, you wait and see. At the same time as we're being told to be concerned about the climate, and to bang our cars off the road, what are we going to do? Frack our own fucking community! What sort of damage will that do? It's a frightening world we live in.

What I learned is: opposition to things you don't agree with is for life, not just for one election. Also, that politics is all bullshit. What you need to get ahead in politics is to be a good liar, full of promises and full of shit. It's driven by the banking system, and the International Monetary Fund, and Masonic forces. In that sense, it has nothing to do with politics, and the matters that directly affect everyday people's lives. It doesn't matter what you stand for politically, you're just doing the bidding of these dark, unknown figures behind the corporations. You're just their puppet. That's why one of my policies was to end money, and the influence of money, and the influence of these shadowy people that control the money. When I said I wanted to make everything free and end money, maybe I didn't realise how right I was.

These money people don't give a shit what happens in the world so long as they're financing it. So what I was saying is, we have to end this tyranny under the financial rule of law. If we truly want to have change, that's where you'd have to start. That way we could look at gaining some sort of freedom, and maybe get some fucking sense back into our lives – end money, end the banking system and make everything free – but nobody could imagine their lives without money, and how it would work. For real freedom to occur, we'd have to break from that conditioning, but it's so thick and layered in our society that it's surely impossible to achieve. The control over the populace's minds is complete. You'll never ever be able to undo it.

None of this stuff ever really occurred to me as a kid. It's only through getting older and reading and finding these things out that you become aware of it, but I'm afraid I don't think that that awareness actually does you any favours either. I think sometimes you're better off living, if you can possibly do it, in ignorant bliss - like I was going into *Celebrity Big Brother*! Only this is obviously much bigger - it's about your happiness and sanity in a crooked world.

That's why, at this very moment, I don't think that I'll dabble in politics again . . . but I would never say never. There may be a point where I decide, if I'm needed, that I may raise my head. Not because I could ever win it, because it's impossible to win, but for raising awareness it was one of the best things I've ever done, because the attention I got from the world press was incredible. It blew my mind just how worldwide the coverage went - the world's press waiting to talk to *me*!

Around the time of my first jaunt out to the Barton Moss fracking protest site, I was falling under the spell of an amazing book called *Return of the Warriors: The Toltec Teachings, Volume One* by Théun Mares.

I'd stumbled upon it purely by accident in a bookshop in Hay-on-Wye, and it first caught my eye because the title really appealed to me - the 'warriors' part. I was just about to set up in politics and start the fight for freedom, so I guess it resonated, and reflected my mindset going into the campaign. Once I'd got a way through actually reading it, though, it became clear that it wasn't quite the warrior idea that I'd imagined: the fight the author guy was talking about is with yourself, and it's really a kind of psychological self-help guide about achieving a state of total awareness in your life.

I read that first volume and I was completely hooked. Then I moved on to the second one, *Cry of the Eagle*, and I became even more hooked, because that one teaches you how you can become a master sorcerer in the Toltec way, and how you can manifest anything you want on this earthly plane and create anything in your own reality. After that, I wound up reading all seven books, and I wouldn't hesitate to say that *The Toltec Teachings* as a whole were the most life-changing books I've come across in the last seven or eight years, and that they've had a massive influence on my view of the world.

The author guy was from South Africa. Apparently you pronounce his name 'Tay-oon Mah-riss', but I've always said it the Mancunian way, like 'Thay-un Mayors'. There's not even a Wikipedia page on him, which is almost perfect in its own right, because he's that much of a revolutionary with his thoughts and his teaching that the powers-that-be don't even want you to know that he exists. He talks a lot about social conditioning, and opens your eyes to the enslavement of your mind – a lot of stuff that the establishment don't want you to know.

He published the first book in 1995, after getting inspired by Carlos Castaneda's *The Teachings of Don Juan: A Yaqui Way of Knowledge*, from 1968. Castaneda was the first writer to document the shamanistic tradition among Mexico's Toltec people who, in the ascendancy around the turn of the second

223

millennium, actually predated the Aztecs. Mares spent years investigating Castaneda's leads on the Toltecs. Connecting with their shamanistic practices, he began to have flashbacks to previous lifetimes where he was training as a warrior, and eventually decided he had to write the seven books because he knew he was dying, and he felt that he didn't have time to pass on his findings to an apprentice.

He's dead now, but he was hoping that his apprentice would find him, like I found him, so I sort of became his apprentice, if you know what I mean. He wanted to pick up random people like myself, as novices to his teaching.

The mad thing he says in the middle of the first book is that he was channelling all this shit from an Atlantian priest called Ibez, and on the cover there's like a chequered chessboard in the middle, which says 'IBEZ . . . IBEZ' all around it in tiny letters. As you can imagine, that properly freaked me out because I only noticed that after reading all seven of the books. From the beginning, it had my name on it, and I never realised!

I consider these books to be filled with important information, and I've personally found so much that applied to my own life. He uses the phrase 'petty tyrants', for instance, and I came to realise that there are always a lot of petty tyrants in life, behaving disagreeably, trying to control you and push your buttons. You meet them in families, business, schools, in any circumstance. It's about how you deal with them, and how you cope with them. I learned that these people cause a lot of pressure on your impeccability. They're sent to test you, and I know I will be judged on how I deal with certain people who are difficult.

At that time, it was all the people I was meeting doing politics, even members of my own party while I was out canvassing - the whole thing was a minefield from that perspective.

As an aside, at one difficult moment during the Reality Party campaign, somebody said to me, 'Why don't you I-Ching it, mate?' I'd been given that ancient divination text as a gift a few years previously, but had never read or used it before. I thought, 'Fuck, I've never asked that Chinese thingy for anything in my life – maybe now's the time!' Some people I-Ching everything they do, so I decided, 'Alright, I'm doing it,' and it was great advice that it gave me.

'Stop trying to be the big island,' it told me, 'and become the little island.'

Genius! It was really sound guidance at that particular moment in my life, not to get into power battles with the petty-tyrant types who'd somehow infiltrated the political party that had been my very own idea from the outset. In that world, I had to deal with those fuckers on a daily basis, one in particular. In that instance, I took a step back, and it got much better. Getting involved would've given the guy power.

Now I can spot one instantly, and I try to avoid the traps and deal with the person with humour and patience. Since I've read *The Toltec Teachings*, I've come to understand that life throws back at you what you give out. If you go around grumpy and drunk, then that is what you'll get in return. I'm now more aware of the consequences of my behaviour and can improve it accordingly. These Toltec books teach you to live in a constant state of awareness.

The final two volumes are called *The Quest for Maleness* and *Unveil the Mysteries of the Female*. I'm not sure if Mares wrote them as an afterthought, or whether he intended them to be at the end as the ultimate wisdom that he'd managed to uncover, but I can imagine that the feminists in the world would hate them.

In these last two instalments, he talks a lot about natural order, and to boil it down, he's saying that the male's job is to make a woman feel like a woman, and that the woman's job is to make their male partner feel all male, which I guess is returning to a very traditional view of maleness and femaleness. Even I found that to be a bit shocking in this day and age, but I actually do agree with him. Indeed, this is the way that Frou and I choose to live - we have a male role and a female role, and we each accept them. We don't ever stray from them, and it really works in our relationship. I make her feel all woman, and she makes me feel all man.

The gender issue runs deeper, though, because he talks about how the Abrahamic belief system has always been centred on a Male Redeemer, but the Toltec thing says that God has to be a hermaphrodite, because you can't be a creator if you're only male. Mares says that the nearest any religion touched on this otherwise was with Mary, the Virgin Birth, and the creation of the Holy Trinity, where the male (i.e. Joseph) wasn't involved in the procreation. But he says you've got to be a hermaphrodite, both male and female, to be a true creator. Having said all that, I can see him being quite a womaniser in real life.

Overall, I felt like reading Théun Mares's books imparted to me the most information I ever received in my life. I consider it to be so important that I'm going to get my youngest son to read them all, because I feel like he needs that information at his disposal.

It is intense reading, and a lot of it is quite repetitive, drumming it into you over and over as a teacher would. But lots of things he says are a total mindfuck: in one of the books, he claims the human race dates back 18 million years - way older than it has always been thought to be, which kind of fits in with my theory about UFOs, that they are actually us humans time-travelling from a distant past to the future.

Looking back now, I can see how *The Toltec Teachings* were my dream read, because they propagate this idea of living your life as impeccably as you can, and to the fullest that you can every day, because every day might be your last. The books were a fitting reminder after my bike crash at the turn of Y2K. I'll never take life for granted again, and I'll live as impeccably as I possibly can. That's the way I live my life, bearing that in mind, how precious life actually is. You can be here, and then any moment you can be gone. It only takes a second, and it's all over. When you wake up in the morning, this could be your last day on earth, so you've got to live each one to the fullest.

I practise the Toltec way now. At that time of reading, and still today, I feel like I am his apprentice - an apprentice to Théun Mares's whole thought process, and I want to follow that path of what I've been shown over the course of the seven books for the rest of my days. I think the most I paid for any of them was about £30, but unfortunately some of the later volumes in the series have become very expensive and highly sought after: they're out of print, but they contain important knowledge, and that knowledge is going up in price!

Around the same time as I discovered Théun Mares, I found out about another South African called Michael Tellinger, who quickly became one of my personal heroes. Someone mentioned him to me while I was in politics, because I was talking about many of the same things as this fella - ending centralised banking and making things like electricity in the home entirely free for every citizen.

Part of his thing is making these amazing archaeological discoveries – as big as discovering the pyramids of Egypt. He claims to have found the exact spot where Man was created, with Adam and Eve, and he's developed this whole new map of Gaia, bringing in the pyramids and other key sites on earth.

Tellinger started out as an author and a songwriter, but actually formed his own Ubuntu Party and ran in the South African election of 2014 – a year before I did in the UK. Fucking hell, though, if I could have been anything like him – he took it to a whole different level, challenging the banking system in loads of practical ways.

For instance, he showed people how to write promissory notes. That's the basis of money: on a UK banknote it says, 'I promise to pay the bearer the sum of . . .' and he said that you can legally write your own version, to pay for your supermarket shop, or to pay off your mortgage! Because paper money isn't based on actual value, it's all promissory notes, so why not just write your own? He shows you how to get your promissory note accepted, and once they have accepted it, they can't take you to court or anything, because the whole financial system of money is based on the same principle – although they stopped him in the courts. For that, Michael Tellinger remains my true hero of the moment.

His books are pretty mad, too, and I have been known to pay mad money for such information. The most I've ever paid is £350 for the five volumes of *The Hidden King of England* by Gregory Hallett. They talk about how the Rothschilds usurped the Bank of England and the breeding rights of the royal family, in a kind of Templar takeover of the country. It's an incredible read, and it's five fucking volumes of *proof* in a box set, all on quality paper with hand-stitched binding and a ribbon for a bookmark.

I have weird taste in books, but reading is important to me. I have bouts of it, but it's normally a bad sign with me, because it means I have some sort of depression, and this is how I deal with it. When I enter into low-level mode, it can sometimes last a month where I just go into my books. I enjoy it, but it's normally at some iffy juncture where I go down that road. I'll maybe not go out for two weeks, lock myself away and just read prolifically.

I haven't got any favourites per se. I read all sorts. I go everywhere from motorbike gangs to conspiracy books. I love a bit of history, like Adrian Gilbert's *The Holy Kingdom*, a great book about the Arthurian legends, and *The Jesus Gene* by Patrick Byrne, Enrique Bozzo and Ray Hudson, which gives the whole story behind Freemasonry, but then there's Johann Hari's *Lost Connections*, about how the pharmaceutical industry pumps us full of harmful psychotropic drugs, and *Not in his Image: Gnostic Vision, Sacred Ecology and the Future of Belief*, by John Lamb Lash. I like any shit!

I'm just going through a few on the shelves here: Alan Moorehead's *The Fatal Impact*, about Captain Cook and the British Navy in the South Seas, and then *The Admiral Benbow: The Life and Times of a Naval Legend* by Sam Willis, about Britain's greatest sailor, even greater than Nelson and a hundred years earlier. I love a maritime chronicle, me.

Where I live nowadays, we have Hay-on-Wye just along the road. It's like the kingdom of books, and I love going up there on my motorbike, a twenty-mile ride on beautiful B-roads to pick my next stack of literature – and sometimes I can spend three or four days picking 'em! I'll sit in each store, going through all these ancient tomes. You name it, any subject in the world, anything you can think of on this planet, they'll have a book on it. If you like your reading, it's the most incredible place to go in England - there can't be anywhere that matches it.

I've got that many books now, I haven't even got enough bookshelves to put them on. Loads are in cardboard boxes. The thing is, I've got time. I've got more time on my hands than most men. I'm really fortunate that way, and I use it to go on many explorations - gardening, beekeeping, reading books.

It's like binge-reading, what I do, but I definitely take everything in. I'm quite a sponge. I've got a really good memory of everything I've read. I can remember them all, in detail.

I can't really describe what reading does for me. It's just where my mind goes. It wanders.

Chapter 9

FROM ES TO BEES: SORTED, AT LAST

After getting involved in the protest against fracking and then standing for Parliament, my eyes were well and truly open to political evil. I'd woken up to the fact that how things are governed by big business has such a detrimental effect on the environment we inhabit and the air that we breathe.

After living on Godfrey's farm for a few years, I was more and more sold on the idea of permaculture - producing your own power, eating natural foods, making your own medicine, and returning your body to an alkaline state.

I know what you're thinking: it's quite a leap from acid house to an alkaline state, but falling in with these rebels living beyond the fringes of society was like being ushered into a whole parallel universe which exists in defiance of the mainstream's despicable norms.

I couldn't believe that I'd got to the age of fifty and I was suddenly feeling that my life was just beginning. Rather than sliding into dreary, pointless old age, the opposite was happening to me: I had acquired a new sense of purpose. It was a godsend, because I'd been spending more and more time worrying about the future, and how I was going to fill the rest of my days. The Mondays never felt like it'd last for the next two weeks, let alone forever, and it entails a lifestyle which isn't necessarily sustainable going into your twilight years.

I also didn't want to become dependent on the state to provide for me, and I didn't want to grow old and start suffering from Alzheimer's in the city, with nothing to do.

This new lifestyle provided the answers. I craved an alternative that wasn't money-based. The idea of living on the land and growing my own food was really appealing.

A couple of months after my Reality Party campaign, I got a place in this amazing spot, out in the sticks in Herefordshire, near the border with Wales. I didn't have much choice in location: that freedom had been taken from me, as I continued to exist off-grid in my battle against the system that imprisoned me. I had to do it like you pick an apple from a tree - you do it where you can - so Frou and I took up an offer from another aristocratic renegade called Johnny to move into a cottage on his estate.

We're at the beginning of the Black Mountains, in a spot where it's really rural, but also where civilisation is only twelve miles away in either direction - not that far out in the wilds, yet it's a place of outstanding beauty. What's more, within the area of the estate, it has everything - pub, restaurant, basic corner shop, church (and, against the odds, that last one will come in useful very soon). It's a one-stop venue with everything you need on your doorstep.

The great thing about it as well, is that the people who live here are people who *want* to be here. It's literally on the commute to nowhere, which makes it a positive choice.

Johnny himself is a really good friend, and we spend a lot of time together. I've got a lot of posh friends, these days. I used to think South Manchester was posh at one time! Little did I know. They always say, never judge a book by its cover, and I think there is no truer saying spoken. There are good and bad people in every walk of life. You know within seconds, a lot of the time. If you follow your heart, your heart tells you straight off whether people are right or wrong.

I immediately loved the country life here more even than Godfrey's farm over near Swansea. Growing up in Salford, we were surrounded by small pockets of countryside, but being somewhere proper rural - I fucking love it, me!

From the off, I really got stuck into the lifestyle. I do a bit of everything - gardening, beekeeping and going out for long walks. I must've planted a thousand trees since we got here, and I like helping neighbours out. My original intention was to keep a low profile, but I found myself naturally getting involved with the local community, and I feel like I know everybody in every boozer within a twenty-mile radius.

At one time, there were a few of us Mancs living on the property, and the funny thing was, we've done a pub quiz, where they had pictures of pubs in the vicinity and you had to name them, and we actually won the quiz! We could name more pubs than the locals could. I don't know if that's a good thing or a bad thing.

I love the lifestyle, but I'm not a hippie, so I have a different idea of how it should be done. I do it in a city sort of way, having parties and making sure I'm having a good time. My lifestyle has always been based around the party, so I'm looking at permaculture through that lens, if you like, and building up a community based around keeping the campfire burning.

Our place is only a couple of acres, but on and off I have mates staying on the property. There's the house, and then there's the field where we party, and another bit where we grow vegetables, keep bees and stuff.

We keep the campfire burning in Joe Strummer's honour, and in summer we have the odd party, sometimes 300 people, other times maybe a hardcore of twenty-five. We've taken his whole campfire ideal to heart. I got all my ideas from him, but I do it in my own way because I grew up with the acid-house era, so I like to have people with decks DJing and I have a bar called The Shack, and once you light the fire, you never know what's gonna happen.

We normally open up for my birthday on 18 April, and after that we hardly ever let the fire go out before early November, because I'm surrounded by woodland, with more than my fair allocation of dead wood to burn. I actually enjoy going out in my own garden more than anywhere else in the country, because I haven't got to do smartphone photos every five yards and all the other shit I get when I hit the town these days. For those reasons and more, it's the best place for me at the moment, and we've had some of the *best* parties I've ever been to, often going on for four or five days – proper parties of old, with 24-hours-a-day music. Really fucking great times! My friends will travel from all over the country to be there – a top party space, with the bar on one side, the decks on the other and a miniature dancefloor in between, which looks full with six people on it, but we've crammed in thirty or forty on some of our crazier nights, with loads of others staggering around waiting to come in.

The Shack is made from reclaimed wood, because we live in the middle of two woodlands, and there is a milling yard next door to us, so we built it out of all the bits and bobs left over, and the roof was sourced from blown-down barns around the area. Looking at it, it could be a shanty-town shack on a beach anywhere in the world, but it's ours, on our land – a beautiful bar, with the campfire going outside, a perfect arena for music, drinking and merriment.

We've been in Herefordshire for seven years or so now, and it's hard to imagine moving. We're so fortunate to live somewhere like this. The middle of the cottage dates back to 1645, with a more modern extension at either end. The kitchen is pretty cavernous, but all the other rooms have low ceilings. I'll have to get my books shelved up one day!

One of my favourite reads in my new rustic guise is a book called *The British Oak* by Archie Miles, a beautiful picture book of all the most famous oak trees in the country. Some of them I've actually visited, through reading about them in there. One is actually close by where we live and it's linked with Owain Glyndwr, the Welsh freedom fighter from the Late Middle Ages, who was also believed to have inspired the mythical Jack o' Kent, who roamed Herefordshire and Monmouthshire. Many of these oaks have a tight connection to British folklore. Robin Hood was linked to Jack o' Kent, too, and I'd love to be a Jack o' Kent myself, to have that kind of energy.

The tree near ours has a girth of twelve feet, maybe more, and is hundreds of years old. I've spoken to that tree a lot, and I've spent time sitting in it, pondering the world. When I set up the Reality Party I sat in there, because I knew that Owain Glyndwr used to hide out from the English in its branches. In a similar spirit, I'd sit plotting, planning my revenge, and asking the tree to give me the strength, because I had no idea what I was doing, and I needed somebody or something to help me. I hoped it would pass on its energy to me to go forth and take down the fucking government for what they'd done to me.

I've also got a house in Manchester, because a lot of my work is up there. I share the house with a couple of other people, and it's slightly like *Man About the House*, if you remember that TV sitcom from the 1970s, but without George and Mildred as the landlords. I'm Richard O'Sullivan, that kind of scenario.

The way I see it, I'm lucky because this way I get to live both lives, the best of both worlds: I get the country life, and a taste of the city as well when I fancy it, with all your choices of food and takeaways and the great things that the city offers which you don't get in the middle of nowhere. In Manchester, I'm right in the middle of the hood. A whole different viewpoint to life.

I enjoy both sides of life, a bit of living in the hood, and a bit of being a fucking country squire! These days, however, I soon tire of the city. It's good for going out at night, and for work, but when you've got nothing on, you can't beat being surrounded by beautiful countryside. I'm always blown away by its beauty, and it still takes my breath away. Plus, I've got a lot of friends living here on our patch, so I'm never bored or short of company.

My three sons and my grandson all spend a lot of time with me, and I have a great relationship with them all. Some people are surprised when they hear that I'm a hands-on dad. I have an ideal in life. I set myself quite high standards. They wouldn't always quite come under the definition of respectability for the norm, but I do have a real idea of what is right and wrong.

I was at all my kids' births. The first one, I had to come home from touring in Germany. The second one, I had a broken arm from Barbados, so I was in one part of the hospital getting my mangled arm from the four-by-four crash fixed, and my missus was in another part of the hospital having the baby. I just hopped across for the birth, and then went back to my bed.

I never cut the umbilical cord for any of them, as I'm far too squeamish for anything like that. Eating the placenta and all that shit - I know some people do it but that's out of my league.

My middle son, Jack, had his fourth birthday party at Strummer's place, with a campfire, and it went on for five days! Jack is now thirty, and the nice thing about it all is that all our kids who were dead young back then, and who grew up around the campfire - at Joe's, at mine, wherever - are all still great friends to this day. That's his kids, my kids, and all the Strummerville mob. They all knock about with each other, and so it will continue through the generations.

Three or four years ago, we took my grandson, Luca, to Glastonbury, his first visit, aged four or five. A few weeks after, he went to hospital to have an operation on his ears under anaesthetic, and when he came out of the anaesthetic, he was talking about Grandad Bez at Glastonbury. I got a phone call saying, 'Luca has just woken up talking about you to all the nurses.'

Luca is a really good kid as well. He is an Aries Dragon, the same as me, born in the Year of the Dragon, which might be a bit of a nightmare for his dad Arlo, because he just got rid of me, and now Luca's coming into it, so he's shot by both sides. I just tell him: it was meant to be!

I've been really lucky with my kids, because unlike me they never misbehaved. They don't have to, because they've got nothing to prove to me. They can't do anything that I've never done, and they all love me.

My other responsibility is looking after the bees. I quickly installed a couple of hives in Herefordshire, and I've still got

237

another three hives at the farm near Swansea where I first started keeping bees - Hive Number Seven and its descendants - and I still go down there to check that they're alright. As soon as I get a spare day at home - maybe when Frou goes off on tour with her band - I'll go down there and spend a couple of days sorting the hives out, and do a quick harvest when the time is right.

I know it's really bad, but I do it for the honey. I like to think that I'm ethical about it. They've spent all year collecting honey, so I never take all their honey off them. I always look after them like that. Some beekeepers take all of it and feed them sugar throughout the winter as a substitute. I don't do that, I always leave them a full 'super' for themselves - a super is the box that you keep the honeycomb frames in.

Each super could produce up to twenty-five pounds of honey, so you can end up with a lot of honey, if you're not careful. I've never actually counted how many jars we produce each year. I normally keep my honey in big tubs at home, as I can't be arsed to jar it up. Mostly I just produce it strictly for myself. I'll go through a full jar's worth a week, and I'll give the odd jar out to friends as well.

I love doing it, though. It's lucky for me that I have a beekeeping partner called Sari, because there are times when I'm that busy, I can't actually get to the hives to do the job properly and look after them. I'm highly dependent on her, and I feel really bad sometimes, especially when she pleads with me to get down there and help her out. One time recently when I was on telly, she went to the trouble of making up a jar with a 'Happy Honey' label in the style of the Happy Mondays logo, all for the cameras, because I didn't actually even have any honey left. She obviously doesn't get through as much as

I do! She probably doesn't give as much away as I do either, so I was lucky she still had some left over.

On the positive side, I'm always there to help financially with new bits and bobs for the bees, and to be honest I can't wait to get out there and get active on the hives. Harvesting is quite hard work because we do it all by hand. It's a labour-intensive job and it can all take quite a while, probably because I eat as I harvest.

With the bees near Swansea, they're kept in fifteen acres of common land, and the farm is on the edge of it, and it's never been pesticided in over a thousand years. It's up a mountain and it's *glorious* fucking honey you get from there. According to the shamanic way of the bee, it's very good for your virility. Honestly, it's better than Viagra. Your manhood is in perfect working order after a session of harvesting and eating shitloads of that honey.

My energy brought beekeeping into the community in Manchester. Somebody heard that I'd been keeping bees out in Herefordshire, so I got asked if I'd do something on the roof at the Printworks building in the city centre. I obviously jumped at the opportunity. We ultimately put a whole perma-cultural garden up there, with beehives, chickens, wildflowers and vegetable patches. The produce, like honey and eggs, was either given direct to charity, or sold off and the proceeds went to charity.

This was quite early in my beekeeping journey, though, and we had a swarm because we didn't manage the hives properly. On a Saturday afternoon, slap-bang in the middle of the city centre on Market Street, we had swarming bees causing chaos at the busiest time for shopping, which didn't go down well at all. Whoops!

Another idea was then to turn inner-city parks into urban farms, where instead of people growing ornamental plants and all that, you could actually farm the land to serve the community. You could have a small number of animals, you could grow food, make cheese, and ultimately provide for the community through the park, because I really do believe that everything should be free to the people. Of course, you could do that anywhere – on a rooftop in a city centre even, as we'd already proved (with one slight hiccup). There is nowhere that can't be turned into a productive landscape.

Once I'd got the ball rolling with projects like this, I started getting bees into schools. We've only managed to get them into one place in Chorley so far. To finance the project, I was auctioning my maracas off, painting them up and putting them in a frame, and the first piece I did went for £1,400 on eBay. With those proceeds, we bought all the bee suits and a hive, then I got a pamphlet through the door about two inches thick, all about health and safety. You try to do something positive, which would help bring kids into learning about the natural world, and there's always some part of the establishment trying to stop you.

One thing I successfully got off the ground unhindered was planting an orchard in the middle of Salford – another example of where things can be free. Apples deliver food, medicine and booze all in one hit – a three-in-one package, all for nothing. You've heard the expression, an apple a day keeps the doctor away – that's just from eating them. I've been producing cider, too, and cider apple vinegar, which has healing powers for the gut. Alan McGee, who manages the Mondays these days, says we've sorted his digestion out!

I got involved in a homeless charity in Manchester called Coffee4Craig, too, because I know everything about homelessness – from the ages of sixteen to twenty-two, that was my life. My website provides opportunities to give a donation, 100 per cent of which goes towards providing hot food, showers, food parcels, medical support and mental health crisis intervention for those in need living on the streets in my native city.

These projects were all opportunities for me to present myself in a positive manner, and in a gentle way. You can't fight capitalism with violence, you've got to do it gently. If it comes to a violent battle, they've got all the tools, and you ain't gonna win. They will win that kind of stand-off all day long. That's what they want, to fight on their terms, so when you are taking on the system, you've got to do it in a manner where they can't respond to you violently, because they don't know how to deal with gentleness.

Most mornings, I wake up early, rip open the curtains, look to the skies and say, 'How fucking lucky are we?' The life I was leading in my teens, I was never going to go anywhere with it, except a lengthy prison sentence. It was always there, the danger of going that way, but I've had an element of good fortune to the nth degree. I'm extremely grateful that I was able to turn my whole life around through the ramshackle band known as the Happy Mondays.

It wasn't my intention to join a band and make a career out of it. I got in there because I was a blagger and a chancer. I'd love to be an artist, but I'm not. I always admire people who are artistically talented, like Frou. She's an amazing singer and can play a few different instruments. She has the kind of talent that I can only dream of, but given my elevated status in the Mondays, I always feel a bit bad for people who have actually got it properly going on, and would dearly love to be standing on the same stages that I am.

What I do really well is to live in ignorant bliss. I don't read anything about myself, either positive or negative, because I'm sure there's been an awful lot of both. I have totally no awareness of what anyone thinks or says about me, and that's how I like to proceed. Even though I've got social media now, I haven't got a clue what's on there, apart from the little film clips I make for it. I walk through life utterly unaffected, completely oblivious of what the world may think, and I'm quite happy to carry on that way.

What I've always had is the Happy Mondays. To this day, that's my thing, and what I've always been able to count on, which is pretty funny when you consider how recklessly we went about things.

We had no money back at the start, and it took about five years before we saw any, but never anywhere near as much as we would have if we hadn't been ripped off so bad. We've always suffered with poor management and untrustworthy people. We've obviously got more money now than when we first started, but we are mostly skint all the time. That's the great thing about the band: we've never had it, so we've never lost it, if you know what I mean. We always financed our own way, and we still do.

When we first set out, if I tried to picture how I would be in middle age, I could never have imagined this. It's truly unimaginable! But the lifestyle is full of insecurity. You can never say it will definitely always be there, so you've never got a solid base to build a secure future on. You constantly feel like you're living on the brink. In that sense, it hasn't changed a bit from the mid-80s, where you thought it could all end tomorrow. It's been like a huge rollercoaster ride, with massive ups and downs, and it's incredible that we're still able to go out and play.

We're all old men now so it's not quite as wild as it used to be, and I don't know how much longer it can go on for because we're all in our fifties and sixties – the danger years!

I always worry about Shaun, because he's not the healthiest man in the world. It always amazes me how he's still there, clinging on. There've been a few times where I've thought, 'Wow, he's a goner this time!' But he's still hanging in there – falling to pieces but still in the game!

It couldn't go on without Shaun, otherwise you get into Clone Roses territory. That shit amazes me. I recently DJed at Spike Island, where the real Roses played their most famous gig back in the day, but there were actually more people who came out for that than for the original gig – 30,000 people watching a fucking tribute band, reliving this moment in musical history. It blows my head off, that.

Shaun has never been the healthiest individual. Put it this way: Shaun has never been a sportsman. I think he's always quite surprised that I'm not in a worse state myself. Everyone's always amazed when they see how fresh-faced I look, and that I'm not actually falling to pieces, or dead. Shaun, by contrast, has a medicine cabinet jam-packed with all the pills he's got to take to stay alive. He's had his hip replacement, his thyroid problems, and his hair has all fallen out. Health-wise it's like he's on the edge. However, he might not look so well, but he is always as funny as fuck and he has completely made a success of himself. We've both been on a long journey together.

*

SHAUN: I'm alright at the moment, but there have been some weird developments. In 2006, my testosterone disappeared, around the time that my thyroid packed up. Although I have actually got a thyroid gland, it's underactive, which means that even if I only ate lettuce, I would be eighteen stone. If it goes the opposite way, you can have an overactive thyroid like my nana, who was pruning the roses at three o'clock in the morning and going on ten-hour walks through fucking forests at seventy years old, because she was basically whizzing her tits off.

I copped for the underactive one, which makes you fat and bald, and they give you testosterone supplements to level you out. One time, they took the testosterone off me to see how I managed, and within a few days I got total body alopecia. Up till then, I had all my hair, I had a beard, and at fifty-seven years old I didn't have a grey hair on my head . . . Then, all my fucking hair fell out.

Recently they did it again for a fortnight, and what I found out is that you basically go through the menopause. It's like taking oestrogen off the female. I became a completely different person: I didn't want to go out of the house and couldn't talk to anybody. Testosterone is what makes a man a man, and because I don't produce that and I have to have testosterone gel, when they take it away, in a matter of a day I turn into this quivering nervous wreck. Eventually I copped for more gel: it took about two or three days to start kicking back in, and I was fine again.

Whereas, Bez: his constitution, right? There's no long-term damage to his liver or to anything, while I've had all this shit to contend with, plus a hip replacement because I got a gammy leg. I also had a fucking great big lump on my testicle that was pressing on a nerve, which caused me screaming bloody agony.

I'm falling to fucking bits, but these days I've got both the Mondays and Black Grape on the go. When it was the twentieth anniversary of Black Grape's *It's Great When You're Straight . . . Yeah*, there was a reissue and I was asked by our people in America if we were going to do something to coincide with it. I hadn't thought of it before, but that's how we ended up coming back together, regrouping as straight, adult, nearly normal men. Not chemically influenced!

That's just me and Kermit, without Bez. You see, we've got to keep them in boxes now. Bez does Happy Mondays, and if we had him doing Black Grape as well, it would conflict. It's about business: why pay top dollar for the Mondays with Shaun and Bez, if you can have them both together for cheaper in Black Grape? So that's how it is now: you're not having Shaun and Bez unless it's on television, or it's in Happy Mondays.

People have asked, why don't we do Black Grape stuff in a Mondays set? Well, then my musicians in Black Grape would soon be out of work, because we'd be doing all that stuff that people are prepared to pay for with the Mondays anyway. So, Black Grape shows and Mondays shows are completely separate. It works for us.

In my lifetime up to now, I've entered into a number of different shamanic journeys, like taking ayahuasca, not just to get off my head (or in hospital), but 'properly', with guidance from a guru. I've done a few lesser-known ones, too, but the only thing I ever took from the whole journey was the experience of doing the drug, and maybe a bit of spirituality.

That one in Panama, for instance, actually left me mentally disturbed for a bit. I made realisations about the cycle of life and how the spirits are everywhere, and these certainly were hair-raising discoveries, but not rewarding in the long term. In the cold light of day, I got absolutely fuck all that did me any good out of any of them shamanic things.

The only one I've taken anything positive from is a Native American journey-into-manhood ritual called the Vision Quest – the irony being that it involves no drug-taking whatsoever.

The idea is that you withdraw into the semi-wilderness with a load of water and the most basic survival equipment – a big plastic bag, made into a kind of bivouac, and a mat to lie on. Once installed you fast there for four days and four nights. It's a bit like a Jesus Christ thing, but without any Messiah involved. It's also a form of self-psychology, without recourse to a psychologist.

I did mine about four years ago, before the pandemic, in a remote place near where I live. To prepare, I went on a ten-day Vision Quest course with a fella called David Wendl-Berry, the UK's pre-eminent Vision Quest guide, who trained in 'Wilderness Rites of Passage' at the School of Lost Borders in eastern California, as well as holding an eight-year apprenticeship under a genuine Chippewa medicine man known as Sun Bear. He basically tours the country during the warmer months, teaching wherever the landscape is sufficiently wild and remote, like the Cotswolds and Dartmoor.

I was really lucky because I found a magical spot in which to do my quest. I strung up my makeshift encampment between the overhanging branches of two vast, ancient trees – a yew and an oak. In Greek mythology, the yew is associated with Hecate, the guardian of the underworld, while the mighty oak is ever a symbol of strength (this one a hollow oak, too - though not the Jack o' Kent one). It was a very powerful location.

While conducting your fast, you have no watch or phone, you haven't got a clue what time it is, or any contact with the outside world. The one thing you have is an agreed meeting spot, where you build a little tower out of stones so that a designated buddy who drops by there at various times knows that you're okay. They knock the tower down, and then you see on your next visit that they've got your last message that everything's going fine - but you never see them or make any other communication. Apart from that safety provision to let people know that you're not in trouble, you're entirely on your own for the duration.

I brought a maraca in with me, and I took it with me everywhere I went - this one special accessory that's meant to be part of the trip. I was doing all these Native American moves, chanting 'oooo waaaay', and walking around shaking my maraca at everything. I felt like I had to introduce myself to all the trees around me, so I was shaking my maraca to them, doing my little Bez dance, explaining who I was, what I do for a living and what I was doing there.

You can feel the wisdom of these ancient trees. You know, to be hundreds of years old - that's fucking old. I was in this yew's space, so I felt obliged to say hello and show it some respect.

In the four days and four nights, as instructed by David Wendl-Berry, you do all this self-psychology work, these various tasks, using the four points of the compass to spread them across the four daytimes.

On the first night, you send your old self to the death, so you build this thing called a death lodge - like an altar with a little fire. On bits of notepaper, you write all these aspects of your old self which you want to do away with and hold them up to the setting sun in the west, which represents death. That way you're sending them out of your life, and you burn the pieces of paper on the fire to complete that process, and when you pass over the threshold into the new day, you leave all the stuff you wrote down behind.

While I was sending my old self to the death in this manner, I actually fell asleep on my mat. In a dream, somebody had entered my camp, and I ended up having a fucking fight with this geezer, and I was thinking, 'Who the fuck are you?' I was looking into this fella's eyes, thinking, 'I fucking know you from somewhere!' I eventually managed to plunge my knife into him and stab him to fuck, then I woke up from this dream, sweating and confused, like, 'What the fuck is going on?' I realised the intruder was me - I was having a fight with my own self.

The next day was about doing all this work with the south, which is the direction where you deal with all your problematic issues, from your childhood right through to the present day. For this task, I was facing towards this beautiful mountain, Skirrid, which has become really important to me in my life since moving to Herefordshire. It's weird to look at, like a witch's hat with a little bit on the side that has split off, but I've built a strong connection with it.

I also had a labyrinth that somebody had made near my camp. It's like a walking puzzle, with loads of paths within a circle, and only one path leads to the centre. Labyrinths are supposed to be really magical, in a witchy type of way, so I spent the second day dealing with all my issues, facing towards Skirrid, walking the labyrinth and shaking my maraca.

After sending your old self to the death, and raking through troubled parts of your past, on day three you face the north and bring in discipline and responsibility. Lying in that direction from my spot in the middle of nowhere, there was a giant seven-foot crystal buried in the ground, so I did my north work with my head resting on the giant crystal.

On the last day, you go around collecting stones in the east, and at night you build your rebirthing lodge, which I constructed around the giant crystal, and you cry for your vision. By this time, you've done four days and three nights of fasting and you're pretty fucking out there, indeed in a visionary state.

As well as the core thread of self-psychology, I had some other stuff going on during the quest. I'd not long before finished reading the seven volumes of *The Toltec Teachings*, and that knowledge was still very much bubbling around in my brain. Here, I had ninety-six hours in solitude to contemplate their meaning and reflect on their application to my own life. In a way, Théun Mares presents a different version of the same self-psychology, setting you into an alternative way of thinking and view of the world.

My favourite book, the second one, *Cry of the Eagle*, teaches you to become a master sorcerer in this state of awareness, and how you can bend awareness to your own purpose. It talks about social engineering and social conditioning, all this stuff that we go through, and it makes you look at how life mirrors back to you the energies you give out. My time in retreat only reinforced my belief in the Toltec system.

At the same time, I was doing a 'pure water cure' devised by one Dr Richard Schulze which entails drinking a gallon of pure water every day - a lot of water drinking, believe me. You're supposed to follow that procedure over five weeks, so I continued with it after I'd completed the quest. Schulze reckons you can cure anything by this method, because it flushes anything that's not organic out of your body. It's meant to decalcify the pineal gland in the centre of your brain. It's apparently great for arthritis, and it clears all the shit around your joints that causes joint pain.

Schulze claims that he can cure schizophrenia through water alone. He talks about Alzheimer's, dementia and all these modern-day curses of the human mind as similarly preventable. He believes that most of this stuff is basically down to dehydration of the human brain. The problem is, people don't drink enough water, the brain dehydrates and shrinks, and it starts firing faulty electrical signals around the whole of your body, causing all these seemingly insoluble problems.

So, the 'pure water cure' is a bit of wizardry, which combats all these things, and I started that process on my quest. The brilliant thing was, every time I felt hungry, I drank a glass of water and the cravings disappeared instantly. I didn't suffer from hunger pangs for the whole four days - until the last night, when I ran out of water.

That last night, all I could think about was food. It completely took over my whole being. I was dreaming of it all night, and I couldn't wait for the sun to come up, when I could get off, finish the quest and get stuck into a serious plate of nosh.

By this time, I was well out there. It was mirage-y, very like hallucinating. You could see the milky light of the aroma, with proper hazy visions going on, and there's another level of exhaustion because you've been pushing your psychological boundaries, doing all this work on yourself. You've not spoken to anybody for four days and four nights, and with the fasting, you get yourself to a level of consciousness you've never been at before.

What the Vision Quest has over all the more psychedelic shamanistic journeys is that it's not about drugs, and you go deep inside yourself unaided. I got so much out of it. I don't really want to discuss what I dealt with, but it was all sorts of shit going back through my childhood and some band issues from the early days, right up to some crises in later adulthood.

Everyone I know who has done one of these quests has benefitted from it massively. For me, it was fucking incredible, unreal, and truly life-changing. After all that time out on my own, I came back with an unbelievable amount of energy. Just from the thrill of company, I was shaking with excitement. I couldn't stop talking. Everyone was telling me I should rest, but that night I went out and did a DJ gig, babbling on the mic the whole time I was onstage.

ARLO: Obviously nobody had been able to contact my dad, but it was agreed beforehand that he would go and do the Vision Quest, then he would come out and that night we would go and do this gig. So I'm sat there in the house in Hereford, all packed up and ready to go, and I remember saying to everyone, 'We're not doing this gig, are we? He certainly won't want to do it.' Then he walked in and he was absolutely *glowing*, head to toe, looking really healthy, bouncing around. 'Come on, let's go and do it!' It was a massive turning point in his life.

*

I had this extreme overload of energy and it lasted for about a week afterwards. I didn't sleep for seven nights because I was processing everything that had happened.

There were many immediate and fundamental consequences of the fast: I didn't eat meat for twelve months afterwards and, perhaps a little more surprisingly to the world at large, I gave up all the drugs for a year as well, and pretty much stopped drinking, too. I had a complete cleanse - purged my body of all the baddies. I stopped everything.

When I got to Glastonbury that year, I met up with an old friend who has since passed away from a cancerous brain tumour, and unfortunately I fell off the wagon. I realised that Glastonbury ain't the same without the Persians. I also started eating meat again, but the thing that stayed with me from it all was perhaps the one I least expected.

I've been smoking cannabis in some form or another since I was fifteen. That's the one I gave up long-term, and I still haven't gone back to it in the four years since the quest. Anyone who knew me from before simply cannot believe that I'm Bez, but *without* a spliff in his hand. It was such a big thing in my life: in the old days, I would drive 3,000 miles to get a proper bag of weed.

With me, it was like every fucking day, from the moment I woke up - before I got out of bed, it'd be, 'Let's have a spliff.' The days go by fucking daft quickly these days - it's unbelievable how fast time goes by when you get older, so I was just thinking, 'How can I slow down time?' I guess my answer was finally to crawl out of the ganja haze. It's hard to say if it has really worked on that level, but I do feel much better for it, and I get a whole lot more done.

The change that the Vision Quest brought in me prevails: I'm still off the marijuana and I've still got that energy of being able to completely drop everything if I want to. The Vision Quest has given me the strength to stop on a sixpence and leave anything I want behind.

I'm now ready to do another quest, to go on another self-analytical journey and see how deep it can take me. I've spoken to many people who have done the vision quest, and the vibe is usually like they've cured themselves when they come out of it. There was one girl I spoke to who had post-traumatic stress disorder, and going on her Vision Quest helped her get over that horrible experience she was suffering from. I've seen one person studying psychology, who's now writing a book about how beneficial the whole ritual is from that angle.

Me, I'm just itching to have another bite at the cherry.

Chapter 10

BUZZIN' THROUGH COVID

On Boxing Day 2019, I took myself off to hospital, because I'd spotted some blood in my urine. I was also suffering from shortness of breath, a persistent cough and a high temperature – those last three factors, obviously, were soon to become the familiar and much-feared symptoms of Covid-19, but this was two or three months before it was announced as a thing.

In terms of how I was feeling, the main issues were difficulties breathing and a tightness in the chest, so when I checked in, I told them, 'I think I've been having a heart attack.'

They gave me a cardiogram, and it turned out that my heart had swollen up due to 'a virus', and I'd duly sprung a leak from the bottom valve, which was manifesting via the red streaks in my piss. Thankfully the doctor said it was nothing to worry about, as it's quite a common problem. He also maintained that I was otherwise fighting fit, and that my standing heartbeat was that of an athlete. I was packed off with some paracetamol to reduce the fever and discharged. It was only a few weeks later when the scaremongering started, that I realised I'd very likely had an early dose of Covid.

In the first months of 2020, once I was feeling better, we went on a snowboarding holiday in France with my three sons, and while we were out there the spread of Covid was just beginning to get reported and was slowly becoming the topic of general conversation.

When we got back from there, I dropped the kids at home, and we pretty much went straight off to Amsterdam for our annual bender in the Dutch capital in celebration of Frou's birthday. On this occasion, it just so happened that we had a Happy Mondays gig there, so this one was a busman's holiday - a debauched long weekend in 'Dam built around a party onstage. We even got the promoter to pay for all our hotel costs.

We'd already been there for a day or two when a call came in saying that the gig was cancelled because of this virus that was sweeping through Europe. Everything was closing down, flights were getting cancelled, and even without the benefit of hindsight you could see that something major was happening.

'Bez,' everyone was shrieking, 'you'd better get home!'

'Fuck that,' I calmly replied, 'I'm not leaving until I've had my weekend!'

I resisted panicking and carried on partying with Frou, but maybe I did push it rather close to the edge. Come the Monday or Tuesday, we were on one of the last flights out of Europe back to England.

Before our departure, we were talking to loads of Dutch people who were all concerned about going into a lockdown, and what it would mean to their businesses. Even back then people were concerned about the economic impact it would have and, sure enough, that weekend was the start of the suspension of all gigs - first it was Amsterdam, then it was this one, that one, like an avalanche of cancellations.

I was really angry about it at the time, thinking, 'What the fuck are they doing, cutting off my income?' To my mind, it was just a type of influenza. Of course, you have to look after the elderly and vulnerable, and those people should've been encouraged to stay at home and generally protect themselves, leaving the rest of us to get on with it. As with flu, most people survive it, with or without jabs.

When Boris Johnson first announced that we were going to deal with the problem by aiming for herd immunity, I thought, 'Fucking hell, it's the first time I've ever agreed with the fella in my life!' Then almost immediately he reversed the decision and went for lockdowns, hysteria and destroying the economy.

It should've been handled very differently, in my opinion, because the lockdown didn't work from the point of view of keeping down the number of fatalities, and in the process they've also caused a financial crisis for us all, with raging inflation, people losing their jobs . . . it's criminal, in my eyes.

As I was heading home from Amsterdam, I started getting desperate phone calls off mates from Manchester and London, going, 'Boris is shutting everything down, please can I spend lockdown at yours?' After five or six years in residence on this beautiful private estate, everyone knew that we live in a good little spot. They were obviously thinking, 'Oh right, we're going to be locked down for a couple of weeks, let's spend it at Bez's and have a good time with it!' Me being me, I was saying, 'Yeah, yeah, get down here, we'll do lockdown together!'

As it turned out, I had a fair few people turning up from around the country. I had members of my family including my three sons, a few lads from Salford - Will Skills, Dom and another lad we know and his girlfriend - and some of Johnny's mates made camp in the woods, all converging to share in this plentiful space that we have, far from the madding crowd - and that's when the party started! Pretty much the first night of official lockdown, we had twenty-five people on site for a shindig, and that's the way it stayed through most of spring and summer.

At that stage, nobody knew how long the measures would go on for. It started as a few weeks, then it kept getting extended till it was three or four months, and the longer it went on we felt more and more fucking lucky to be where we were. We had a little community going on in our garden, all in tents and caravans and what have you, and the weather was unbelievable.

The kids really embraced their freedom and went totally feral on our private land. They had the motorbikes out, they were making dens in the woods, having an amazing time, but us adults were possibly enjoying it even more.

In April, we started the campfires – it was minus-four on the first night, but it soon warmed up – and we had lovely nights, a load of us all sat around the blazing embers, and that's when the cider drinking started. We have this cider farm near us called Gwatkin's House of Cider, and we were getting through two boxes of their scrumpy a week – 33 pints in each box! We're talking the very finest Herefordshire cider, like a spiritual experience. You can almost taste God in there, they're that wonderful.

Every night, we were all cooking outdoors on the campfire, and we were getting really experimental. One night, we had a paella with rabbit, duck and snails in it, like a proper Valencian peasant meal. We were eating pheasant and even muntjac, because the local gamesman was dropping them round for us. We ate all sorts. We were having fried-chicken nights, marinating the meat days before to get it juicy. We were using the slow cooker a lot, putting a whole chicken in there for these big communal meals. Somebody would decide that they were going to cook that night and, like a proper cooperative in action, every mouth would be fed. The food went exponential!

We had this beautiful kitchen table that my son made set up in the garden, and we would all sit out there and have huge banquets, fucking stuffing our faces out in the evening sunshine, campfire going, tunes on . . . We ate like kings, to be truthful, every night.

What's more, my garden was looking mint. We were growing all our own veg, as I'd had all that going on for a while beforehand, but suddenly I had loads of extra pairs of hands working on it. There were big wood piles in the woodshed, everything was in tip-top shape and trimmed down, because I had three months of grown men with not much else to do but tend the garden with me. It was looking the best it's ever been.

Gaz Mayall was both the hardest-working and smartest gardener I've ever come across in my life: he had a hat, a three-piece suit and shiny shoes on, while tending to the beds. When not accessorising with green fingers, he was running around hunting pheasants. He definitely got stuck into the lifestyle here.

Everything that wasn't actually grown on site, I was going out to buy on my new motorbike, which was another of the great joys for me. Twelve months previously, I'd gone on the waiting list for a bike off this company in Greater Manchester called CCM. It's a British bike, made in Bolton, because I'm proud to support British engineering and manufacturing, and it arrived at the very beginning of lockdown. You were only allowed out to do essential shopping, so, right in the middle of the most beautiful heatwave, with the roads practically empty, I'd zoom off on a 28-mile round trip to the supermarket and back.

I had my shopping bag on my back, doing the legal essentials, but I was having this unbelievable time, riding some of the most beautiful B-roads in the country, twisting, turning, taking the scenic route. I've ridden motorbikes all my life, and I've never had it like that on the roads. It became like every day I had an excuse to go to the shops.

During lockdown, The Shack was open every day and every night – religiously. The only bar in the area that was open was mine, strictly for our little bubble of garden-dwellers! Most nights we were out till 4am, maybe half-four or even five in the morning before we were going to bed.

One evening, Gaz was doing a live stream from our party around the campfire, because he was celebrating his fortieth anniversary in music, but Facebook grassed us up. They gave the coordinates of the property to the police, who duly turned up late at night. I was shocked by it, but the funny thing was, they'd come to shut us down because they'd been told there was a rave going on, and one of my mates went out and said, 'Listen, there's no rave, it's just a load of old people sat around the campfire listening to music!' Which was true, unfortunately.

During this time, I discovered a new drink: Calvados. It's apple brandy that takes up to twenty years maturing in the barrels. In the run-up, I'd been a big fan of Patron tequila, but a mate started me on this Calvados stuff. I've heard it said that it's a bit rough on the throat, but to me it's smooth, top-quality brandy, quite mature in flavour. Maybe it's an acquired taste. I must be moving into the Calvados phase of life!

It's seventy-five quid a bottle, not cheap, but at least you know it's not shit if you're paying that much. It originates from Normandy, and you know how the French are, they're quite snobby about their beverages, it must have to reach a certain standard to pass their quality control.

It wasn't all party-party-party, though. I remember one day taking a long walk up the foothills of Skirrid. I had my binoculars with me, and we ended up filling the box with wild blueberries. They're usually quite scarce, but they were out growing wild in abundance along this mountain-top path, and on the return walk we had black lips, because we were all eating as we were picking. But we kept enough to have blueberry cobbler on our return - home-made by Frou and fucking delicious! Frou makes lots of different cakes for me, like lemon drizzles and Victoria sponges. Once on Valentine's Day she made me the best Vic sponge ever, with chocolate-coated strawberries on top. My all-time favourite is Frou's banana bread though, which I love eating with peanut butter and halloumi cheese - strange but delicious.

In short, these were the best of times for all of us. My youngest son Leo said to me when the first stint was coming to an end, 'Dad, I reckon we've had one of the best lockdowns in the country!'

I know that elsewhere millions of others were having terrible times, and my heart went out to them - single people in cities locked up on their own, made to suffer in an unnecessary lockdown. It was like human cruelty. We often sat there talking about all the poor souls stuck in high-rise buildings who couldn't get out. Others were fined for getting together with their friends, with the Covid police banging on their door, and they didn't have any rights to turn them away - they could just barge into your house and fucking empty everyone out onto the street. It was like the Gestapo or Stalin's Russia, people grassing each other up, and the heavy mob storming into your home to stop you socialising. For me, it was disgusting, the fear that was rife in the nation. The lies and the fear.

If we stopped to think, it was really upsetting, but our little community carried on pretty unaffected by it all. For me personally, I've never had that long where I wasn't on the road in the last thirty-five years. I'm always going somewhere, either with the band or DJing with Arlo. Usually I'll spend three or four days at home, then I'm off out again, so it was extra-special for me to spend such unlimited quality time with family and friends.

I'll remember that period with fondness for the rest of my life, and everyone who was there says the same thing – how fortunate we were, just because Frou and I happen to live in a fucking *mega* corner of the beautiful garden that is England.

On the downside, for most of those two years I was prevented from plying my trade as a Happy Monday. Our government's prohibitive strategy for handling the pandemic completely fucked us touring musicians financially, as they have millions of others across all areas of working life. I considered writing a letter to Boris Johnson, telling him, 'No wonder people don't respect you or take you seriously. You do these televised addresses about saving lives, but the reality is that you are destroying lives and livelihoods on a huge scale beyond comprehension.'

Because of his policies, I was looking down the barrel of the gun. They stopped the government support, they wouldn't help the gigging economy get insured against cancellations and they were even telling me to go and sign on, or retrain to do summat else! Why would I sign on when I could be working? I wasn't unemployed because I couldn't get a job, it was just that they were stopping me doing the one I'd done all my life. It was a fucking joke – fearmongering, causing hysteria, just to keep the people in their homes, under control.

During our enforced lay-off from touring, I was lucky enough that I found other ways to make money. Initially, I built up my Facebook and Instagram profile and for the first time ever set up a merchandising company to sell Bez clobber. I was so taken aback by it: I never realised you had to do all these things to keep the money coming in.

It was really TV that came to my rescue, however, and provided me with a much-needed income. In winter 2019, Shaun and I had chanced upon this cushy little earner appearing on *Celebrity Gogglebox* as a kind of double act, sitting in Shaun's living room in Manchester talking shit about random telly programmes. Me and Shaun are tighter than ever. We natter away like an old married couple, and you could see that on the programme. At that stage, it was just a laugh, and a bonus to be able to make extra pocket money out of alternative mediums, other than music.

Once the pandemic hit, *Celebrity Gogglebox* kept on running. I suppose everyone was just stuck indoors watching all the same light entertainment on TV, so it connected more than ever, and we became mainstays through the various series.

All it takes is a couple of hours each Monday, over seven weeks. I'd just turn up, banter with my best mate, go home and get paid for it. They're not bothered if you don't even talk about the shows. They just want anything! Half the things we say could obviously never make it onto national television. We get really carried away with shit, going places that definitely aren't fit for broadcast, but if they ever did an out-takes special showing the stuff they couldn't use, after hours, I reckon it'd be pretty funny.

I enjoy doing *Gogglebox*. I enjoy the wages, and what a great job through lockdown! Sat having a laugh with your best mate, watching telly on the settee and getting pissed! It doesn't get better than that. At that stage, nobody could go anywhere, and the Covid paranoia about social distancing was reaching mass proportions, but because it was for Channel Four, it was all okay. Me and Shaun were saying at the time, 'We've been sharing germs for fucking years, you know what I mean? A bit of Covid's not gonna make much difference . . .'

The only thing about it was, it wasn't the healthiest show you could do: we'd obviously have a few Guinnesses, Shaun would crack the Jameson's open, and all the sweets and cakes would come out. You're just sat there getting pretty slaughtered watching telly.

Like everybody else, there had generally been a lot of sitting around doing nothing during the pandemic. In the first lock-down, all I did was eat and drink myself into oblivion, and as much as I revelled in all that, it wasn't good for the waistline. The overindulgence was outrageous, and you wouldn't believe the weight I put on, drinking cider, eating cake, just living the good life for three months, and not really exercising apart from dancing in The Shack or doing a bit of gardening.

Once we were all roaming a bit more freely after the end of the first lockdown, I decided that I couldn't go on like that and started thinking about creative ways to fight the flab. That summer of 2020, I was really fortunate to be asked by this production company if there was anything I'd like to do, and I came up with the idea of an online fitness instruction programme. Basically, I was coming after Joe Wickes.

At fifty-six years of age, and as a grandad, I set up 'Get Buzzin' With Bez' on YouTube, and invited people to come and join me on my trip – a different trip. The concept was that I got a PT instructor called Andy, and he was showing me a very gentle introduction to exercise. I did some yoga, got some hypnosis, and set about kicking that sugar habit. There was even an ambitious plan to give up the booze again, which just about came to pass. Goodbye ciders, hello fruit smoothies!

I hoped it would be useful for people watching who'd maybe been thinking about doing it but could never be arsed. Because for myself, I hadn't done anything for about two and a half years. I was getting really worried, like I was in the last-chance saloon, and if I didn't start doing something, in the last throes of my youth (!), then I was gonna miss the boat before that slow deterioration into old age.

When filming commenced that autumn, I was aching in places I didn't know you could ache, but it was kind of a nice ache. Some mornings, I really didn't feel like doing it, I was really struggling, limping down to the park, thinking, 'It's sleeting, this is horrible. What am I doing?' But once I got started and got through the first few exercises, I warmed up and felt really good.

Almost immediately I started sleeping better. Usually I have disturbed sleep in the night, but exercising really changed that. After only a week, the feelgood factor, the natural high of all the endorphins rushing, was unbelievable. The reaction was incredible from the general public, from friends and people I know in the music business, and in the media - I was on BBC One's *Breakfast* talking about it. It was just the motivation I needed to keep going and see what I could achieve in the longer term.

We were getting over 250,000 views per episode, and I managed to lose a substantial amount of weight, and improve my fitness levels a hell of a lot. Perhaps even more importantly,

I had loads of telly coverage: the idea of Bez cleaning up his act got picked up on by all the main channels, and that put me in the running for more TV work.

As we were shooting through the second lockdown in autumn 2020, another positive was that it was getting me out of the house, because I had to travel to Manchester for the filming. At one point, I actually had the Covid police around to the house, because somebody had grassed me up for travelling and having a personal trainer, neither of which were allowed at that point. However, because we were working for a proper production company, we were deemed 'essential workers' bringing entertainment and wellbeing to the public.

To be very honest, I hadn't even noticed the second lockdown in November '20. We still had a load of my mates staying in the garden, so life never really changed for us either way. In Manchester in the run-up to Christmas, it didn't really affect me. Each area had its own rules: in the city all the restaurants were shut, but just over the county border in Cheshire, different guidelines were in place and the restaurants were open.

It was fucking mad having all these different restrictions going on in different areas, depending what the R rating was. It was the lockdown that wasn't really a lockdown. In some places pubs were shut, in other places pubs were open, and everybody was just nipping across borders to where things weren't so tight. It was like, 'Fucking hell, what is the point of this?' I didn't get it at all. It would've been comical if it wasn't having so much impact on people's everyday lives.

Every year, I normally take all of Frou's family out for Christmas dinner in Manchester. Needless to say, we changed things up for Christmas 2020 and dined in Cheshire.

The intensity of the attention I received after *Big Brother* had effectively driven me away from the world of television celebrity. I hated that level of intrusion on my privacy, so I'd been routinely turning down stuff where I thought there was a danger anything like that might happen again. These were clearly different times, though, and I was in no position to look any passing gift horses in the mouth. I'd entered into the 'smash-and-grab' mentality that had always served the Mondays so well, and by January 2021 I was filming as a contestant on *Celebrity MasterChef* – another great job that chased the wolf from my door and kept the lantern burning.

I wouldn't be revealing too much if I confessed that I'm not a natural cook. Frou won't even allow me in the kitchen at home, largely because of the mess I leave in my wake when I try and put a meal together. As part of my new permacultural diet, I take a juicer with me everywhere I go, along with my own fruit and vegetables, and it could be anywhere – a friend's place, a hotel room – but there'll always be utter destruction, just to make a pint of juice.

I do make a decent old-school breakfast and I have a few stock dishes I can scrape together, but generally I regard cooking as something that other people do. As my two older sons will tell you, the first time I ever cooked was when their mother started work again, and by default I had to take charge of feeding them. For months we had takeaways every night, then one day Jack and Arlo just stood there with their arms folded, shaking their heads, going, 'Please, Dad, not another takeaway!'

The first thing I cooked was lime and coriander chicken, which is lime caramelised with sugar in a pan, with chicken and butter, sitting on a bed of rice, topped off with coriander. When it all got eaten, I was so pleased with myself that we had it constantly, for days on end. I only found out recently that the youngest lad, Leo, who's not had it yet, really wants to experience this culinary treat, but I've put the elder two off it for life. Obviously, I made it a few too many times.

It wasn't like my gourmet side was ever stimulated while on the road with the Mondays. I wasn't picking up tips from the cooks backstage, because catering never worked for me at gigs. With all the Persians going down, I never ate a morsel.

I'd certainly never cooked to a high standard like I had to on *MasterChef*. I know that Shaun recently did a cooking programme too, but that was a show for people who *can't* cook! In fairness, that was definitely the category I fell into beforehand, but I was actually on the series for people who supposedly know what they're doing. For me, it was a whole new experience, a mission into the unknown, pushing my limits of cooking knowledge to the very max.

The way it happens, you never know exactly what's coming in each programme, but you get told that you will have to cook, say, a spice dish, and about certain specific tasks that you may have to perform. Those bits of the show you can prepare for; the rest, they just throw at you on the day.

In order to give myself some chance of competing, I went to get some advice from a local Michelin-starred chef called Stephen Terry who runs the Hardwick gastropub in Abergavenny. Before the show started, I went down there to get some practice in his kitchen, and he helped me out with some of my dishes.

I have to come clean here: the presenters Gregg Wallace and John Torode kept on complimenting me on my 'big flavours'. Taste-wise I was killing everyone! My instinctive mastery of flavours stunned the various guest chefs, but they weren't mine at all – they were Stephen's! It was him that came up with all the combinations of ingredients, and I was just taking the credit for them. In fact, I was completely ruining all his best dishes, which are out of this world, or should be, but my special take on his recipes somehow got me through the early rounds.

The problem was, my presentation was shit. Everything I served up looked like slop on the plate, and I was the messiest contestant they'd ever had.

In the early part of the contest, I kept not believing my luck. In the first heat, we had to rustle something up using rhubarb, which just happens to be one of my favourites. We grow it in the garden, so while some of the other contestants didn't even know what it was, I knew straight away what to do with it – a ginger-infused crumble with creamy vanilla custard. Then we had to make a pasta carbonara, and I was the only person who knew that you do the sauce with egg and cheese, *not* cream – it's literally one of the handful of things I do know how to make – another mad stroke of luck.

Once I'd made it through to the last eight, we had to create our own 'super-sandwich'. As kids growing up in the North, you had bread with every meal, and whatever was on your plate – bacon, cheese, all kinds of vegetables, even a whole pie – you'd throw it into your bread and make a sandwich out of it. You could go through half a loaf of bread with your dinner, making butties. For the cameras, I made a posh one, with battered cod and tempura whitebait, but my deployment of a pickled egg, like any northern chippie, got me hailed as a 'legend'.

I made a point of ensuring on camera that the cod was line-caught, as opposed to caught in nets, which kills lots of other species unnecessarily, and causes mass destruction of the seabed. Everything I cooked on the show was sustainable, like organic wild vegetables, and organic meat from my new local providers Black Welsh Mountain Sheep, who refuse to slaughter young lambs, only hogget and mutton. It was important to me to get that message over.

Filming in January/February 2021 was an absolute treat because you got to socialise at a time when nobody else was allowed to, and I was spending the day with some right characters, like Joe Swash off *Eastenders*, who was a lovely lad. My favourite was Su Pollard, because she's just nuts, she is who she is, and I really enjoyed her company. Some people didn't get me liking her, but she has so much energy for a woman in her late seventies – she's absolutely non-stop! She brightened up any dull day, and she was texting me rubbish jokes for weeks afterwards.

The thing about *MasterChef* is that it really takes it out of you, constantly cooking against the clock. When you cook at home, it's a relaxing thing because you've got your missus doing the commis-cheffing for you, you've got your tunes on, you're quaffing glasses of wine, and time isn't much of an issue. The air of competition, and always having the clock ticking on you, were the things I struggled with.

Where I eventually came unstuck was on the show where you were one step away from the grand final. The day before was actually a day off for me in London. I got a little bit bored sitting around and being well behaved, and some friends who run a Japanese promoting firm invited me down to a little gathering they were having at their place under the Westway. All my buddies in the capital found out I was there, and it turned into a bit of a do, shall we say, everyone partying in this covered outside area.

I didn't get home until the early hours, and then I was picked up at seven to go to the television studios. Predictably, I worked a little slowly in the kitchen that day, got flustered and ended up making soggy flatbreads for a dish of party nibbles, which put me out of the game just before the final hurdle.

I was really dejected about fucking up that way, but I'd probably got further than anticipated because, as everyone could see, I was no Gordon Ramsay.

Cooking at home, I'm not as untidy as I used to be, but I still always panic trying to get the timing right at the end. That's when the mess occurs, when all the pots and pans go everywhere, and the food is flying all over the shop.

For me, the whole pandemic period blended into one. Half of the lockdowns, I didn't even realise we were locked down. I was missing some of them altogether, because I stopped watching the news. I'd fucking had enough of it. I decided that I wouldn't participate in any of the fear they were feeding me. We went into our own bubble and didn't have the foggiest what was going on in the outside world.

Money-wise, I was lucky enough to find different ways to get by. I wasn't a meek mouse, locked up in self-imprisonment. I was out there, taking advantage of the moment – doing TV, buying and selling shares, and basically having a right old party.

During the sharp end of that gruelling first half of 2021, I got an opportunity to make a single with the acid-house DJ/producer Doorly. He's a really lovely kid, originally from Huddersfield, and has become massive in the field of dubstep, especially in America. Deep into the period where nobody could travel, he very kindly offered to put us up in his beautiful villa in Ibiza. With all scheduled flights grounded, we managed to fly out there on a little four-seater private jet – who could turn down a once-in-a-lifetime opportunity like that?

I can't tell you how many times I've been to Ibiza to party. About five years ago, I went out there for the filming of a Julien Temple movie about Ibiza, where I was playing Bez, the God of Dance. Frou came with me, and it turned into a mega trip. We started in Barcelona, where Frou DJed with me. Then we hired a car and had three weeks travelling all over Spain, visiting friends. We flew to Ibiza for four days' shooting and had a night out on Halloween. I even got dressed up, which I rarely do, with all the fake blood and white face make-up, but not many other people had bothered. Typical!

After all the visits there over the years, I've never seen Ibiza the way it was under Covid. It was like a ghost island. Frou was along for the trip again to provide some vocals, and I wanted to show her San Antonio and the West End where all the mad English go fucking crazy in summertime, but it was empty, dead, shut down.

All the Spanish beaches were quite busy with locals, however, and the restaurants were open, so we managed to cram in a bit of sun, sand and sangria, while up at the villa we were putting this 'Flying Bus' tune together in an old-school acid-house style. I don't think it has done exceptionally well, but it's the joining in that counts! And we got an amazing five-day holiday out of it, when such things were prohibited.

The only thing about a private jet is, it ruins everything – how do you go back to normal passenger planes after that? When we got back to England, the bags got loaded straight off the plane into the back of my car, and we were gone.

By the time the restrictions were finally lifted in the summertime, it was like we'd had this gang of people living in my garden forever. The moment had arrived for people to return to their own homes, and Frou and I were quite pleased when we got a bit of normality back.

Professionally, everything went into that limbo period, where public events were allowed to go ahead, but many punters were too afraid to risk venturing out, leaving promoters with little option but postponement. That summer, I signed up to take part in October's Celebrity Boxstar at Manchester Arena, and duly went into eight weeks' training. I'd never done boxing before, so I did some intensive sparring with a pro boxer, and I was getting beaten up on a regular basis.

Come the big day, there were maybe twenty fighters – reality-TV stars off *Love Island* and what have you, a few footballers – and I was up against Clayton Blackmore, an ex-Man United player with lots of boxing experience. I was fighting an elite sportsman at least two or three weights above me. After the fact, a couple of the organisers admitted to me that it was something of a mismatch, but that's no excuse.

I came into the arena to the strains of 'Step On', maracas in hand, and all the papers said it was the best ring walk ever seen by man. It was two three-minute rounds, and I really thought I was going to win it. I didn't have any pre-bout nerves, but I probably should've been a bit more apprehensive. In the final round, he caught me with a belter. I took an eight-second count, and I didn't even know I'd had one, and he won on points, so I have to congratulate him.

I still really enjoyed the whole experience, and I'd do it again even though nobody around me wants me to. I guess I'm a sucker for that edge of danger, but I'm probably the wrong age to become a prizefighter at fifty-eight – it's really no time to take up boxing.

That night, I DJed at Bowlers over in Stretford and had a great night out with my mates. It was only when I woke up the next morning that I realised I had double vision – it went by completely unnoticed throughout the previous evening. It's possible I did some damage to the nerves behind my eye, but luckily there were no symptoms of concussion. The blurring lasted for about three months, and I got used to it after a day or two. I'd walk about with one of my eyes shut, sometimes even both.

Undeterred, I was back in the big arenas in the run-up to Christmas, as the Happy Mondays were opening for our Mancunian contemporaries James on a seven-date tour – a great opportunity to show how good the band is to larger audiences who'd probably never seen us before. We were just glad to be out playing, and earning a wage. At Wembley, I fell over a monitor and almost pitched headfirst off the stage – I blamed the double vision.

To try and prevent anyone in the entire crew catching Covid and thus scuppering the tour, there were strict regulations barring outsiders going backstage. For the others, that was nothing out of the ordinary, as they tend not to have people back before and after the show. Nobody likes having a party any more. For me, however, it was completely different from any other tour we've done in recent years, because instead of having my own changing room, which this time would've involved me sitting there on my own twiddling my thumbs, I hung about in the band's room, and I think in the circumstances they quite enjoyed having my company.

The nice thing about the band at the moment is that it's not like the old days - we're all getting on great - and we were all very thankful to get to play all seven shows and bag the money for them. It happened just in time, as within a few days new restrictions came in for Christmas around the Omicron variant.

After the announcement, I lost almost six grand in one phone call, thanks to the cancellation of a TV thing with the scouse comedian John Bishop (who often gets mistaken for me on the street, the poor fucker!) and a DJ gig at the Lowry Hotel in Manchester.

I shouldn't answer the phone, should I?

I wasn't at all happy.

My belief is that we're governed by a bunch of Masonic wrongathons.

Luckily, I still had the prospect of an exciting TV project in January 2022, as well as ongoing commitments to *Celebrity Gogglebox*. While the way I live my life and the work I do may have evolved in latter years, it's all down to being a Happy Monday, and my friendship with Shaun William Ryder.

SHAUN: More than ever, me and Bez have a really good thing going together, doing *Gogglebox*, as well as other one-off TV and radio appearances, which all contribute to bringing in new fans for the band. At this point, we've got a couple of our own TV productions in the pipeline, which will hopefully come good in 2022/23. The two of us see more of each other than ever.

I've always known that the public love him. Dude, I was aware of that from street level, back when we were teenagers, when I'd not even met him, just heard about his legend. Everybody knew who Bez was, and just because

I didn't want him around at my flat the very first time, that didn't mean I didn't realise he was a cool cunt. I brought him in the band because I knew what he had.

There is no one like Bez: you could literally throw him out of a helicopter at 60,000 feet and he would land in somebody's extra-deep swimming pool, get out and they would cook him Sunday dinner – *and* let him stay the night!

Some of his ideas are way out there, even by my standards. You know, I reckon I'm quite normal in thinking that we are not alone in the universe, and that other lifeforms exist out there somewhere. Bez, on the other hand, has got conspiracy theories coming out of his arse. Some of the things he believes I tend to think are just too far gone.

But I totally understand Bez – his personality, what he is, how he is – and I accept it, for all the chaos it entails, because that's what makes him who he is, and that's why we've remained friends for nearly forty years.

I'll give anything a go, me. I've never been known to shrink back from a challenge. As my participation in *Celebrity MasterChef* and Boxstar amply demonstrated, I'll sign up for as many of these things as will come my way.

I'm like the character Yosser Hughes in Alan Bleasdale's TV drama from 1982, *Boys from the Blackstuff*: I can never say no to any offer that's on the table.

'Gizza job! I can do that!'

The thing about *MasterChef* is that any fool can cook: you just follow the instructions. You might argue that I was on the wrong side of fifty to start taking up boxing, but I like anything with a little bit of danger in it. If I was going out to undertake a project and I thought there was no danger involved, it would be pretty boring for me.

Such impulses probably drove my involvement in the January 2022 series of ITV's *Dancing on Ice*: a bit of 'I'll try anything once', mixed with a cavalier and possibly foolhardy physical risk, and as always a strong flavour of not being arsed what others thought if I came a cropper on live television. It goes without saying that my decision to enlist was also greatly influenced by the financial reward I'd earn from doing so.

I first got asked about going on the 2021 series during lockdown in 2020, at which point I'd never ice-skated before in my life. It was never something I thought I'd do. Seeing as no public rinks were open then, I ordered myself a pair of rollerblade boots online and tried to teach myself the basics of skating that way. I later found out that I'd got my technique all totally wrong, even after watching umpteen YouTube videos of all kinds of ice-skating manoeuvres.

After some auditions, I didn't get the job, but then they phoned me up a few months later about the following year's contest, and said if I wanted it, I'd already got the job, without the need for any more auditions. While it was obviously going to be a challenge in that I'd never ice-skated before, what the show's producers probably assumed was that, since I'm always credited as the dancer with Happy Mondays, I'd have that half of the show's title nailed.

What these people don't realise is that I wouldn't actually call myself a dancer – I'm a raver, which is a totally different skill set.

I've not been classically trained in any way at all, whereas, as it turned out, there were skaters on the show who had done ballet, you had Brendan Cole off *Strictly Come Dancing*, and professional sportsmen as well as pop stars fresh from being drilled in step routines, all of whom seemed to pick up the skating skills really quickly. I was just a 57-year-old raver, with loads of injuries from my turn-of-the-millennium motorbike crash.

Most people who know me wouldn't big me up on account of my gracefulness: I'm heavy-handed in everything I do, and that manifests in everything from putting food on the plate right through to doing a bloody pirouette on skates. Neither of those are my strong suits in life, and from the off I was like an elephant in a china shop on the ice.

I was the most accident-prone entrant they'd ever had on the show, to such a point where I was the first ever to be allowed to wear a helmet on competition days. Initially, though, there was a reason why I had so many falls, and some pretty spectacular ones to boot: I still had my double vision from the boxing, so at the beginning I couldn't tell which ice rink I was on – the top one, or the bottom one. I was learning on two parallel rinks.

On the very first training day, I had one of the worst falls they've ever seen on the programme, all mercilessly captured on camera: I fell backwards and smacked my head that hard on the ice, my helmet flew off yards away. I was kitted out with all the padding known to man: padded shorts, padded pelvis, padded thighs, padded arse, pads on my knees, pads on my elbows, and extra-strong wrist guards.

They were apparently worried that I might actually be unteachable, because they'd never seen anybody looking so 'not right' on the ice, with absolutely zero coordination and balance completely off.

With one fall, I damaged my knee, and by the next morning I couldn't bend my leg. Luckily I knew a physiotherapist in

Didsbury, who'd sorted my back out with acupuncture and deep-tissue massage one time when I slipped in the mud in my garden. I thought it was game over for this lucrative venture, but the miracle-worker physio actually got my knee moving in just one session. Still, with the double vision and the knee, I missed a bunch of training, which didn't help my cause. And then I got Covid midway through, which also wasn't ideal, but did at least prompt *Billboard*'s memorable headline 'Happy Mondays drummer tests positive'!

I was like Bambi on ice, crossed with Frank Spencer, but with time I managed to overcome some of the difficulties. I got better at falling, if you get my drift, and I had a huge amount of fun doing it. I had a brilliant coach called Lindsay - a local woman from the very same estate in Boothstown where Shaun and I lived in the late 80s. I'm not sure I ever quite mastered gracefulness, but along the way I mastered nearly all the basic moves: pirouette on the spot, hockey glides, going backwards, and backwards doing half-melons - or lemons, should I say!

For the show itself, I was lucky to be allocated a brilliant dancing partner called Angela Egan, a Scottish girl who was very understanding, and I came on leaps and bounds. She was a no-nonsense type of woman, but we had a lot of laughs together - well, I made her laugh, but I couldn't say whether she was laughing at me or with me.

My first competitive skate was to 'Step On' (what else?), and ITV really pushed the boat out on the production: they lowered me down from the ceiling on a giant pair of maracas, after which I hopped off and went into some basic moves, while the audience shook the normal-sized maracas they'd been equipped with, and loads of twisting melons pirouetted around me.

All I had to do was remember my routine, and luckily, because it was primetime TV, it wasn't the full song, just a ninety-second edit for me to try and stay upright throughout, and thus impress the judges.

I think the fun element saw me through that first week, and after that the public kept voting me in because they wanted to see me wipe out and make a dick of myself. It wasn't like I ever thought I'd be in the running for winning it, with pipe dreams of me doing the 'Bolero' like Torvill and Dean in the final show.

I had a lot of fun trying not to tumble, and somehow made it through to the last eight. I entertained the masses variously dressed up as Indiana Jones, a Scotsman, a beekeeper and a biker, until I quite rightly got booted out once the competition started hotting up. All but crippled with terrible soreness in my feet, knees, back, calves, bum – you name it, there was pain in that region – I was ready to leave.

Back home in Herefordshire, when the final Covid restrictions were lifted in February 2022, we had a big old party which doubled up as a birthday bash for one of my boys. After that, everyone went off the property back to their own homes – the grown-ups back to work, my kids back to Manchester, and us back to normal at last. It wasn't long, of course, before my birthday came around on 18 April, and the lighting of the first campfire of the year, and we've been partying with guests, with renewed vigour, throughout the summer.

The whole pandemic phase seems to have come to an end now, almost like it never happened, and I'm right back into DJing and the band and appearing on mad TV programmes like *Would I Lie To You?*, *Blankety Blank* and *Pointless*, which bring with them that high level of privacy intrusion. When I was in town last weekend, every five yards I was getting stopped for a photo. It is what it is, and you can't look a gift horse in the mouth. Ultimately, it's whether you want the dough or not, and right now I'm into taking the dough. When I decide that enough is enough, I'll leave and be forgotten in a matter of weeks, which will suit me fine.

ARLO: It very much goes up and down with my dad. When the Happy Mondays were at their peak, he was getting recognised, then there was a lull until he did *Big Brother* and got recognised *all* the time. Then it dipped off again, and now he's back doing TV, it's serious recognition.

I've never minded people coming up to him. The only time it bothers me a little bit is when they don't even know his name, like this woman the other day who goes, 'Ooh, it's him from *Dancing on Ice* . . . him!' She wasn't even a fan of who he is or what he does, she just had to have a picture with him because he's someone off the telly. That's the only time I think, 'Fuck off, you don't even know who he is!'

But Dad stops and talks to them all. He has never said no to anyone for a photograph. He really is the most kind-hearted man I know. He always says that he makes the bed he lies in. It's part of his job, and he doesn't mind it at all. Actually, I'd say it goes completely the opposite way: I think he quite likes it. In fact, I know he does.

Among his fans from the music, a lot of those people still have him boxed in as this 'king of drugs' character, and they don't see anything past that image of him when he was in his twenties and early thirties. The general consensus on him is that he's just a rock 'n' roll fucking drug-taker, but there's quite a bit more to him than that.

*

For the past two years, TV came to my rescue when millions of others weren't able to earn a wage, and I'm grateful for the opportunity. To be truthful, I haven't worked out why they want me on there. I'm still an old-fashioned rebel at heart, but sometimes now I'm not quite as loud about it. I don't want to upset the powers-that-be and kill off my own business. At the present moment, people who speak out are getting sacked and fucked off.

Right now, we're going into a bit of a dictatorship, aren't we, and the nation has been divided. There is a massive gulf between the haves and have-nots, and we may possibly lose all our freedoms, thanks to voters backing a tyrant regime, and willingly accepting the consequences. It's dangerous times, so you've got to tread carefully.

People of a certain mentality - like most people I know - we managed to get through the Covid situation, living our own lives as we saw fit, but nobody was unaffected by it. For instance, in my game as a live performer, there was another group of people that was buying tickets for gigs, then not actually turning up, presumably because they were living in fear of the virus as it was being presented to them through the media.

In that way, the governing forces have skilfully split the country. Even though the whole thing seems to have ended now, you see these scared people all still walking around with masks on, uncomfortable at the prospect of giving up the fear.

I read a lot about what's going on with the corporate strategy for mankind - fracking is just the tip of the iceberg, believe me. None of this reading has helped my state of mind one bit - it can ruin your life, as well as being a positive, educating force. I almost wish I didn't know about it all. It's so unbelievable that when I tell people about it, I can see them looking at me like I'm crackers.

Just Google the 'Great Reset' – this agenda from the so-called World Economic Forum, where all the biggest players in global business are pushing for their ultimate goal by 2030, just eight years away – a new world order, one world government, and one currency. It's all fucking going on, and the more people wake up to it, the more hope there is that the collective consciousness might actually be able to stop it.

Even the weed now has been taken over by the giant agrochemical and agricultural biotechnology corporation, Monsanto, who manufacture this Frankenstein weed which makes people mentally ill. That's another reason why I don't smoke any more. After waking up to that reality where you think you're rebelling and you're really just conforming, the whole thing does my head in.

I find it's more rebellious to be staying straight most of the time, rather than getting off my nut. It's a bigger rebellion to refuse to be drawn into the world of psychotropic medicines, painkillers, and all the other prescription drugs that they've got everyone on. In America, it's a huge problem; now it's hitting the UK. These enormous companies who run the show want to turn everybody into zombies. They've got half the world popping psychotropics, readily plunging themselves into mental illness.

All this awakening started when I went into politics and tried to fight the revolution. That's when I woke up to what exactly I was fighting. When I decided to fight the cunts, I realised how totally they control the populace. It blew my head off, and I wished I'd never even taken on the struggle. I realised that the fight is everywhere, and that I had to move on and, like Théun Mares taught me, occupy my own world.

High-ranking officials like head teachers and corporate bosses apparently get trained in a thing called 'common purpose', and you quickly get disposed of by these people if you speak out of turn. I can't afford to get common purposed out of the game, so for the time being I'm keeping some of my more controversial views to myself and moving about under cover of the night.

That may be a bad thing, because I feel a little bit like I'm being controlled, by not being able to speak honestly, but sometimes you've just got to be cautiously aware of your own situation, and this would be the wrong time and place for me to be too opinionated.

If I was a multimillionaire and didn't have to give a shit about the rest of the world, there'd be no holding me back! But I'm having to play the safe game at the moment, and hopefully people who matter can tell from the twinkle in my eye what I'm thinking.

Chapter 11

FULL CIRCLE

In David Mitchell's excellent novel from 2004, *Cloud Atlas*, the lives of characters from six separate stories start crossing over across the centuries and into the future. I loved that book, because it makes you think about whether maybe there's a higher purpose to our existence which we don't comprehend, but which maybe guides us in our decision-making, along pre-ordained paths that intertwine over many generations.

A year or so ago, my dad called me up, because he'd been digging into our family tree. He loves all that stuff, and he goes, 'You'll never believe what I've just found out!'

In 1705, it transpires, my great-great-great-grandmother on my nana's side was born pretty much exactly where I'm living now in Herefordshire. She lived less than half a mile away from our house and worked on the estate. She probably used the same roads and paths that we do, and doubtless visited the house where I reside.

Her father and grandfather are actually buried in the church nearby, so it's pretty damn freaky that I've come to settle there 300 years later - and that, like a scene from *Cloud Atlas*, I'm now going to marry Frou in the very same place of worship where my ancestors are laid to rest.

I feel like I've worked my way back home again, and that it was all meant to be.

By autumn 2021, Frou and I had been together for eight years, and she was saying to me, 'You must know by now whether you want to be with me all your life or not.' I kept pretending that I was still thinking, but I'd already decided to take the plunge because I wanted to make her really happy.

I've never been married before, and, to me, it's a one-time-only thing. I've left it till I'm fifty-eight, and I reckon Frou's getting me at my best, at my most mature and considerate, and I'm confident that it will work out.

I arranged to pop the question on top of that favourite mountain of mine. We've had some really good forage off that mountain - wild blueberries, all sorts - and I feel powerfully connected to it. I had both of our families and a few friends go on ahead to a pre-arranged spot up there.

When we reached the little summit, Frou was totally surprised to find all our nearest and dearest waiting for us there. I dropped to one knee, asked for her hand in marriage, and we had a mini-party to celebrate. That mountain just keeps throwing up good things.

As the pandemic rolled on, we set the date for September 2022, so it'll have happened by the time you read this, and the advance for the book will have contributed to the cost of Frou's dress. Thanks for that, readers!

I have to say that wedding preparations are really not my thing. Frou has done most of the organising, and I just pretend to be listening to all of her plans. She has obviously got into it in a big way, along with her sisters, and I think it's all coming along quite nicely. It's a great idea, getting married, but I didn't anticipate the amount of planning that needs to go into it! I'm really just looking forward to getting married, and being married.

The things I've sorted out: I've got a great keyboard player, Ace Face, playing a *Blues Brothers*-style jazzy version of 'Here Comes the Bride' on the church organ. Rowetta is singing for us, too, and all our friends will be there.

Shaun is going to be my best man. If me and him really are in some kind of weird sexless marriage, we've actually been together longer than most proper married couples - almost forty years - so maybe his official capacity is a good omen for me and Frou.

I've tried to persuade Shaun to come down and stay with us countless times since we moved down to Herefordshire. All the other members of the band have been, but Shaun still sees me as his worst influence. I'm his biggest fear, but I've always wanted him to visit me at home, to see how much my life has changed, and how I've left all that shit behind.

He's a changed man, Shaun, not the party animal he once was. He always goes on and on about our old lifestyle being repetitive. 'It's fucking Groundhog Day, B, I can't do it any more!' He's always worried about losing control. He's trying to cling on to his sanity, and be as normal as possible, and he knows it could easily fall by the wayside. He's not that strong-willed, and he knows that if it goes, it'll go with a bang!

Now I've got him captured for the wedding, I can show him how I live my life and open up his eyes to it all. I'm sure he'll love it.

FIROUZEH: It's going to be the greatest party ever. The wedding itself is in a beautiful church, where Bez has family buried – it's such an amazing coincidence, we just had to get married there. I'm going to have a horse and carriage bringing me to the church, and we'll have the traditional ceremony in there with the wedding rings exchanged.

We're being greedy, though, because afterwards we're having another ceremony where we give each other honey, which is part of the Persian tradition, because I'm half-Iranian. We're having a Sofreh Aghd, where a table is laid out in front of the couple and everything on it has a specific meaning, like the honey is for a sweet life. There's the Mirror of Fate, where the bridegroom sees his bride's face once she's lifted her veil for the first time, and then all these different herbs which each represent something.

We're doing it with a slight twist, though. Like, we'll feed honey to each other, which is amazing for Bez, obviously! Also, instead of exchanging the rings which we will have done already, we're doing a hand binding, where your hands are tied together to seal the union, which is what they did many centuries ago, before religion took over. That will happen in a little wood henge we've built from which we can see the mountain where Bez proposed to me in the distance.

For the food, we'll have ribs of beef, lamb and chicken barbecued over open fires by our friend Simon Morley, who's a famous 'Puppeteer of the Penis'. He has flown all over the world doing shows, but he's given it up now to run the restaurant he set up in his back garden during lockdown, with open-fire cooking. Whenever he invited us over for dinner, we were really happy because he's the best chef. To go with the barbecued meat, there'll be baba ghanoush, loads of different dips, specially made pita breads, and loads of different salads with fruits.

At night, once the party's rocking, we'll have a pizza

oven on the go in case anyone's still hungry. In the next field, we'll have some giant tipis set up, with dinner service, a bar, and a stage for live bands and DJs, and we'll party into the night. We've got Doorly and Leeroy from The Prodigy DJing, and Gaz Mayall's eleven-piece band, The Trojans, playing with a full horn section.

It should be a great day, and it'll be the hottest day of the year, obviously! It's the final step for me and Bez – not to prove our love, but the final stage in our union. Together we are stronger and nothing can break us. And maybe it's going to be a new beginning for Bez, because now he realises that he's found the love of his life! It will only get better and better, and we're ready for the next adventure. That's so cheesy, isn't it?

Frou's great, she looks after me. I love her very much, and we get on really well, even though she's nineteen years younger than me. We've obviously lived together for most of our time, so she gets involved with my lifestyle, the occasional little parties we have at home, acting as my official driver for Happy Mondays gigs - doing everything together, playing tennis, walking the dogs and going on lots of lovely holidays together.

We've thought about moving on somewhere, but we could never replace the house we have now. We've looked into finding a bigger smallholding farm, to take the way we're living now to the next level - maybe eleven to fifteen acres, where we could create a space for a small sustainable community. We'd make our own booze, keep bees, and all that shit - like my version of *The Good Life*! We could build glamping sites with yurts and other structures, and put on small birthday parties for people, offering accommodation, toilets and all that – to bring the party to *me*.

We also had an idea for a market-gardening venture – I'd offer my land to maybe a young couple just finished with studying at university somewhere, and give them a place to live and land to do it on. Because it's a lot of hard work to do yourself, and I'd labour for them. That way we'd look at building a small community way of life, being self-sufficient on a bigger plot of land, and do parties! What could possibly go wrong?!

We've looked at all these different options, but we keep coming back to the fact that the place we have now is a total one-off, and you'll never get anything even nearly as good anywhere else, for any money. So we plan to stay where we are, and maybe get my books out of boxes at last.

We're lucky, because we've got people close by who look out for us 24/7, and we've got two dogs now, Yoko and Snoop, who are also good for security because they're yappy – they've definitely got a bark on them. I never thought I would get into having dogs. Earlier in my life I never had them, because I suppose I was here, there and everywhere. When I lived in Glossop, I had a cat named Kipper. One day I was away on tour and I suddenly got a vision of Kipper in my head, which wouldn't go away, then five minutes later I received a phone call saying Kipper had died. Psychic connection.

Fast-forward to Herefordshire, and we got Yoko two years ago just before lockdown, then Snoop followed a year later. They're both miniature dachshunds, and they don't know it yet, but it's an arranged marriage.

Yoko has been a source of amazement for me. She's really loving, but she's no lapdog. She's out hunting every day, and she's got pure kills to her name – pheasants, rabbits, rats, squirrels and voles – I'm so proud of her. She eats everything she catches as well! She'll spend seven hours a day out digging holes and chasing prey. Frou is like the real master, they adore her. The way they look at her is unbelievable! I'm definitely second-best when she's about.

Truthfully, I can't believe how fortunate I've been in life. I really do throw back the curtains in the morning and say to the missus, 'How fucking lucky are we?' Because I've never had a normal job, I've had a lot of time on my hands to ponder shit, and take it all in. I've had this charmed life where I've had the freedom to go down exploratory paths and do loads of different things. I'm not forced into a nine-to-five exist- ence, so I can think outside the normal box that people get trapped in, and reflect on life more. I can lie about and let my mind wander.

I've lived a good life, but I still wouldn't say that I've lived anything that amazing, different or untoward. I'm not a lone ranger, in that regard. I know a lot of people like myself, who just get on and live similar lifestyles, and probably do it better than me.

I don't ever dwell on that thing of 'what ifs', or regrets that keep you awake all night. You know, I could've gone with Julia Roberts! In the car park in Los Angeles, it was like she was asking me back to hers, but I didn't go for it. For all I know, that could've been a whole different crossroads in my life, but I don't regret my decision in any way at all and it's not something I brood on – never any 'what if *that* had happened?'

Equally, I could've been shot and chopped up that time I got kidnapped, or I could've died from the hospital superbug after my bike crash, so you could say I'm lucky to be around still anyway.

When I'm walking the dogs on my own, I still fantasise about a whole different reality to the one we ordinarily inhabit. I dream of having five thousand acres of my own, where, as Lord of the Manor, I could secede from the union and set up an independent state – a self-sufficient fiefdom where I could pursue my ideal of ending money and making everything free for everybody living there. We could do industrial-type farming, set up workshops where you could make anything – woodwork, engineering shops, everything – and have no need for the outside world.

I'm pushing sixty now and I *still* believe that there's something amazing waiting around the next corner. I hope that I can live a long and healthy life, and that I'll be able to wangle my way around what I see coming, swerve the worst of it and carry on in my own merry way.

You just never know.

You've got to keep on believing.

Around the next corner . . .

Acknowledgements

Bez would like to thank:
All of my band, Happy Mondays.
All of my fans, who have supported me through thick and thin.
My family and friends.
Everybody who has worked with me, past and present.
Nikki Mundy and Peter Eatherall at Howards Solicitors.
Orion Publishing and White Rabbit Books.
And my loving wife, Mrs Firouzeh Berry.

Andrew Perry would like to thank:
Victoria, for putting the life and the love back in me, while putting up with the 'moving-carpet situation' of writing a book; Rose and Georgia, my little chicas, for running the show on cheese; my mum Pat for ongoingly being 'la jefa'; and my brother Jimi for advice 'as my attorney'.

For *Buzzin'* itself, boundless thanks go to: Alan McGee, an inspiration for almost forty years, for having the idea of writing this autobiography, and putting me forward to co-write it; Natalie Galustian, for brokering our deal, and for sorting legal entanglements at the eleventh hour – trooper!; Lee Brackstone for signing us up and remaining cosmically unflappable; and to everyone at White Rabbit, especially Georgia Goodall in the labyrinthine editing.

Endless gratitude, finally, to the mighty Deano Hamilton, for his unflagging dedication to the project, above and beyond (often actually at 30,000ft, aboard one of his private jets); to

ACKNOWLEDGEMENTS

Frou, for cross-checking, guarding everybody's safety and a cracking Bonnie Tyler cover; and to Bez, for giving me this opportunity and generally being ace . . . here's hoping the two of you ride off into a sunset untroubled by man-made clouds at the horizon.

Picture Credits

Plate 1: © Getty/Ian Dickson (*top*); © Alamy/Stephen Parker (*middle, bottom left, bottom right*)

Plate 2: © Getty/Kevin Cummins (*top, bottom left, bottom right*); © Getty/Paul Bergen (*middle*)

Plate 3: © Getty/Steve Pyke (*top*); © Jules Annan (*bottom*)

Plate 4: © Deano Hamilton (*top*); © Jules Annan (*middle right, middle left*)

Plate 5: © Jules Annan (*top*)

Plate 6: © Jules Annan (*top, middle left*); © Firouzeh Berry (*middle right*); © Alamy/PA Images (*bottom right*)

Plate 7: © Alamy/Dave Ellison (*top*); © Alamy/Rachel Megawhat (*middle*); Jules Annan (*bottom*)

Plate 8: © Shutterstock/Matt Frost/ITV

Where not mentioned, images belong to the author.

Credits

White Rabbit would like to thank everyone at Orion who worked on the publication of *Buzzin'*.

Agent
Natalie Galustian

Editor
Lee Brackstone

Copy-editor
Ian Allen

Proofreader
Sue Lascelles

Editorial Management
Georgia Goodall
Jane Hughes
Charlie Panayiotou
Tamara Morriss
Claire Boyle

Audio
Paul Stark
Jake Alderson
Georgina Cutler

Contracts
Anne Goddard
Ellie Bowker

Design
Nick Shah
Steve Marking
Joanna Ridley
Helen Ewing

Finance
Nick Gibson
Jasdip Nandra
Sue Baker
Tom Costello

Inventory
Jo Jacobs
Dan Stevens

Marketing
Tom Noble

Production
Paul Hussey
Katie Horrocks

Publicity
Virginia Woolstencroft

Sales
Jen Wilson
Victoria Laws
Esther Waters
Group Sales teams across
    Digital, Field Sales,
    International and
    Non-Trade

Operations
Group Sales Operations team

Rights
Barney Duly
Flora McMichael
Ayesha Kinley
Nathan Kehel
Marie Henckel